Lorne Greenaway
From Horseback to the
House of Commons

LORNE GREENAWAY
From Horseback to the House of Commons

Lorne Greenaway
with
Kate Greenaway

CAITLIN PRESS
HALFMOON BAY, BC

01 02 03 04 05 06 17 16 15 14 13 12

Caitlin Press Inc.
8100 Alderwood Road,
Halfmoon Bay, BC VON 1Y1
www.caitlin-press.com

Text design by Kathleen Fraser.
Cover design by Vici Johnstone.
Edited by Patricia Wolfe.
Printed in Canada.

Caitlin Press Inc. acknowledges financial support from the Government of Canada
through the Canada Book Fund and the Canada Council for the Arts, and from the
Province of British Columbia through the British Columbia Arts Council and the
Book Publisher's Tax Credit.

Canada Council   Conseil des Arts
for the Arts   du Canada

BRITISH COLUMBIA
ARTS COUNCIL
An agency of the Province of British Columbia

Library and Archives Canada Cataloguing in Publication

Greenaway, Lorne, 1933–2010
    Lorne Greenaway : from horseback to the House
of Commons / Lorne Greenaway and Kate Greenaway.

ISBN 978-1-894759-80-9

    1. Greenaway, Lorne, 1933–. 2. Canada. Parliament. House
of Commons—Biography. 3. Legislators—British Columbia—
Biography. 4. Veterinarians—British Columbia—Biography.
I. Greenaway, Kate A. II. Title.

FC3828.1.G74A3 2012   971.1'04092   C2012-900546-0

Lorne Greenaway

1933—2010

"The ties of friendship,
stretching far,
Link days that were
with days that are."

CONTENTS

EARLY DAYS

My father, William John Everett Greenaway, was born in 1907 in Holland Centre, near Owen Sound, Ontario, where his family owned a farm.[1] Sadly, at the age of six, Dad was orphaned after a house fire, separated from his four siblings, and shipped out to BC to live with his Uncle Dick and Aunt Nellie in the Fraser Valley. He never felt welcome there. Dick and Nellie were only subsistence farmers, with their own large family to support, and resented being burdened with another mouth to feed. At some point, he was passed along to another uncle, Chris, and his wife, Margaret. Uncle Chris was the black sheep of the family, a ne'er-do-well and a drunk, but Aunt Margaret was a saint and made ends meet by teaching school. At some point, she left Uncle Chris and got a job teaching school in Bella Coola. She took Dad with her and he received most of his schooling there.

Dad was called "Jack" in Bella Coola, but later in his adult life he made the switch to "Ev." Dad had his heart set on becoming a mining engineer but, with no money to pay for his education, he left Bella Coola and headed north to take various jobs in logging camps and the like.[2] When he had saved $1,000, he headed down to Vancouver to see if he could begin his university education. Arriving in Vancouver, he found his sister Ann seriously ill and, sadly, the money he'd saved went to cover her medical bills. She subsequently recovered, but Dad had to change direction and decided to go to Normal School to become a schoolteacher.

Dad supported himself by working nights so that he could attend school during the day; it was tough. He lived in a boarding house in Marpole, attended classes at Eleventh Avenue and Cambie, and worked at a service station downtown near the Hotel Vancouver. He frequently worked the late shift and had to walk home, which would take him about two hours, often in the rain. He persisted though, and successfully completed the two-year course. Certificate in hand, he headed north to his first teaching job in the small community of Alice Arm, and later worked in Hazelton and Kispiox. In the early 1930s, he returned to Bella Coola to teach.

My mother, Olivia Nygaard, was born in 1911 on a homestead near Chilanko Forks, about seventy miles west of Williams Lake. Her parents, Ole and Sophie Nygaard, had seven children: four boys and three girls.[3] Like my dad, she relinquished her childhood name when she got married—she started out as "Livia," but for most of her adult life she was known as "Pat."

Mom was less than a year old when her parents decided to sell their Chilcotin homestead and return to Bella Coola. They took to the two-hundred-mile trail on foot, with three small boys and Grandma carrying my infant mom on her back in a papoose bag given to her by a Native woman. It must have taken several difficult weeks to make the trek back to Bella Coola. On the trail, they ran into the Knowles family, the people who had purchased their homestead. Mrs. Knowles had a baby about the same age as Mom, and Grandma gave her the papoose bag as, by then, the Knowleses had a longer journey in

My parents, Olivia Nygaard and William John Everett Greenaway, were married on June 30, 1932.

front of them. Soon after their arrival in Bella Coola, Grandpa purchased a piece of land in Hagensborg on the Bella Coola River. He cleared the land and established a farm, but it was always difficult to make ends meet.

Mom started her education in Bella Coola and completed her Grade 12 at Magee High School in Vancouver. She went on to take a business course before returning to Bella Coola in 1930 or '31, where she and Dad soon became sweethearts. They were married in the Hagensborg Church on June 30, 1932, by Reverend Kelly, a United Church minister, the first ordained full-blooded Haida Native. They honeymooned in Tweedsmuir Park, going in on horseback with a guide, and spent three weeks venturing into some of the farthest reaches of the park. Mom was apparently the first white woman to make such an extensive trip and Olivia Lake in Tweedsmuir is named for her. She and Dad spent that first year living with Aunt Margaret in a small, Norwegian-style house.[4] These houses were beautifully crafted and built of hand-split cedar planks with dovetailed corners.

I WAS BORN ON May 8, 1933, in the Bella Coola Hospital. This was a small outpost facility that catered to the white and Native populations. As in so many communities at that time, tuberculosis (TB) was raging through the area, especially among the Native population. Many TB patients were confined to the hospital and, unfortunately, while Mom was in hospital delivering me, she contracted the disease, which settled in her uterus. She didn't show any symptoms until about Christmastime but by then she was seriously ill.

Dad could see that the only way to save her life was to get her to hospital in Vancouver. The Union Steamship Company's boat came once a week to deliver supplies and mail, and it also carried passengers. Fearing the worst, Dad gathered Mom up and made the journey to Vancouver where he had her admitted to St. Paul's Hospital. With nowhere to stay in Vancouver, a small son at home, and with Mom obviously needing several months of hospitalization, Dad had no choice but to come home and go back to work. Still only months old, I was cared for by my aunts, Thelma and Helen, who were still living at home with Grandpa and Grandma. They nearly lost me once, though.

They used to take me everywhere with them and one day, meeting up with friends, they put me down on the bridge railing at Snootley Creek while they chatted. I fell off and landed in the river but somehow I stayed afloat. They ran down alongside the water and waded in to fish me out. It was several years before they told my mom.

Mom very nearly didn't make it. At one point, she developed peritonitis and her abdomen became very swollen. The doctor drained fluid from her abdomen on a daily basis. Years later, she laughed as she told me that the doctor kept a piece of string in his pocket and used it to measure the girth of her abdomen every morning. The swelling gradually went down and, after nine months, she was finally discharged. Dad travelled to Vancouver to get her and they returned together to Bella Coola.

Mom's illness had far-reaching implications. First, and probably most heartbreaking for both of them, she could not have any more children. Second, they were left with a huge medical bill. It took almost twelve years of making monthly instalments to finally pay it off.

At that time, the treatment of TB was mainly palliative: there was no real cure. People with TB were advised to move to drier climates, which makes some sense when the respiratory system is involved. In Mom's case it made no sense at all but, nevertheless, they decided to move to Naramata where Dad had secured a job teaching in a two-room school.

L–R: Me, Mom and Aunt Thelma, who, along with Aunt Helen, cared for me when Mom was hospitalized with TB.

With Dad on my fifth birthday in Naramata.

Dad had a 1928 Model T Ford that he had adapted into a kind of pickup truck. The cab held a driver and a passenger. Aunt Thelma was delegated to accompany us and help Mom look after me and she volunteered to sit in the back out in the open. It was a muggy August day in 1935 when the four of us left Bella Coola on the boat to Vancouver. Our car-truck was unloaded there and we headed into the Interior. The best way to get to the Okanagan Valley by car at that time was through Washington State. As there were few motels and we had little money, Dad had rigged up a sort of tent in the back of the truck, where we slept.

The trip took at least a week. As we travelled inland, the humid

warmth turned scorching hot and dusty. Aunt Thelma held me in her
lap most of the way, trying to keep me cool while avoiding the dust and
sun. As the afternoon temperatures climbed past 100°F, Dad's biggest
worry was keeping the car running. Our Model T had wooden spokes
that dried out in the heat, and they started to rattle in the rims. If the
rims collapsed, we'd be in real trouble. The only way around this was
to drive into a creek or a lake at every opportunity, stopping for long
periods to let the wooden spokes soak up the water.

We arrived in Naramata in early September, just a few days before
school was due to start, and moved into a small house. At that time,
Naramata was a very small community of three hundred people from
"the old country" (the British Isles). There were two small stores (one
with a gas pump), a post office and two churches, United and Anglican.
The nearest centre of any size was Penticton, ten miles to the south along
a rough dirt road. People with cars travelled to Penticton once a week to
shop but most patronized the two local stores, Dudley's and Billy's.

The local economy was completely dependent on fruit growing
and, in those Depression years, orchard owners were in dire straits.
That fall, the growers threatened not to pick their fruit; their slogan
was "two cents a pound or on the ground." They begrudged every
nickel, dime and dollar that had to be spent, especially on taxes. In
fact, it was during this period that producers started looking to the
government for support. Dad's salary was only $80 a month but people
resented him for having a regular salary at all. This was very hard on
Mom, who was trying to make friends in our new surroundings.

My earliest memory occurred in Naramata, probably when I was
about three years old. Some neighbourhood boys came by our house
with a pony and put me on its back. I remember burying my face in its
mane and breathing in that wonderful, earthy aroma of horse that has
remained with me these many years.

MY DAD HAD SPENT much of his life trying to further his education, as
he always felt his simple teacher's certificate was inadequate. In the
summer of 1938, Dad and Mom decided to go to Victoria so that Dad
could go to summer school for teachers. We rented rooms in a house
on Hillside Avenue. It was very, very hot and sometimes we would go

to Crystal Pool to swim or to Beacon Hill Park. I have vague memories of going down to the Inner Harbour one warm evening, amazed to see a British warship with huge guns and many sailors.

Years later, much to his credit, Dad earned a Bachelor of Education from the University of British Columbia (UBC); it was a real struggle. The same year, Dad bought a very small house on an acre of land on the north side of Naramata, about a hundred yards from Okanagan Lake. It came with a sizeable asparagus patch, and Dad planted a small peach orchard and supplemented his income by selling asparagus and peaches. During asparagus season, Mom and Dad would get up early in the morning to cut and crate it. Every day, Dad would find ways to send asparagus to the Penticton grocery stores with anyone who happened to be going in that direction. Even more amazing, he had an arrangement with someone in Summerland to sell asparagus there. He would get up even earlier on those mornings and row across the lake to deliver it. All of this before heading to school for a nine o'clock start.

Like many of the houses in our neighbourhood, ours had no insulation and was heated by a wood stove and heater. Every autumn, Dad would take his old truck partway out along Chute Lake Road and fall dead fir trees with an axe and a crosscut saw. He would cut them into lengths he could handle, load them onto his old truck and haul them home. Then, of course, he would cut those lengths into smaller pieces that would fit into the stove and split them, all by hand. Life was hard but we were in the same boat as most of the people we knew.

In June 1939, it had been four years since Mom had seen any of her relatives and friends in Bella Coola. This time, rather than taking the boat from Vancouver, Mom and Dad decided to drive overland from Naramata in our 1929 Model A coupe. It had two seats in the front with the gearshift in between and a rumble seat in the back that could be closed. Dad put our one suitcase and two spare tires and tubes with the jack and all of the patching equipment in there, and we started off as soon as the school year ended. It took three tough days just to reach Williams Lake. There was no pavement but many potholes and lots of washboard stretches and dust. The sidewalks in Williams Lake fascinated me: they were made of planks and I remember the jingle of spurs as the cowboys walked by.

Mom's side of the family was still well known in the Chilcotin from their homesteading days at Chilanko Forks. News travelled fast that Ole Nygaard's daughter would be passing through, and there was no way to avoid visiting. It took us another three days to travel from Williams Lake to Anahim Lake.

Leaving Williams Lake, we had been prepared for the road to get worse but when we got to Tatla Lake, there was no road at all so we began to follow Stanley Dowling's freight truck tracks along the shore of the lake. The water was high that year, right up to the jack pine treeline and, at one point, the tracks simply disappeared into the water. There was no choice but to follow the tracks, drive into the lake and hope it wouldn't get too deep. We crept in, but before long water was coming through the floor into the car. Luckily it didn't get much deeper, and after a few hundred yards we came back out onto dry land. We then drove on to Grahams' ranch house, where we were warmly welcomed, and stayed overnight.

We left the next morning, still following truck tracks on a newly slashed trail through the jack pines. This narrow right-of-way had been cleared in a hurry and the stumps that were left were not at ground level. The clearing had been done by axe only—no saws were used—so the tops were pretty ragged. The big wheels on the freight truck provided enough clearance but our Model A coupe was much

Age 6 at Atnarko, on the way to Bella Coola. Dream was a gentle horse with an infuriating lack of enthusiasm.

lower to the ground. Dad tried to manoeuvre through the treacherous maze but we hadn't gone very far before the front end of the car was hung up on a stump. Not having anticipated this particular hazard, Dad had packed only a hacksaw so he had no choice but to crawl under the car and use it on the stump while Mom and I waited in the shade.

We drove on for a while and things seemed to be smoothing out, until we came to a great bog hole. There was no way to go around it, so Dad and Mom finally conceded that they had no choice but to turn around and go back to the Grahams'. We decided to have something to eat first and, as we sat there, we heard voices coming from the bush on the other side of the bog. It turned out to be a small group of Native people, mostly on horseback, moving to their summer camp along the same trail. They were a friendly bunch and soon realized our predicament. Three or four of the men hooked their saddle horses to the front of the car with lariats and in a few minutes, with very little to-do, they had pulled us through the mud to the other side of the bog.

When we got to Anahim Lake, the Bowser family welcomed us. They owned the only store there and had two teenaged daughters. The girls had saddle horses tied to a hitching rack in front of the house, and as our parents visited, one of the girls offered to take me for a ride. She boosted me up behind her but I was too shy to hold on to her so I tried to get a grip on the cantle of the saddle. I was barely seated when she kicked the horse into a dead gallop. I remember being scared half to death, hanging on for dear life with my small hands. At some point, she must have slowed down because we got back to the house without my falling off.

After almost a week of travelling, we were ready for the last leg of our long journey. We met up with a big, tall cowboy named Bert Lehman, who had been hired to take us on horseback to the head of the Bella Coola Valley, a three-day trip. We left the car with the Bowsers and rode out behind Bert, Dad on one horse and Mom and I on another. Our horse's name was Dream, a gentle creature but lacking in get-up-and-go: Mom had to keep prodding her along. There were two or three packhorses that carried tents, our suitcase, bedding, food and cooking gear. Towards evening, we stopped and made camp, and the next day we started down the narrow trail that clung to the side of the mountain, a

Grandpa made me pose with the grizzly carcass. "Is it really dead?"

drop-off that was known by the locals as "the Precipice." The trail was extremely steep with many sharp switchbacks, a barrier to the valley for many years. It seems much more scary these days to drive the Precipice by car than it was to ride down it then on our sure-footed horses.

We spent the second night camped outside a trapper's cabin. His wife was kind enough to provide a salmon and rice supper for us. Soon after we went to bed, all of us were deathly ill with diarrhea and vomiting, but luckily we'd recovered somewhat by the morning.

That day we continued down the valley to Atnarko where Grandpa, Grandma, and a huge crowd of uncles, aunts, various cousins and friends were there to meet us. Grandpa had the only truck in the valley and he delivered freight once a week when the boat came in. His truck was also the area's biggest people-mover, and that day, Grandpa had collected almost everyone we knew and brought them to Atnarko to welcome us home. We said goodbye to our guide, Bert, and Dad made arrangements for him to meet us there with the horses at the end of August. We piled onto Grandpa's truck with everyone else and drove down to Hagensborg.

I WAS SIX YEARS old that summer and those two months in Bella Coola were truly memorable. Grandpa was busy putting up hay and delivering freight. He was a big man, over six feet tall, and he probably weighed at least two hundred pounds. With a big walrus moustache, he scared me a little but he was a gentle giant. Grandma, Mom and my aunts, Helen and Thelma, seemed to spend most of their time in the kitchen cooking and making Norwegian delicacies like flatbread, lef-sa, and shingles. Flatbread was made in large sheets on top of the big wood-burning stove in the kitchen. When it cooled, it was broken into smaller pieces and we ate it with all our meals. When they weren't cooking, the women were outside tending the productive vegetable garden.

Aunt Helen and Aunt Thelma had a following of young men who were forever calling in at the house. They had a deal with these boys: if the boys would go up a nearby mountain and bring home ice, they would make ice cream. There was ample milk and cream, fresh every day, and so I spent many mornings turning the crank on the separator. Helen and Thelma also got up to their own brand of mischief. Knowing

In 1938 we rented rooms in Victoria so that Dad could go to summer school for teachers.

the boys were gluttons for candy, they cut bars of Fels-Naptha soap into little squares and dipped them in chocolate. At church on Sunday, they put on their most innocent faces as they lured one boy after another into trying their "candy."

At that time of the year, some of the Chilcotin First Nations[5] would come down the valley on their way to trade with the Bella Coola, exchanging buckskin, moose hide and furs for oolichan grease.[6] Grandpa had a small cherry orchard of which he was very proud, and the Natives would often camp near it. Invariably the kids would sneak into the orchard at night to raid the cherry trees. Grandpa got so upset that he emptied the buckshot out of his shotgun shells and filled them with rock salt. He would shoot the young rascals in the backside to scare them off—fortunately no serious injuries occurred.

The Stranaghans[7] lived just down the road from Grandpa's place. They had two boys, Vernon and Ken, and we hung around together all summer, often getting into trouble. Sliding off the haystacks was a favourite pastime, although not popular with Grandpa as we wasted a considerable amount of hay.

We spent long days at the river with our fishing poles (long willow sticks with a hook and a line tied to the end) and a can with smelly fish eggs that we used for bait. Almost every time you dropped your line into the river, you could count on pulling out a Dolly Varden trout. Some were three or four pounds and we would take them home for supper. Sometimes there were so many dead salmon in the creek that we used them for fertilizer. I would help Grandpa and Dad fork them into a wagon so that we could spread them on the fields. I don't think I wore shoes the whole summer long.

Probably the most exciting thing that happened that summer was the raid on Grandpa's steers by a grizzly bear. Grandpa had twenty or twenty-five big steers that he was hoping to fatten up and then butcher in the fall. His plan was to sell the meat locally and this would have been a considerable percentage of his annual income. One night a grizzly got into the pen and killed seventeen steers—just swiped at their heads with his paw and broke their necks. Only the hindquarters of one steer was eaten.

The next morning, of course, there was hell to pay. Grandpa summoned some of his friends in the valley and they all came with their rifles, and some with dogs as well. They were able to track the bear to an island in the middle of the river, where he was unceremoniously shot and killed. When the men came back, they were still marvelling at the size of this bear. Grizzlies were very common in the valley but no one had ever seen one this size. Dad had a camera so he, Grandpa and I went back to take pictures of it. Grandpa sat me on the bear's neck, and staying put was a real act of courage on my part. With gas escaping noisily from various orifices—making the carcass move a bit—I was not at all convinced that the bear was actually dead!

Towards the end of August, Grandpa, Grandma and the rest of the entourage returned us to the head of the valley, where we were met once again by Bert Lehman, and after tearful goodbyes, we headed home. The trip home was hot and dusty but, outside of a few flat tires, uneventful. We arrived back in Naramata on the very day that World War II broke out and I remember how concerned Mom and Dad were.

There was a twelve-foot sunflower in our backyard. The next day I started Grade 1.

MY "FREE TO ROAM" CHILDHOOD

THE BEGINNING OF THE school year in 1939 was overshadowed by Britain's declaration of war on Germany and Canada's alignment with the Allied Forces only a week later. It was a scary time to be a kid: although we didn't understand most of what was happening, the adults in our lives were tense, spending evenings huddled around the radio and speculating about what the war would mean to the young men we knew. But oblivious to most of it, I began Grade 1 in the two-room school where my dad and a young "lady teacher," Miss Cavanaugh, taught about fifty kids from Grades 1 to 6. Dad always left home early, leaving me to walk the mile to school with Paddy Wheeldon, who lived next door. Paddy's mom, with seven kids, was famous in our neighbourhood for her unique approach to doing laundry: rain or shine, she'd hang all the dirty clothes on the clothesline and give them a good spray with the garden hose, leaving them there to drip-dry. My mom was not impressed but I actually thought it was a pretty good idea.

I have fond memories of that school with its beautiful acacia-treed lawns at the front and huge open playground at the back. I was lucky to start out with Miss Cavanaugh, a warm, gentle teacher who taught Grades 1 to 3 in "The Little Room." Dad taught Grades 4 to 6 in "The Big Room," while kids in the higher grades went by bus to Penticton. The Union Jack went up the flagpole every morning and down at

Mom and me with the twelve-foot-high sunflower on the day Germany invaded Poland, starting World War II.

the end of the day. We started our days with a Bible reading and the Lord's Prayer, and a picture of King George in his Royal Navy uniform looked down on us from behind the teacher's desk.

Just off the dirt playground behind the school were two strategically placed outhouses, one for the girls and one for the boys. At recess, the older boys would terrorize the girls by peeking through the knotholes, threatening to tip the outhouse over and even rocking it back and forth. If they were caught, they would be summoned into the

cloakroom, where Dad would administer a stern lecture and six stinging cracks of The Strap.

To his credit, Dad was pretty straight with kids so I didn't take a lot
of abuse about being the teacher's son. It wasn't until I was in Grade 4
that I tangled with him in a serious way and had my own first encounter with The Strap. Every spring, the Doukhobor people arrived from
Krestova to work in the orchards and they would put their children in
school with us temporarily. When the wind was right, we could hear
their parents singing Russian folksongs in multiple harmonies as they
worked. I don't remember much about the girls but the boys were big
and strong, top-notch ballplayers, and they taught us a few words in
Russian every year.

In school, we had just begun to learn to write in ink, using inkwells
and pens with detachable nibs, which were perfect for jabbing into the
bottoms of the kids sitting in front of us. We were sneaky enough to
make sure the teacher was out of the room—we all knew that jabbing
was a strapping offence. At one time, I found myself sitting behind a
Doukhobor boy twice my size, who kept putting his big hairy elbow
on my desk and "inadvertently" ruining my work until finally I gave
him a good poke in the elbow with my pen. He let out a squawk and
bled a bit where the pen had made its mark. It didn't take Dad long to
figure out what had happened and he hauled me up to the front of the
class where he administered six of the best on each hand. It always
seemed vaguely unfair that my antagonist, Alec Makortoff, got away
scot-free, though I'll bet he still has a small ink spot on his elbow.

BY THE TIME I got to Grade 4, the war with the Japanese was in full
swing. At home we were under strict blackout rules at night. From
the playground, we would see airplanes flying overhead and, although
they were a long way up, we always watched closely in case they
dropped any bombs. Warnings of incendiary balloons and bombings
manifested themselves in regular fire drills when we crawled under
desks and tried (not always successfully) to sit quietly until we were
told to come out. This was serious stuff!

The war had a visible effect on Naramata—most of the young
men enlisted and were gone for the duration. Dad went to Penticton to
enlist but was turned down because of his varicose veins. Undaunted,

he took the Kettle Valley Railroad train to Vancouver to try enlisting there but, when he was turned down again, he joined the reserve army (the BC Dragoons) at home. Training took him to Penticton once or twice a week with Mr. Grant, who had been in World War I and was now called *Major* Grant. Dad soon came home in full kit, complete with a Lee-Enfield .303 rifle, which, of course, fascinated me. I took Dad's rifle and traced it on a pine plank and carved out my own rifle with a handsaw and a jackknife. We boys started up our own little army, each of us with our own homemade weapon. Little David Grant was especially creative: he made a machine gun out of an old car muffler. Our moms made hats or caps and we marched around town pretending to shoot German soldiers; we were, no doubt, a very formidable part of the war effort. No casualties either.

From time to time, sad news arrived about a husband or a son who had been killed, injured or taken prisoner. By then we had a radio at home and suppertime was overtaken by lessons in history and geography as Dad listened to the CBC news (with clips from the BBC), map in hand, plotting the course of the war. The voices of Churchill and Roosevelt—even Hitler's ranting and raving—were our regular suppertime companions. It made a lasting impression upon me.

I got my very first paying job when I was eight years old, delivering the *Toronto Star* weekly newspaper. I covered all of Naramata, so it took me two or three nights after school to make the weekly deliveries along my ten-mile route—fifty or sixty papers for two cents each! In the summer, I dragged the papers around in a wagon and when there was snow I used my sleigh. I didn't enjoy it much, especially in the winter when it was cold and dark. I got quite a scare late one afternoon, on a shortcut through Percy Hancock's orchard, when I stumbled into a squad of soldiers in uniform with rifles—Germans for sure! I ran to the Hancock house in a panic where Miss Cavanaugh, who had by then married Percy Hancock, reassured me that these soldiers were not Germans after all—they were trainees from the Vernon Army Camp, on manoeuvres.

MAY 24 WAS ALWAYS one of the most memorable days of the school year. The May Day celebrations were carefully staged and well rehearsed and, unless it was raining, brought the whole town out to watch.

Our junior army on patrol with homemade guns in Naramata. I'm in the middle.

Dressed in white with a royal purple cape, flanked by her princesses, one lucky girl from Grade 6 would take the crown from the previous year's May Queen on the lawn in front of the school. Ten boys were selected to serve as guards, decked out in white shirts and purple hats with matching capes and carrying silver-painted wooden staves. After the crowning ceremony, the May Pole was erected on the lawn and, to the music from a gramophone, we escorted the girls in the traditional May Pole dance.

We had practised this every morning for several weeks leading up to the twenty-fourth and, although we boys were a bit bashful about it, our parents loved it. Afterward, we all walked together to Manitou Park by the lake, where the real fun began—a picnic, races and games.

The other festive event was the annual Christmas Concert, staged in the Community Hall. Students in Grades 1 to 6 prepared an elaborate concert and the whole town came to celebrate. A large Christmas tree, covered with candles, stood in one corner of the hall and when the candles were lit it was the most beautiful sight. I can still smell the fragrance of the tree mixed with the aroma of burning wax. It's a wonder the whole place didn't go up in flames! Of course, Santa Claus always came to distribute gifts to the younger children and everyone joined in the carols.

BUT MOSTLY, WE *weren't* dressed in good clothes—we were dressed for mischief! One of our favourite pastimes was sliding down the clay banks behind our houses. There was no way to avoid getting filthy dirty, and we all knew our mothers had absolutely forbidden it, but we did it anyway, as often as we could. If it was warm enough, we would shake out our clothes and jump in the lake to wash the clay out of our hair, but our mothers would alway spy dirt in the corners of our eyes and we would get soundly scolded. Occasionally we'd choose to do something stupid, like the time several of us rolled around in poison ivy to see what would happen. "What" did happen, and boy did we suffer. The treatment was calamine lotion and confinement in our darkened bedrooms for several days.

We also entertained ourselves by smoking monkey weed, which grew up the cottonwood trees. We would cut a piece of dead vine into pieces that looked like cigars and pretend to be big shots. It was easy to light and smoke but had a very acrid smell that made us cough and choke. Our clothes and hair would reek of it, advertising our mischief to all when we got home. We graduated from smoking monkey weed to chewing tar after the power line came in. The crews had heated tar and used it to preserve the poles, and someone figured out that these shiny black chips of leftover tar got soft if you put one in your mouth and worked on it for a while—free chewing gum!

On the slightly more dangerous side was playing with rattlesnakes. There were many snake dens above the orchards and in hot weather the creatures used to crawl down into the irrigation ditches. We came across them almost every time we went hiking. We usually killed them and cut off the rattles to take home unless we found an unusually large one, which would have to be shown off. One summer, someone read in a Zane Grey book about teasing rattlesnakes with a piece of stewing beef tied to a stick with string. Supposedly, when the snake struck the meat, the venom would turn it green! This was an experiment too good to pass up, so we found an old bathtub that we dragged into the bush behind our houses. We captured several snakes, pinning their heads down with forked sticks so that we could grab them, and brought them home in a gunnysack. In the backs of our minds was the tale of the old hermit who'd been bitten on the thumb while chopping wood. The story goes that, without missing a beat, he'd chopped the end of his thumb clean off, cinched it up with a rag, got in his boat and rowed across the lake to the doctor in Kelowna. Not being keen to follow his example, we were pretty careful unloading our snakes into the bathtub to try our stewing beef experiment. The snakes, however, were pretty uncooperative—striking half-heartedly only if we stirred them up—and to our great disappointment, the meat never turned green. Being enemies of the state, of course, they all had to be killed, so eventually we disposed of them. And although we had a few close shaves with snakes—at least we thought we did—no one ever got bitten.

AT THIS TIME MY very best friend in Naramata was Garnet Grimaldi. His dad, Charlie, a World War I veteran, taught us how to handle a .22 rifle. Garnet and I had a lot of fun shooting squawfish and suckers in the creek behind his place. Mrs. Mahoney lived next to the Grimaldis. She kept goats and when she went to town we would sneak into her pasture to ride them. This was great fun for a while but, inevitably, we got caught and our dads were both really cross.

We also got caught in the attic over Billy's Store. Garnet had heard that Billy had a German machine gun up there from the war and one Sunday afternoon we snuck up the outside stairs into the attic. Sure enough, amongst all the other stuff, there was a machine gun. Of course, we had to install ourselves behind it and practise gunning down imaginary Germans, complete with sound effects. The store was closed on Sundays, but Billy was downstairs doing his books and he heard us up there. Our hearts stopped when we heard him coming up the inside stairs and we high-tailed it out the way we had come in, but Billy spotted us and, of course, told our dads, who gave us a good dressing-down.

We were all at pretty loose ends after school, especially in the fall when most of our mothers worked at the packing house. We used to hang out at the Earles' place, and we found a box of shotgun shells in the shed there. We experimented by putting shells in the wood stove in their kitchen but luckily nothing happened. Another time, we put a rifle shell in a vise and pounded a nail into the end to see if we could make it go off. It did go off, with a satisfying bang, and the lead slug went out the back of the shed. We only did that once.

At some point about half a dozen of us decided to start collecting birds' eggs. We scouted for nests and became pretty good at identifying birds. We could slide one egg out of a nest without disturbing things too much and when we got home we would blow out the egg's insides and add it to our collection. There was a keen competition between us to see who could collect the most or the rarest eggs. By the time we left Naramata, I had almost a hundred eggs in my collection, each carefully labelled.[1]

DAD HAD ALWAYS BEEN interested in fishing but could never afford a boat of his own. Percy Hancock had built a boat that had fallen into disuse and was pulled up on the beach near our place. It was a flat-bottomed, ugly old thing about fourteen feet long, with most of the paint peeled off and cracks in the bottom that you could see through. Percy gave it to Dad, along with an old Briggs & Stratton two-cycle engine. Dad brought it home and spent hours caulking and painting it. He installed the engine, a steering wheel and an old Ford windshield across the front, and made floorboards out of an old cedar packing case. I don't know how he got it into the water but there was a great celebration when he finally fired it up. That summer, and many summers thereafter, Mom and Dad and I often went camping along the lakeshore, sleeping in a tent on a bed of fir bows that smelled so good.

Dad was offered a better position with more money at a school in Kelowna so, in August 1943, we packed everything we owned in the Model A and Mom drove it to Kelowna while Dad and I took the boat. He and I ran into a terrible storm off Squally Point and nearly lost it all. Waves were coming up over the gunnels and I bailed like crazy while Dad tried to hold us on course. Since we had no life jackets, Dad emptied the spare gas can into the water, put the cap back on, and told me that, if we sank, I should hang on to it because it would float.

LOOKING BACK ON THOSE DAYS in Naramata, I realize that it was an idyllic time to be a child. Our parents had no worries about child safety—everybody knew everybody—and we were simply allowed to run free. There was a single policeman stationed in Penticton, but we never did see him in Naramata. In the summer we swam practically all day and would dive off the barge wharf from a ladder that we had built ourselves: no lifeguards, no supervision! We would get up in the morning, put on our bathing suits, and off we would go, taking care to only show up for supper and at bedtime. We learned to be self-sufficient and creative, to survive and to thrive. All in all, it was a very memorable time for me and my pals, an unforgettable period of my life. When we left, I was heartbroken to leave all my friends.

AN EXTRACURRICULAR EDUCATION

WE ARRIVED IN KELOWNA in time for Dad to take up his job teaching Grade 6, and I started Grade 5 at the same school. We stayed in the Rainbow Auto Court for a while and I settled into school, still pining for Naramata. Mom was pining too, but for Bella Coola, so just after Christmas, she and I set out on our own for a visit. We took the train to Vancouver, stayed overnight at her cousin's house on West Pender, and then boarded the Union Steamship *Cardena* to Bella Coola. It was pretty exciting for me and much easier than going by car. The war with Japan was a palpable threat on the West Coast, so the *Cardena* had a four-inch gun mounted on the deck. The food was wonderful—fresh fish every day—served on Union Steamship china with fancy cutlery by waiters in white jackets. The trip took three days and when we arrived at Prince Rupert we had to be let through a submarine net to enter the harbour.

We stayed in Bella Coola for almost four months. I missed a lot of school but had the time of my life. My Aunt Helen was married by then and her husband, Uncle Bob,[1] gave me my own set of traps. He taught me how to use them and I was soon catching squirrels and weasels. I skinned, stretched and dried the skins, and Uncle Bob sold them for me (seventy-five cents for a squirrel and two dollars for a weasel skin) to the fur buyers who came through. I was on my own in the forest a

L-R: Aunt Helen, Grandma, Grandpa Ole, Mom and Aunt Thelma. I'm in the front with the appendectomy scar!

lot of the time—a very dense and dark rainforest, completely different from the BC Interior woodlands I was familiar with—but by some miracle, I always managed not to get lost. Uncle Bob also let me use his .22 rifle and I learned to shoot grouse and squirrels.

I had my appendix removed during this time too. Apparently it was pretty dramatic but I don't remember anything about it.

Uncle Bob had a successful trapping business in the winters, but he was a fisherman at heart. He had a good-sized boat with a crew of three or four, and they fished mainly for halibut. The best fishing seemed to be off the west coast of the Queen Charlotte Islands (Haida Gwaii). Very sadly, a few years following our visit, he and the boat and crew were lost, perhaps after hitting a deadhead and puncturing the hull— no one was ever sure. A mayday call was the last communication from them and the boat was never found.

During our stay, Mom spent her days visiting and cooking up a storm with Grandma. We had lots of the best Norwegian food. It was fortunate that we made this trip because Grandma died a year later and the family started to disperse. This was my last visit to Bella Coola for a very long time—I didn't go back again until 1974.

AT HOME IN KELOWNA, we were feeling more established and moved from a small rented house on St. Paul Street to another rental on the lakeshore, on Manhattan Drive. Not long afterward, we heard the sad news that our next-door neighbours, Mr. and Mrs. Bath, had lost one of their three sons in the war. They wanted to sell their house and leave memories behind, so Dad bought it for $3,000 and we moved next door to 998 Manhattan Drive. The house was on a double lot with a fair bit of lakefront. At about the same time, Dad was promoted to vice-principal and started making a bit more money. The war ended around this time and, in general, things were looking up.

Life was simple then, predictable even. Dad now had a 1930 Model A sedan, which he sometimes drove to work, but usually he walked or rode his bicycle. Mom worked at the packing house every fall to help make ends meet. In the summers we usually had two or three weeks off as a family, taking our boat to Wilson's Landing or down towards Squally Point. We would camp out there, sleeping in a tent, fishing and picking berries. Mom canned fish and made jam, and I swam and collected arrowheads. I made a good friend, Bill Maxwell, whose family came from Vancouver every summer to rent a cabin on the lake not

At 8 years old with Mom and Dad.

far from our house. He and I scoured the beaches for Indian artifacts, often finding mint-condition arrowheads and other implements to add to our collections.

MY FASCINATION WITH HORSES had never waned and, around this time, the most amazing thing happened: I won a horse of my own! Byers Flour Mills of Camrose, Alberta, manufactured a breakfast cereal called Sonny Boy, similar to what we call Red River Cereal today. They sponsored a contest, offering the prize of an Indian pony to one winner in each of the four western provinces.

To enter, you had to write to them requesting a map of Canada that showed most of the main Indian tribes. Each box of cereal came with a stamp showing the chief of a particular tribe, which you pasted onto the map in the square with the right name of the tribe underneath. I announced that I was going to win the horse for BC and Dad promised that if I won he would build me a barn to keep it in. It took me months to collect the stamps and fill in all the spaces as required. I traded stamps with kids at school and we ate a lot of Sonny Boy cereal. I finally sent the completed map to Camrose and a week or so later, much to everyone's complete astonishment, we received a telegram informing us that I had won the horse! BC Rail would ship it out within the month.

True to his word, Dad started right away remodelling an old boat-house on our property, making it suitable as a barn. The day finally came when we were notified that the horse had arrived and I walked by myself over to the railway yards. A freight agent and I found the car, opened a door, and there she was: a bay pinto, 14.2 hands high with the Indian Department brand (ID) on her left hip. She was tied in one corner of the boxcar, in the dark, on quite a long rope with no support, and no doubt had been thrown around a good deal on the long trip. She was frightened and skittish as we brought her out onto the freight dock and into the bright light. I led her home gently and put her in the barn. I fed her and gave her water, and sat with her all that afternoon. I named her Lady.

Our neighbour Jack Colton lent me an old stock saddle and bridle. The saddle was too big for me and the seat had been patched with a piece of tin, which made it pretty uncomfortable to sit on, so I rode

Mrs. Rankin with Howard and one of his friends enjoying a hot drink after a long day's ride.

Howard Rankin, my riding partner, whose mother took us on week-long riding adventures.

Me on Lady, heading out for a long day's ride.

A horse of my own! I won Lady in a Sonny Boy cereal contest when I was twelve.

bareback most of the time, although Lady had a very rough trot. Grandpa came to visit us soon after and brought me a bridle. With Grandma gone, he used to come down every year from Bella Coola, stay with us for a while, and then take the bus to Calgary to go to the Stampede.

My friend Howard Rankin also had a horse, and he and I soon began spending our spare time together riding in the hills behind his family's orchard in Glenmore. I did odd jobs wherever I could find them—I needed the money for hay and oats and equipment. I ordered a pair of cowboy boots out of the Eaton's catalogue and when they arrived they were too small, but I didn't let that bother me. I wore them for a couple of years until it was impossible to get them on. They did permanent damage to my feet.

WITH LADY, MY SUMMERS were now completely different. As soon as school was out I would go to Naramata for six or eight weeks to stay with Phyllis Coleman and pick fruit in her orchard. To get there, I would ride Lady out through Okanagan Mission, up the West Kootenay power line, on to Chute Lake and down to Naramata. It was a long day's ride, forty or fifty miles, and Lady and I were always pretty worn out by the time we got there. Mom and Dad didn't seem to be worried about my riding there alone, although Phyllis always phoned them when I arrived.

I loved it there. As soon as I arrived, I was happily reunited with my pal Garnet Grimaldi and we spent our days together in the orchard.

I kept Lady tethered on the road allowance and every night, with Garnet sitting behind me, we would go riding with a few other boys who had horses. The orchard work was difficult: the cherry trees were huge and often we had to use sixteen- or eighteen-foot ladders to reach the higher branches. The ladders often fell over and left us dangling from the nearest branch that we could grab, but someone always seemed to come to our rescue. We got two cents a pound for picking cherries and on a good day I could pick eight twenty-five-pound boxes. The evenings were fun, more than making up for the days and, of course, we ate pounds and pounds of cherries.

Back in Kelowna, I continued to spend most of my spare time riding, but I also developed a keen interest in playing basketball at school, coached by Mr. Larson. School was uneventful for me. I didn't get into too much trouble and got reasonable marks in spite of the fact that I didn't do any work. Mom and Dad also had me taking violin lessons, which were a complete waste of time since I only practised the evenings before my lessons. I regret that now.

ONE EASTER HOLIDAY, MRS. Rankin (who loved to ride) took Howard, his brother Douglas, and me on a five-day ride around the top end of Okanagan Lake. We had a packhorse to carry our food and sleeping bags, and camped out every night in the woods, tethering the horses. The days were great fun but I dreaded the nights, which were too cold for my thin sleeping bag. Our packhorse was a rapscallion, getting away from us several times with his pack on and dumping our supplies all over the ground or rubbing the pack off on the trees. We learned a good deal about going on trips with horses on that ride.

Mrs. Rankin was a strong, outgoing woman with a real sense of adventure. That summer she also took us on another, much longer trip. It was a hot day in late July when we started out from Glenmore, near Kelowna. We rode up the east side and around the top end of Okanagan Lake, then down to Whiteman's Creek, where we took the trail into Pinaus Lake. We had a Forest Service map but found it pretty tricky making our way through the mountains and trees. After four days—much to everyone's relief—we finally reached the lake! From there, we followed a road down to Westwold, where we turned towards Douglas Lake.

When we arrived at the Norfolk Ranch (one of Douglas Lake's main properties), they were putting up hay, using horsepower, and stacking it the old way with buckrakes and a wooden stacker. Foreman Finley Anderson invited us to put our horses in the barn and sleep in the loft on the fresh hay. He kindly welcomed us into the cookhouse for a hot supper and again for breakfast the next morning. We must have made quite an impression—a woman and three boys riding through on horseback.[2]

After we left Norfolk Ranch, we passed the main Douglas Lake headquarters, on to Pennask Lake and then to the headwaters of Trepanier Creek just north of Peachland. This last leg of the trip was very difficult. With no trail to follow, we were forced to pick our way through the trees and windfalls as best we could. All in all, we covered about 150 miles in about ten days. It was a great trip and something to remember.

HOWARD RANKIN AND HIS dad, Percy, were great hunters and they always went out deer hunting in the fall. Percy also went north to hunt caribou, moose and sheep. He was an avid gunsmith and had quite a collection of rifles. He reloaded ammunition and would give it to Howard and me, and we often went to the rifle range to test out a new gun or some type of ammunition. I soon developed a keen interest in hunting and Mr. Rankin gave me a Winchester .32 Special lever-action rifle. I thought I had died and gone to heaven.

I went hunting with the Rankins several times up at Wilson's Landing. Howard's grandfather came along and told us endless stories about the Klondike gold rush, the trials and tribulations of the Chilkoot Trail, and so on. Howard remained a great friend and has spent most of his life as a big game guide in Alberta, northern BC, and Yukon.[3]

Dad and I also hunted at Wilson's Landing; the second or third time we were there we shot a black bear, which was pretty exciting. We skinned it and had the hide tanned and made into a rug. We even ate some of the meat though none of us really liked it. In order to make the rug, the feet had to be skinned out so we sold them to a Chinese man for five dollars apiece. They considered bear feet a delicacy. We considered them a windfall! By then I knew some of the Chinese men quite well because I used to catch squawfish and carp near our place and they would buy them for twenty-five cents each.

At that time in Kelowna, quite a few kids had horses. We tethered them on vacant lots and road allowances, and rode together most evenings and weekends. We didn't get into too much mischief but we used to stand on our saddles and pick (steal) cherries during cherry season. We got chased out of the orchards several times but never got shot at.

One of the funniest things that happened was when four or five of us were riding up the back alley between Bernard and Leon Avenues. We were going past a rickety old apartment hooked onto the back of one of the stores, with stairs up the side of it and a small landing at the top. Tom White bet Wally Fuller twenty-five cents that he couldn't ride his horse up the steps. Wally had a good little mare and he took her up to the top in no time flat. Unfortunately, there wasn't room on the landing to turn her around to get back down, so his only option was to knock on the door and ask permission to bring the horse inside. Worried that the rickety landing would give way altogether, he quickly summoned his courage, and an unfriendly woman opened the door. She glared at Wally as he begged her to let him lead the horse into the kitchen so he could get turned around. She was very cross, shouting at him as she let him in and chasing him out with a broom as he made a hasty retreat. Wally came down those stairs like a scalded cat with his horse dutifully behind him, collected his twenty-five cents and we all rode away laughing until we nearly fell off.

THE WINTERS WERE COLDER then and the lake almost always froze around the shore, sometimes right across. We would rush home after school and play hockey in front of our house, staking out a goal with rubber boots and using the one real puck we had between us. Every so often the puck would slide out and into the lake at the edge of the ice, shutting the game down completely until we could retrieve it. Being careful not to let Mom see us, we would wriggle out on the ice on our stomachs with two hockey sticks to where we could see the puck in the water. If we were lucky we could catch it between the two sticks and bring it back onto the ice. We fell in more than once but the water was usually only waist deep. It was cold, though, and always difficult to get volunteers.

It was about this time that Mom and Dad adopted my sister. Mom went to Vancouver and came home with a tiny baby, only three or four

days old. They named her Wendy Margaret Evelyn. I was excited to
have a little sister and Mom had always wanted a girl, so she was in
seventh heaven.

IN JUNIOR HIGH SCHOOL, the end of Grade 8 was marked by the election
of an incoming Grade 9 student as president of the Student Council. I
can't recall how I got involved but we had to campaign, make speeches
and so on. I won the election and, at the age of thirteen, unwittingly
embarked on the first leg of my career in politics.

*Mom and Dad adopted my sister, Wendy, from Vancouver when she was just
days old.*

I got through junior high with a minimum of effort and spent most of my energy honing my basketball skills. I was also doing a lot of riding with my soon-to-be-best-friend, Tom White. Tom and his sister Lorraine had taken riding lessons from Mrs. Davis, who had a riding stable on Mission Road and taught them to ride in the English fashion. I was still riding Western. That changed, however, when Tom introduced me to the world of horse shows and gymkhanas. I sold Lady and bought a horse from Tom called Monte. Tom and I started riding out to Paddy Cameron's place almost every night after school and on weekends.

We loved Mr. Cameron and he took us under his wing, lending us each an old military English saddle so we could practise the various show events. Tom had bought a pretty little mare called Query, an ideal gymkhana horse. Monte turned out to be too slow for me so Billy Atkinson generously lent me Flurry, a mostly thoroughbred mare, who turned out to be the perfect starter horse. I sold Monte to our local forest ranger, Roy Eden.[4]

Another man who helped me out was a friend of Dad's, Gordon Herbert. He and his wife ran Herbert's Business College and owned several hundred acres of land above Poplar Point. He offered Dad and me the use of that land to pasture my horses. This was first-class pasture land that had almost never been grazed, with lots of original bunch grass, but it needed to be fenced. In the hills behind the Rankins' place, I cut as many posts as I thought I would need and used my horse to drag them down to the road on a rope tied to the saddle horn. Dad hauled them the rest of the way with a trailer behind the Model A. It took me several months of after-school and weekend work, but in the end I had about a hundred acres of good fenced pasture. The land is all part of Knox Mountain Park now. When I was there a few years ago, I could still see places where the fence had been.

In 1948, the new, state-of-the-art Kelowna Memorial Arena opened. In the wake of the coronation of Queen Elizabeth, the city fathers decided that Kelowna should get on the bandwagon with some kind of a coronation pageant in the new arena. Mr. Cameron and Mrs. Davis decided that some of us in the riding club would take part on horseback. Kathy Archibald was chosen to play the part of Queen Elizabeth, riding sidesaddle on Mrs. Davis's quiet old mare. Tom and

I and several others were chosen to be guards on our horses. To be allowed onto the hardwood floor of the arena, all the horses had to be shod with rubber shoes, which we all found to be quite novel. The RCMP in their red coats also participated on horseback. It went off smoothly and was quite a spectacle.

WHENEVER TOM AND I could find time, usually on a Saturday or Sunday, we would take off and go riding in the hills north and south of Kelowna. One fall day, with Tom on Query and me on Flurry, we decided to see which of our horses was faster. We came into a big clear stretch called Hachey ("Hashee") Flats and in a flash we were off. The next thing I remember is Query's hind end up in the air beside me and Tom flying through the air ahead of us. Query had landed her front foot in a gopher hole, had somersaulted and, according to the RCMP officer who later took measurements, had thrown Tom eighty feet through the air. He landed in a heap, not moving, and for a horrible moment I thought he was dead. Query stood quietly, holding up a front leg.

As I leapt off my horse, I could hear Tom groaning a little. I quickly took off Query's bridle and saddle, covered Tom with my jacket and saddle blanket, and headed downhill for help. Luckily the Raymers lived not too far away so I galloped straight to their place to tell them what had happened. They didn't have a phone so Mrs. Raymer drove to the nearest phone to call the police and the ambulance, while Harry Raymer came back with me to Tom. It wasn't too long before the ambulance came and took Tom off to the hospital. He needed emergency surgery to remove his ruptured spleen, and eight pints of blood just to get stabilized; it was touch and go that night. He had other injuries as well, and later developed hepatitis from the transfusions. He was hospitalized for three weeks. I was credited with saving his life, which was an exaggeration, to say the least, since racing across the flats may well have been my idea in the first place. Luckily Query recovered completely, but she stayed out all winter that year because no one could catch her. Tom later sold Query to our friend Alf Fletcher.

THE THREE YEARS OF senior high school were without a doubt some of the best years of my life. They consisted of very little work on my studies but no end of extracurricular activities. Basketball and riding took over my life. Of course, in the fall when hunting season came along, Tom and I and other good friends would skip school and go hunting for deer or pheasant. The main thing was to not miss basketball practice. I also joined a boys' club at school called Hi-Y. Only members were allowed to purchase yellow cardigans, which we wore with our white or bleached corduroys. We certainly thought that we were the cat's meow. In Grade 11, I was elected president of Hi-Y, which was quite an honour.

During my time in high school I started to become interested in girls and, for a long time, went with a super girl named Audrey James. By then, Dad had a 1940 Chevrolet sedan he had bought from Mike Durban, and I was allowed to borrow it to take out girls. One memorable night after a school dance, Audrey and I parked the car on the sandy beach just south of the Aquatic Club. When it was time for me to take her home, we found ourselves stuck in the sand! I had to walk Audrey home to her house near the hospital and then walk all the way home to Manhattan Drive, about four miles altogether. The next morning, very early, Dad hoisted a big plank onto his shoulder and handed me a shovel, and we hiked back to the beach to dig the car out. I'll never forget how kind he was—he never said a critical word. Somehow the story got around town, though, and I took a good teasing. Audrey and I eventually split, and she later married future premier Bill Bennett. I then started going out with Kathy Archibald, who went from being Lady of the Lake in our local beauty pageant to becoming Miss Canada in 1953.

I was lucky to get a well-paying job at McGavin's Bakery, working weekends and some nights after school, cleaning equipment and washing the floors. I moved up to making some of the deliveries, taking the truck to Penticton, Vernon or Kamloops at night. These trips made me pretty sleepy in school the next day, but I earned enough to buy clothes and horse feed, to take out girls and, of course, to put gas in Dad's car.

Once the summer horse show season was over, basketball became my predominant activity. I had made the high school team and played with some guys who became well known later on: Brian Weddel became a prominent Kelowna lawyer; Ross Lander became a judge; Bill Bennett became BC premier; John Ritchie (with his brothers) became a co-founder of Ritchie Brothers; Cliff Serwa became a BC

Social Credit cabinet minister; and Don McKenzie became chief pilot for Okanagan Helicopters. These guys were all committed and competitive, and we took our games seriously. We played against teams from Oliver to Kamloops, as well as some exhibition games with teams from the US. We never made it to the provincial finals, but we were good representatives of our school.

FOR THREE SUMMERS, I worked for the BC Forest Service on a fire suppression crew. There were twelve of us young guys, along with a foreman and a Chinese cook. Our foreman, Harry Murrell, was a World War II veteran; we soon learned to admire him and respect his judgment. We made $200 a month and spent almost nothing. We lived in tents, worked hard and ate very well. I learned a good deal about handling forest fires and in my third year I was made the "straw boss," or sub-foreman.

In my spare time, I began working for the only veterinarian in Kelowna, Dr. Pat Talbot, who had recently built a new animal hospital and a residence just off Glenmore Road. I cleaned kennels and went with him on some calls. He had been raised on a thoroughbred farm at Westwold and really knew horses. He was a first-class polo player and, because of his interest in horses, he and I got on very well. He was later responsible for my being admitted to veterinary college.

At home, I had built a good corral and a proper barn for the horses and I soon had people bringing me horses to break and train. At this time, three young RCMP officers were boarding just down the road from us, at Lloyd and Gwen Robertson's house. This was their first posting and they had all taken part in the musical ride. We became good friends and they taught me a lot about handling horses and caring for tack. One of them was mad about hunting, and in the early morning and the evening he would park the police car in our yard and shoot ducks on the lake in front of our place from behind my barn. No telling what would happen to a policeman if he tried something like that today. I became very interested in joining the RCMP, which was at that time a very highly respected police force.

During these years I really enjoyed going to horse shows, hauling our horses in Mr. Cameron's truck with Tom, and jumping

Mr. Cameron's filly, Merrylegs. I became fairly proficient at most of the gymkhana events but missed a lot of shows because of my jobs.

In my Grade 12 year of high school, I was elected president of the Students' Council, a great honour. My procrastination and lack of commitment to school finally caught up with me in Grade 13, though, and I ended up repeating it to earn enough credits to graduate. Most of what I learned, I learned outside of school: extracurricular activities were much more up my alley than the subjects I was supposed to be studying.

IN THE SUMMER BETWEEN Grade 12 and 13, I was all set to once again work on the fire suppression crew but there was a new foreman—a windbag and a boozer—and I took an immediate dislike to him. I quit after two days and headed home, where I bumped into one of my basketball teammates, Dave Wiens. He had read in the paper about the building of the Trans-Mountain Oil Pipeline that was to run from Edmonton to Vancouver. At the headquarters in Jasper, they were looking for labourers.

In less than twenty-four hours, Dave and I were on the train to Jasper. When we arrived, we found a place to stay—the attic of a house belonging to an old bachelor—and at six the next morning we walked down to the construction yard. There were many of us, so we stood around and waited for the foremen to come out and select their crews. We were passed over on the first morning but were picked on the second, loaded into the back of a truck, and hauled about thirty miles west of town. We were put to work filling old feed sacks with sand, some weighing at much as a hundred pounds. We carried them on our backs up a steep grade on the right-of-way, where they were used to protect the pipe from rocks in the bottom of the ditch. That first hot July day, we worked twelve hours and I could hardly climb into the back of the truck to get back to town, but we had proven ourselves and were hired on by the river-crossing crew.

The river-crossing crew was responsible for building the sections of the pipeline that crossed the rivers, while the main crew kept working on the dryland sections. The engineers calculated the length of the gap, constructed the line on the bank, weighted it down with concrete river weights and dropped it in. Our crew went from river to river, welding these sections into the main line to create one long, uninterrupted pipeline.

As this was one of the first major pipeline projects in Canada, most of the skilled employees were American—Canada just didn't have that kind of expertise. Most of them were World War II veterans, tough buggers from their time in the Pacific campaign, and crack welders. Many came with their families in Airstream trailers, which they set up at the campground just outside of town. We had a great boss from Kansas whose philosophy about work was simple: "If I want you to do something, your job is to run like hell and do it. If there's nothing to do, sit down." The sitting down part didn't happen often. We worked sixteen hours a day, seven days a week, so by Wednesday at noon we were making time and a half. We settled into a routine and it seemed to get easier over time. The money was good, but we begrudged the mandatory $100 a month we paid in union dues, since we never once saw a union rep or even got a card.

I learned a lot about heavy equipment and pipelining in general. We saw all kinds of accidents, one or two fatal, and we learned early on that we had to keep our wits about us. In the middle of August I was assigned to assist a welder on a utility truck. Harry was a Texan, a top-notch welder, and an incorrigible alcoholic. He drank bourbon by the case, starting at six in the morning, as soon as we got in the truck. Harry and I manned a self-contained unit, with a complete set of welding and cutting equipment mounted on a four-wheel-drive Dodge power wagon. My job was to drive the truck and, when we got to a site, to lay everything out so that Harry could get out of the truck and get the job done with as little effort—or opportunity for calamity—as possible.

Harry and I got along well but I had to work at it. My hours increased and often we worked through the entire night, right into the next day. I regularly drove fifty or sixty miles between jobs, with Harry passed out dead drunk beside me and, more than once, fell asleep myself, lucky to wake up just before I went off the road. He took a shine to me, though, and taught me to cut and weld; I even fooled around trying to weld aluminum when we had a little time between jobs. I came home to Kelowna in mid-September with a good deal of money and went on a bit of spree, buying a wristwatch, a pair of field glasses, and a cashmere sweater for Audrey.

In 1952 I was relieved to finally graduate from high school.

I MISSED THE START of my Grade 13 school year and my French teacher, Mrs. Gale, didn't approve of my absence those first two weeks. On my first day back, she asked me to get up and recount what she had taught in French class over the previous ten days. Of course I couldn't do it—and she *knew* I couldn't do it—so I made some stupid remark and she threw me out of the class.

This was a problem because, without French, I couldn't pass Grade 13, so the principal advised me to take German by correspondence. The course was made up of twenty lessons; every time I finished one, it was sent off to be graded and the next lesson would appear in the mail. With nobody to push me, I kept putting off the lessons in favour of riding, hunting and playing basketball, ultimately setting myself up for disaster. By May 1, I started to get worried. When I wrote my final test on June 30 I had completed only seven of the twenty lessons. Some kind soul gave me 49 percent.

Now I was in real trouble. I spent the summer working for Dr. Talbot and he urged me to study veterinary medicine at Guelph. I filled in the application forms and sent them off along with my marks. I also asked Dr. Talbot and several other people to write letters of recommendation to the registrar. Since I believed there was little hope of my getting into Ontario Veterinary College (OVC), I sent in an application to the RCMP at the same time and had my police friends put in a good word for me.

As summer came to a close, Mr. Cameron, Tom, Alf Fletcher and I loaded our horses into Mr. Cameron's truck and headed for the Armstrong Fair. We met up with our good friend Sandy Boyd, and the four of us slept together in a loose box in the horse barn. We did well in the riding events but not so well in the evenings. We somehow got into the local beer parlour and proceeded to really tie one on. Sandy kept himself busy laying out his lariat in the doorway, snagging people as they came and went. An acquaintance stopped to talk to us, and, as we were chatting, Alf surreptitiously nosed his beer bottle into this guy's pocket and poured it all down the front of his jeans. We were making a real nuisance of ourselves until finally the exasperated proprietor called the RCMP.

Just as the police arrived, we escaped out the back door and hid ourselves by lying flat on top of the railway cars that were parked outside. In those days the railway track ran right down the middle of Armstrong's Main Street. After making a few inquiries, several policemen came out of the beer parlour and started shining flashlights here and there looking for us. We were feeling pretty safe until Sandy heedlessly threw an empty beer bottle at one of the policemen below. A shout went up that we'd been spotted, so we hightailed it down the far side

Kathy Archibald: Beauty, Brains and Personality

IN MY FINAL YEAR of high school, Grade 13, I took up with a beautiful brunette, Kathy Archibald. She loved horses, which gave us something in common, and she was interested in becoming a veterinarian. Not long after we started going

together, she was crowned the Kelowna Regatta's Lady of the Lake, a great honour that was bestowed on a good-looking, talented girl every year. Of course, I was expected to accompany her to all sorts of events.

The following summer, Kathy competed in the Miss Canada pageant and won. She was Kelowna's pride and joy, but that didn't faze her a bit—she took her duties seriously and maintained her easygoing, sunny good nature. She moved to Toronto to stay with Miss Canada sponsors and had a heavy schedule of events to attend. I was summoned from college in Guelph to Toronto several times that fall to escort her to large parties of Toronto upper-class types, where I felt like a complete fish out of water. The guys at college were pretty envious and I took a lot of teasing, but I couldn't risk my grades slipping, so finally we agreed that she would have to find another escort.

Kathy started veterinary college herself the following year. She came first in her class in the fall term but decided she didn't really want to be a veterinarian after all. After a brief marriage to a BC Lions football player, she went on to UCLA, received a PhD in Psychology, and became a well-regarded professor there. Years later she left UCLA to get a law degree at UBC. An amazing girl, an amazing career.

Alf Fletcher on Query and me on Merrylegs, at the Armstrong Fair.

of the railcar and took off in separate directions. We all wound up back at the barn and quickly got into our sleeping bags with our clothes on just as several constables entered the barn. We pretended to be asleep, and after shining their flashlights on us, they decided they'd scared us enough and left. It was a pretty stupid thing for us to have done.

When I got home from the fair there were two letters waiting for me. One was from Ontario Veterinary College informing me that I had been accepted into first year, but on a probationary basis because of my poor showing in German. It was September 14 and I was to be in Guelph by the twentieth to start classes. The other letter confirmed my acceptance into the RCMP and instructed me to report in Regina ASAP. I decided that I wanted to be a veterinarian, dreaming, of course, that the rest of my life would be spent with horses. So I packed and shipped a steamer trunk, bought the required train ticket, and left for Guelph two days later. Mom sent me off with a big box of sandwiches and cookies, and Tom drove me up to Salmon Arm where I caught the CPR passenger train at midnight. It was a long, boring, lonely trip—four nights and three days—sitting up in coach class on hard wooden seats.

Little did I appreciate at the time that this was really the end of my youth, the end of living with Mom and Dad, the end of my time in Kelowna, and pretty much the end of my riding days.

COLLEGE DAYS

I WAS WORN OUT by the time I reached Guelph and I have no memory of where I spent that first night. I'd carried a few belongings to tide me over, but luckily my steamer trunk from home had already found its way to the residence. My roommate, John Lantink (from Holland), and I shared a room on the third floor of the "Vet wing" in a huge building dominated by agriculture students (the "Aggies"). In those days, the Guelph campus was a satellite of the University of Toronto, with about eighteen hundred agriculture students, three hundred veterinary students and two hundred girls at the Macdonald Institute. The girls had their own residence and most of them studied Home Economics: we called it the "diamond ring" program, because they all seemed to marry Aggies or Vet students. In 1964 our campus was liberated from U of T and became the University of Guelph, and these days it enjoys enrollment of over twenty thousand students.

There were about seventy-five of us enrolled in the Class of '58 at the Ontario Veterinary College (OVC), with a record-breaking contingent of five women.[1] Day one began with hazing, meted out by the second-year class, which went on all week. We were their slaves, the lowest of the low, fit only to serve the members of the Class of '57 according to their whim. We were dressed up in white lab coats, black hats and ties with "OVC '58" emblazoned on them, which we had to wear all week.

Our animal-handling "practice sessions" were more like impromptu rodeos.

In the first year of our five-year program, we were aggrieved to learn that we had to revisit several of our high school subjects—English literature, physics, organic chemistry—which we felt bore little relevance to veterinary medicine. We took particular exception to our literature professor, Dr. Alva Riggs. He came across as effeminate and affected and his classes brought out the worst behaviour in most of us, until someone found out that he had been a Spitfire pilot during the war and was a highly decorated air ace. That turned us around in a hurry!

As if English literature was not insulting enough to us aspiring young veterinarians, we were also expected to learn how to show various farm animals—pigs, sheep, dairy and beef cattle, and horses. Luckily, I was assigned a two-year-old Belgian colt, which suited me just fine, but some nasty in-charge had assigned all the girls to show large sows and boars. These animals were hard to handle, almost untrainable—and they bite! Preparing our animals for the College Royal Show was a compulsory activity that did have its benefits, though: it gave us access to the barns on weekends.

Weekends in residence were pretty quiet since most of the Ontario students went home. Those of us left behind soon figured out that there was no one supervising the barns on weekends. A few of us decided that an impromptu rodeo would pass the time, so we let some of the horses and steers into the alleyways. We took turns riding the steers, stirring them up and seeing who could stay on the longest—not really in the best interest of their training program! We had great fun at this for several weekends, but were finally caught and threatened with expulsion if we organized any repeat performances. With Christmas exams looming and the weather getting colder, our rodeos were ready to die a natural death anyway.

Personally, I was experiencing an entirely new life. Classes ran from 8:00 a.m. until 5:00 or 6:00 p.m. every day, with additional hours on Saturday mornings. My probationary acceptance was subject to the results of our Christmas exams and I was so afraid of failing that I studied pretty much non-stop. My efforts were regularly interrupted, however, by our continual fighting with the Aggies in our residence.

The Aggies didn't have to study as hard as we did and were forever playing tricks on us. One of their favourite pranks was to take the thirty-gallon garbage containers in our hallways, fill them with water, and lean them against our doors as we slept. First thing in the morning, as we emerged from our rooms to stagger to the communal bathrooms, these barrels of cold water would tip into our rooms, soaking the floors and generally making a mess.

Getting even required a team approach, like running the fire hoses into the Aggies' section and soaking any Aggies that we could catch. Often an entire floor of the residence would be engaged in a fierce water fight, using buckets, fire extinguishers, garbage cans and anything else that would hold water. Of course, the floor deans would be furious and threaten us with dire consequences.

The Aggies had lots of tricks up their sleeves, though. Each floor of the residence had several large washrooms, with eight or ten toilets with black seats. One night the Aggies came up from the floor below and poured thick, sticky syrup on all the seats. That area of the washroom was poorly lit and the first unsuspecting guys to use the toilets that morning stuck hard and fast to the seats, sacrificing dignity and the hair off their backsides to get loose. Planning retaliation—and avoiding it—became such a way of life that we couldn't even remember who started the war or whether anybody won.

All of this served to bond us as a class. I made many good friends, most for life: Harold Johnson ("Coonhunter"),[2] Harvey Grenn

Harold Johnson, a.k.a. "Coonhunter": college roommate, raconteur and lifelong friend.

("Crotch"),[3] Duncan Sinclair, Don Fishman ("Fish"), Harry Bacon ("Bumper"), Neil McKie ("the Senator"),[4] Bob Billin, Rod Davies, Bill Barnes and, of course, my roommate, John Lantink. I played on the intramural football team until the ground froze, and then joined intramural basketball. The first snowfall came in November and with it came my first real bout of homesickness. Mom and Dad wrote me a letter every week, which I faithfully answered. Each of us had our own mailbox and I checked mine every afternoon after class.

Christmas exams came and we all studied as hard as we could, sometimes staying up all night and working right through weekends. We had two weeks off for Christmas and my roommate and I went to London, Ontario, where he had spent several years working in a dairy. The dairy manager and his family had kindly invited both of us to spend Christmas with them. It was a homesick Christmas for me. It was too expensive in those days to call long-distance, but Mom sent a wonderful Christmas food parcel, which was devoured by several hungry boys on the day it arrived.

We returned to Guelph several days after Christmas and spent the rest of the holidays in the residence. We passed the time with the guys from the Caribbean, who had been making homemade rum with some ethyl alcohol they had filched from the chemistry lab. They mixed the alcohol with several pounds of very dark brown sugar, then heated it in a frying pan over a hot plate. After a lengthy process of stirring and tasting, they bottled it—no caps or corks necessary—and we all started drinking as soon as it cooled enough to swallow. Most of us were not experienced drinkers and didn't realize how potent this juice was. About six or eight of us got so blind drunk that it was several days before we were able to eat again. We staggered through the last few days of our vacation until the Ontario boys returned from their holidays with cookies and Christmas cake from home.

Early in the new year, our first term's marks arrived in our mailboxes in sealed envelopes. I opened mine with shaking hands and was relieved to discover that I had passed all my subjects, ranking thirty-ninth out of seventy-four. Probation was lifted!

We settled into the second term, which was much like the first, although we became even more creative in our efforts to blow off our stress with pranks and practical jokes. For instance, Harry Bacon was a nice but very gullible farm kid from Marwayne, Alberta. Harry loved to run around in the residence in just his jeans—no shirt, no socks, no shoes. One Sunday afternoon, about a dozen of us were sitting around in Terry O'Connor's room and someone produced a football. Terry's room was located over the infirmary, with a balcony directly over the infirmary balcony. An old battle-axe of a nurse operated the infirmary and we all did our best to keep clear of her.

With the room full of guys and the window purposely opened, it didn't take long before the football was dropped "accidentally" out the window, landing on the balcony below. Of course, the idea of asking this cranky old nurse for the ball back was unthinkable. The only solution was to lower someone down to retrieve the ball and it didn't take long to get Harry to volunteer. A length of rope soon materialized and was cinched around his waist. The boys quietly lowered him over the edge and as soon as his feet hit the infirmary balcony, the rope was dropped on his head and his rescue squad disappeared back into the residence. It was about twenty below zero with a foot of snow on the balcony, and there was Harry—no shirt on and in bare feet—with no choice but to start rapping on the window. We all held our breath upstairs as we waited to hear what would happen. The old nurse let out a good squawk, cursing and complaining until she finally opened her window to get a better look at this Peeping Tom. She laid into him at the top of her lungs until he finally escaped with the ball and came back upstairs, cold, chagrined and a good deal wiser.

Another classmate who got on the wrong end of a prank was a guy from Edmonton, Otto Radostits. He had worked for several summers for the Rattray brothers, prominent small animal veterinarians in Edmonton, and he would have liked to have skipped right through to fifth year. He particularly enjoyed recounting his exploits in surgery; correcting diaphragmatic hernias seemed to be his specialty. It didn't take long for us to hatch a plot to put his skills to the test. The Veterinary College had an ambulatory clinic, staffed 24/7 by fifth-year students who took calls from farmers and small animal clients. In cahoots with a fifth-year student, the guys arranged to have Otto paged by the ambulatory clinic.

A couple of nights later, the call came through to the phone on our floor and someone shouted down the hall: "Otto Radostits wanted at the ambulatory clinic—diaphragmatic hernia case." Poor Otto was even more gullible than Harry Bacon. He ran to the phone, listened for a moment in stunned silence, and then leapt at the request to help the fifth-year students with a difficult diaphragmatic hernia case. We eavesdropped from our rooms, barely containing ourselves, until Coonhunter stuck his head out into the hall to ask Otto what was going on. When Otto told him about the emergency, Coonhunter whipped him into an even greater frenzy, encouraging him to hurry and instructing him to wear a clean, white lab coat. By then a crowd had gathered in the hall. Someone brought out a clean dissecting kit for him to take along, and we finally sent a properly attired and fully equipped Otto out into the night. Evidently, when he arrived at the clinic to offer his services, he was turned out on his ear.

When it dawned on Otto that he'd been had, he slunk back to his room and stayed quiet as a mouse for the rest of the term, although we continued to harass him. But his passion for vet medicine propelled him into a hugely successful career. He became one of the best large animal clinicians in the world and capped his career as Professor of Large Animal Medicine at the Western College of Veterinary Medicine (WCVM) at Saskatoon. I had the privilege of working with him for a year there, and his ability as a diagnostician was truly phenomenal. He was well loved by his students and often honoured as Professor of the Year. He co-authored the unsurpassed textbook on large animal medicine with Drs. Blood and Henderson—a veritable bible in the hands of veterinary students and veterinarians the world over. He was so highly regarded that, before succumbing to cancer, he was honoured at a special celebratory night held in Calgary attended by hundreds of former students and veterinarians.

THE WINTER PROGRESSED, SPRING finally came, and we busily crammed for end-of-term exams. Dad had a friend in Kelowna who owned the Ford dealership and I was offered the chance to bring out a new car for him.[5] He sent me a credit card and asked me to pick up the car at the Ford plant in Oakville immediately after final exams. I took three Western classmates with me—Harry Bacon, Neil McKie and Keith

L–R: Tom White, me, Mr. Cameron and Alf Fletcher, tent-pegging—Tom and I captured the pegs!

Marling—since we could pool our money to cover expenses and see a bit of the country as well.

We were all packed and ready to go several days in advance, and I'll never forget how I felt as I walked out of that last exam—it was as if I'd been released from prison! We grabbed our suitcases, caught a lift to the bus depot and arrived in Oakville in the early afternoon. We were turned loose in a brand new, top-of-the-line 1954 Ford sedan, in a beautiful cream colour with whitewall tires and a radio. None of us had ever been anywhere near a new car and we kept inhaling, savouring the smell: we couldn't believe our luck! We had been warned not to go over sixty miles per hour for the first thousand miles but, after that, we could go as fast as we wished.

With little experience in highway driving, we thought taking Highway 10 across the northern US would be the most straightforward route. This took us through Chicago, though, and when we got close to the city, we wound up on a twelve lane freeway that went through the city and around the bottom of Lake Michigan. I had never seen so many cars in all my life, going in both directions and all at high speed.

I was next to terrified, just white-knuckling it all the way through, but somehow we made it unscathed. After that, the driving was easy.

We had barely enough money for meals, so we decided that, rather than sleeping in motels, we would drive straight through without stopping. We did a bit of touring, seeing Mount Rushmore and the Black Hills of South Dakota, hearing all about Wild Bill Hickok and Calamity Jane and visiting their graves in the Deadwood Cemetery. We crossed the border back into Canada at Coutts to drop off Harry and Neil in Calgary; then Keith and I re-crossed into the States for the last leg home. We could see the end of the road now, so we spent a few dollars on socks, a couple of shirts, and a case of American beer before heading up to the Osoyoos crossing.

The rule was that we were each allowed to bring $200 worth of goods into Canada if we had been in the US for forty-eight hours. However, the customs official discovered that we had taken a side trip to Calgary and thus had only been back in the US for less than a day. With undisguised delight, he totalled up the duty we owed on everything we had purchased, including the beer. We had just enough money to pay the tax on the small items of clothing, but not on the beer. He gave us two choices: pour it down a storm drain, or drink as much of it as we could. We tried the latter but, in the end, we left most of it behind and drove to Penticton, where Keith spent the last of his money on a one-way bus ticket to Vancouver.

I drove on to Westbank to catch the ferry home, only to find that I didn't have the fifty cents I needed to buy a ticket! Luckily, at a small café, there was a pay phone that I used to call home, and Dad came over on the next ferry to rescue me. By then it was dark, but I was so glad to get home. The 3,300-mile trip had taken us just over four days. The Ford dealer, as far as I know, was pleased with the car.

I DIDN'T SEE MUCH of Mom and Dad that summer. Money was still pretty tight and Dad had summers off, so they started spending their summers away, working for the BC Forest Service's Parks Division. Dad was the foreman of a crew of high school boys who travelled through the Central Interior creating campsites, most of which are still in use today. They spent the summer in tents and Mom cooked for the whole crew. I think they enjoyed the work and they certainly enjoyed the boys. But we saw very little of each other.

After a few days at home, I took the bus to Vancouver where Keith and I had summer jobs at the Lansdowne Track in Richmond. There were eight races every day except Sunday, and our job was to help the track veterinarian, Dr. Joe Lomas, with testing the winners for drugs. I boarded with Keith's family, and we both started looking for second jobs for the mornings and early afternoons. Keith wound up working for Dad's Cookie Company and, after a few days, I landed a job working at a riding stable in Southlands. We took the bus each afternoon to the racetrack and Keith always had a big bag of broken cookies that we ate in lieu of dinner.

I was in my element, being around horses from morning 'til night, until the end of July when the Lansdowne Track closed and the horses were moved to Exhibition Park. That put us both out of work, so Keith went to work full-time at the cookie factory and I hitchhiked home to Kelowna. I spent the rest of the summer working for Dr. Pat Talbot, boarding with him and his wife at the veterinary hospital. It was great to be back on home turf for a few weeks with all my friends, and I got to a few horse shows with Alf, Tom and Mr. Cameron before heading back to OVC in mid-September.

SECOND YEAR STARTED OFF with my being elected class president. This was a real honour, and my return to second year would have been easy and painless except that I decided to join the only fraternity on campus: the OTS, a fraternity exclusively for veterinary students. They put us through a very miserable initiation process that nowadays would generate serious repercussions. We were taken to a vacant service station where we were told to undress. Once we were all securely blindfolded, they poured cod liver oil over our heads and smeared axle grease all over our bodies. They had a culvert about thirty feet long that they filled with old guts and body parts from the post-mortem lab, and then forced us to crawl through it, chasing us along with cold-water hoses and banging on the culvert with sledgehammers. At about midnight, we were finally allowed to dress, loaded into the back of a furniture van, and driven six or eight miles out of Guelph and dumped off at a gravel pit.

There were about twenty of us, cold, wet and miserable, without a clue as to where we were. We decided to split up to better our chances of getting a ride back to town. Three or four of us must have walked for a couple of hours before some kind soul picked us up and gave us a ride all the way to the residence. We were so relieved to be back and could hardly wait to strip down and get into a hot shower. But our torture wasn't over yet. These sons of guns had run the showers on hot until the tanks were empty, so to add insult to injury, we had to wash the cod liver oil out of our hair and the grease and gore off our bodies with only ice-cold water. A night not to be forgotten![6]

Also, by some miserable quirk of fate, the residence was full that year and some of us had been assigned to an old dormitory called Mills Hall. Keith Marling and I shared a tiny room in the basement, next to the furnace room. The ceilings were so low we could barely stand up, and it was noisy and hot because the open steam pipes, carrying heat to the rest of the building, ran just under our ceiling.

But all was not lost. Classes were much more interesting now, as we were introduced to "real" vet subjects such as embryology, histology, anatomy, parasitology, physiology and others. Our physiology professor was the infamous tyrant Dr. Tom Batt. His father had been a physiology professor and had worked with world-famous physiologist Dr. Dukes at Cornell. He wanted his son to follow in his footsteps and after graduating from OVC, our Dr. Batt had been sent off to France to get a master's or a PhD in veterinary physiology. Instead, he had enrolled himself at the Sorbonne in interior decorating. He was eventually found out and recalled to Cornell where he was forced to finish his degree in veterinary physiology under his father's uncompromising eye.

His sexual orientation was always a great point of speculation amongst students and graduates. He had a real flair for drama. On the first day of his lectures, he strode into the room in a great flowing white lab coat, leapt onto the podium, and stood there until there was dead silence. None of us ever forgot his opening remarks and they are always quoted when veterinarians get together: "Look to your right, look to your left… This time next year, one of you won't be here." He warned us that we'd need to study "at least three hours every night and on weekends as well." Then, holding up a textbook, he said, "This is

Duke's physiology text. You're responsible *for every word on every line*."
As we sat there gawping, he added, "Including the footnotes." Sure
enough, when mid-term exams rolled around, the first question was
to quote the opening sentence of the text and then to state to whom
the book was dedicated. To this day, most of us can recall this passage
word for word.

Dr. Batt terrorized us for two years and failed a number of our
classmates. Students did not dare, if they had failed, to ask him to re-read
their papers as he was more likely to give them an even lower grade
than they had already received. Physiology labs were held on Wednesday afternoons, and Dr. Batt regularly kept us at our workbenches until
6:30 p.m., when he knew the dining hall would be closed. For most
of that year, chocolate bars from the student shop were our regular
Wednesday evening meal.

WE WERE ALL PRETTY busy studying and didn't have too much time to
get into trouble. The dining hall cuisine, however, was always a source
of inspiration: it was terrible, and we were hungry all the time. Luckily the Aggies had chicken pens in their poultry division, but multiple
efforts to convert those chickens to an edible meal were doomed. In one
of our more promising forays, someone had finally managed to steal
a nice, fat hen. We killed, plucked and cleaned it, then tried to roast it
on a broom handle over a wastepaper basket in one of the rooms. We
scavenged for paper and cardboard to feed the fire, but to no avail. The
chicken didn't cook—it just turned black—and the dormitory filled
with smoke until someone on another floor, fearing the worst, pulled
the fire alarm. That was the end of that experiment.

Our battles with the Aggies continued and we became increasingly
devious as the year progressed. The dining hall brought us all together,
seating about five hundred of us in long rows of tables, with the Aggies
and Vets at separate tables. We had to line up for meals and this was
the perfect time to create minor diversions, allowing someone to slip
unmentionable bits and pieces of dead pigs and cows into an Aggies'
jacket pockets and cause a ruckus. At the head of each row of tables was
a stand with a twenty-gallon container of fresh milk from the college
dairy, from which we drew milk into the smaller pitchers on individual

tables down the line. One day at noon, several veterinary students slipped some pig testicles into one of the Aggies' milk containers. As a couple of Aggies were refilling their container, they noticed these little floaters in the bottom and, without warning, bedlam erupted. The ensuing food fight, wrestling, and a few actual fist fights brought Administration to the scene with threats of closing the dining hall.

And the Aggies weren't long in getting even. While we were responsible for washing our own clothing, the college laundry service did our sheets and towels once a week. Our individual laundry bags were to be left in the residence foyer by 8:00 a.m.; our laundry was returned, washed and pressed, that afternoon. With only one set of sheets and a couple of towels, this same-day service was important! One cold January day, the Aggies made off with all the Vets' laundry bags and, with some kind of a hoist, hung them from the highest branches of the large oak tree at the front of the residence. By the time we got back from classes, it was dark and we had no end of trouble trying to retrieve our laundry. No one fell out of the tree but, to free some of the bags, we had to saw through several branches with a handsaw that we lifted from a utility room.

Coonhunter continued to entertain us with his antics. He had the misfortune to live just above an Aggie student who played the tuba— badly. Early that spring, as the weather warmed, the tuba player took to playing out on his balcony for all the world to hear. We were all trying to study and went over to Coonhunter's room to see what he was going to do about it. We found him in the process of filling a huge garbage can with water, muttering, "That's about enough of that honking!" He took the water out onto his balcony and poured it into the yawning bell of the tuba… and all hell broke loose below. I hightailed it back to the safety of my room while the Aggies stormed Coonhunter's floor in search of revenge.

My basement room was so unbearable that I finally moved out of residence altogether. Harvey Grenn, Don Elliott and I rented the top floor of a house on College Avenue. It was a better place to study but a fair hike to the college. We still took our meals at the college dining hall. I was quite busy with class politics and the fraternity, and course-work was heavy and took a lot of study time. At the end of final exams

L–R: Alf Fletcher, me and Tom White, on Mr. Cameron's horses. I treated Merrylegs as my own.

that spring, I picked up another new car at the Oakville Ford plant and four of us took off for the West. This time we skipped the side trips and made it home in three days. With Mom and Dad planning a summer away again, I arranged to spend the summer working for Dr. Pat Talbot and boarding at the vet hospital. I entered a fair number of horse shows and had a good summer.

THE THIRD YEAR OF our program at OVC was reputed to be the toughest. We worked and studied day and night to try to keep up. Of course Dr. Batt did his best to make things even more difficult. He regularly tested us with very cleverly designed multiple-choice questions. He provided separate answer sheets with boxes that had to be filled in so that he could grade us quickly by overlaying a piece of white plastic with holes punched to correspond with the correct answers. For a while, some thought they could outfox him by filling in every box, but he quickly caught on and switched to a clear plastic marking sheet.

At the beginning of term, I was very lucky to be invited by Don Elliott and Tom Hulland to share a downtown apartment with them. Tom was a '54 graduate and on staff in the pathology department, and Don, a '55 grad, worked as a clinician at the ambulatory clinic. We cooked our own meals and did our own laundry, and my marks certainly improved.

The event of the season was the College Royal Ball. I invited Nancy Rannard, a really nice girl I'd dated in high school, to come from Toronto for the weekend. The event was held in the ballroom of a local hotel and was very popular. I wore my college blazer, and she was the belle of the ball.

Another incident involved Rod Davies, Fred Bartoff and a '59 girl, Norma Turnbull. Rod was popular and very mischievous, and Fred was one of the few students to have a car. It seems that we were always hungry, so one night Rod and Fred came up with a scheme to steal a turkey from the college poultry department. They captured a large tom and wrestled him into the back of Fred's station wagon. Fred was to hold him down while Rod, with Norma beside him, drove around trying to find a suitable place to dispatch the turkey and get him plucked. They hadn't gotten far when they were pulled over by Pete, the campus cop. Thinking fast, Rod quickly had Norma wrapped in his arms and was kissing her when Pete shone his flashlight in. Pete appeared to be satisfied but, as he was turning away, the half-smothered turkey got loose. Pete had no choice but to turn them in, and the following morning, they were ordered to report to the dean's office where they were all expelled. A day or two later, luckily, their sentences were reduced to a $50 fine and they rejoined their classes.

THE SPRING TERM OF third year finally ended and I headed back to Kelowna for the summer. Don Elliot had decided to pack it in and had taken a job working for a veterinarian, Jack Greenway, who practised in Acme, Alberta. Don had purchased a brand new Ford Thunderbird and the two of us set off on a marvellous trip home. That winter, a '52 OVC grad, Paddy Clerke, had purchased Dr. Talbot's practice.[7] Paddy was a wonderful person and his wife, Sheila, was a jewel. I spent the summer working with him and boarding with them at the vet hospital. I cleaned kennels, bathed dogs, assisted in the surgery, washed and sterilized instruments, handled the phone, accompanied Paddy on large animal calls, and learned a good deal. It was the perfect summer.

Most evenings, I was at Mr. Cameron's where Tom White and I rode his horses, Dusky and Merrylegs. Merrylegs was virtually my horse (since I had broken her as a three-year-old) and Tom and I spent hours training both horses to jump. Mr. Cameron, seeing how committed we were, decided that his hired man should build us a jumping lane. It had two parallel rows of poles set up as a one-hundred-foot runway, with a jump about every thirty feet or so. To keep the horses from knocking off the top rails, they were wired hard and fast to the runway sides. Luckily, no one, including the horses, was injured. We had a bit of a struggle one night when Tom's horse stopped in the middle of the runway, and the only way to get her out was to take the whole thing apart.

Occasionally, we would take off for a long ride north of Kelowna to a large open flat above Okanagan Lake called McKinley's Landing. Wally Bennett's cattle were always on that flat and we loved to chase them. Neither of us knew anything about cattle and didn't realize what a nuisance we were being. Years later, Wally told Tom, "I knew you darn kids were chasing my cows but I never could catch you." One night when we were at this sport, a calf ran between Dusky's front legs and she and Tom took a spectacular spill. Dusky landed on top of him, pinning him down in a bit of a dip, unable to get to her feet. I had to find a pole and pry her off, and, just by luck, neither of them was injured. Most importantly, Mr. Cameron's saddle was not damaged. I got no thanks from Tom, though, because evidently I had been laughing the entire time, which really upset him.

IT HAD BEEN SOME time since I'd had a girlfriend, and, since my life was pretty busy, I'd sworn off the whole idea of "girls," at least for the time being. However, on June 3, 1956, my short-lived resolve came to an abrupt end. I was at work at the vet hospital when Lois Dunlop, my good friend and fellow OVC student, phoned me to set up a blind date. She had met a young nurse who'd just come up from Vancouver and was working at the Kelowna Hospital. I agreed, under some duress, to take this girl to the Saturday-night dance at the Aquatic Club.

That May, I had bought my first car—a '48 Ford two-door sedan—from Mike Durban, for the huge sum of $800. It wasn't in the best of shape but it ran, and Tom and I had installed a radio that I got at an auto wrecker's for $10. Having my own car with a radio was like a dream come true. So that afternoon, I washed the car, organized my best clothes, and finally presented myself at the Nurses' Residence. Little did I know that something was going to happen that would change my life forever.

I remember the next sequence of events as if they happened yesterday. I pulled up across the street from the residence, got out and was crossing the street when I looked up to see this gloriously beautiful woman coming out the front door. The first thing I noticed was her wonderful smile—it seemed to light up the world even in daylight. She had dark hair and wore a pale blue dress with white flowers on it, a white duster, white pumps and large white earrings. I was literally struck dumb. She bounced down the stairs and we introduced ourselves. There is absolutely no doubt that, for me, it was love at first sight. We drove to the Aquatic Club and danced until about 10:30 p.m. when I had to take her home in time for her shift at 11:00.

I didn't get much sleep that night: I just couldn't stop thinking about this girl. I had mentioned to her that I was riding in the Spring Horse Show at Mr. Cameron's gymkhana field the next day and, much to my amazement, she appeared there that Sunday afternoon. She had borrowed a bicycle and found her way to Mr. Cameron's, looking even more beautiful in red pedal pushers, a white blouse and a blue jacket. I nearly fell off my horse when I saw her. From then on, Phyllis McLorg and I were an item. My feelings for her seemed to be reciprocated and my resolve to spend the summer working and riding went out the window.

WHEN PHYL AND I had been dating for about four weeks, Don Elliott (who had come over to do a locum for Paddy Clerke) gave me a ride to Calgary where we had planned to spend a couple of days at the Calgary Stampede. I returned to Kelowna on my very first commercial flight, secretly hoping to find Phyl at the airport to meet me. Much to my surprise, she was there, *with her mother*. Phyl had been giving her mum frequent updates on our friendship, so Mrs. McLorg had driven up from Vancouver to get a first-hand look at me. I can't imagine what went through Mrs. McLorg's mind when she first saw me coming down the steps of the airplane, looking like I'd just come off a ranch in my jeans and cowboy hat... At any rate, our first meeting seemed to go well and we soon became great friends.

OUR ROMANCE CONTINUED THROUGHOUT the summer. One weekend, Phyl and I drove up to Lac La Jeune where my mom and dad were working, and they were as taken with her as I was. The summer flew by with both of us working so much, but we spent every possible moment together. When I found out Phyl's birthday was August 2, I borrowed $300 from my Aunt Helen to buy an engagement and wedding ring set from a local jeweller I had known for years. On the night of her birthday, after a nice dinner out, we drove out to Mr. Cameron's and parked at the end of his beautiful driveway. It was a unique spot, defined by a long double row of huge cedar trees that had been planted by the original owners, Lord and Lady Aberdeen.[8] The trees had grown together at the top so the driveway was like a long secret tunnel. There, at the top of the driveway, I offered Phyl my heart and, to this day, I can't believe she accepted. It was the coup of my life!

A TASTE OF THE UPPER CRUST

WHILE WE WERE AT the Aquatic Club that first evening, I was taken aside by Dudley Prichard, who had been a grade ahead of me in school. His parents owned a large orchard in Westbank. He asked me if I knew with whom I was dancing and I told him, "Yes, her name is Phyllis McLorg—she's a nurse from Vancouver." He puffed up and told me, "My parents and her mother have been friends for years. She's much too good for you."

I think he may have been jealous but it did sting. All those familiar feelings of upper versus lower class flooded back. Dad had always been poor and we had always struggled—we just knew that people with money looked down on us. Mom was particularly sensitive and as the child of Norwegian immigrants from a community like Bella Coola, she always felt inferior. I inherited some of this, along with her shyness, and I know it held me back from some achievements that should have been mine in later life.

In mid-August, Tom, Sandy Boyd and I had a chance to take the horses to the PNE in Vancouver. We borrowed Mr. Cameron's truck to make the trip, and entered individual and team events, doing reasonably well against some pretty strong competition. One of the judges, Larry McGuinness, whose family owned a distillery in Toronto, had a large farm with a string of jumping horses. He and Mr. Cameron got chatting and out of the blue, I was offered a full-time job at the McGuinness Farm working with and jumping their horses. Since I couldn't just quit college, he offered to take me on weekends and holidays but, with the coursework being so heavy, I couldn't swing it. I have often wondered what would have happened if I had accepted.

As the summer drew to an end, it was pretty clear that Phyl and I couldn't bear to be apart and, by the end of August, Phyl had decided to move to Guelph and take a job at the hospital there. As I now had a car, I had to drive it to Guelph. Lois Dunlop (who had introduced Phyl and me) was going into third year at OVC, and Nancy Rannard, who was working in Toronto, also drove back with me.

We started off with about five days to get there, hoping for an easy trip and a day to spare before registration, but coming into Spokane on the afternoon of that first day, we heard a horrendous clattering sound from under the hood. I found a mechanic who felt so sorry for us he could hardly look me in the eye as he delivered the unwelcome news: the wing nut that held on the air cleaner had come loose, causing the rod through the air cleaner to break loose and fall down through the carburetor and into the motor, resulting in terrible damage. He gave me two choices: put in a new motor or burn waste oil until I got to my destination. Because time and money were so short, we elected the second option, so he gave us a five-gallon pail of messy black oil and we started off.

The girls now sat together in the back as the oil pail took up the entire floor of the front passenger side. The trip soon unravelled into a nightmare as we limped along, stopping at shorter and shorter intervals to pour oil into the engine. There was no way to monitor it, as the mechanic had welded the dipstick hole closed. When we finally got to the border at Detroit, our top speed was around thirty miles an hour and the girls had to get out and push the car up the bridge so we could coast down to the Windsor side. They were amazing—really good sports—and never complained.

We finally arrived in Guelph a day late and the sonofabitch registrar, F. Eugene Gattinger, fined us each $50. Fifty dollars was a lot of
money then (room and board was only $40 a month), but "The Gatt"
wouldn't even listen to our story. I detested that man and celebrated
when, not long after that, he left the college. Nancy left on the bus for
Toronto the next day and, sadly, it was the last time I was ever to see this
lovely girl. I heard several years later that she had committed suicide.

Phyl came out by train and had arrived in Guelph ahead of me. She
had found a small apartment not far from Guelph General Hospital, on
the second floor of a house owned by a couple of old spinsters. They
were serious about protecting the virtue of the young maiden Phyl and
frowned on my visits, allowing me no further into the house than the
front hall.

The previous spring, our fraternity—with the help of some former
graduates—had purchased a large house about a block from the college. During the summer, with a minimal amount of work, the house
had been converted into a dormitory, with room for about eighteen or
twenty of us. It was a very old two-storey brick house with a full basement, and a kitchen with an old fridge and stove for making breakfast
and coffee. It was pretty unsanitary, but we were made of sturdy stuff.

I roomed there that fall with my good friends Coonhunter and
Harvey, a noisy time but lots of fun. We spent the first few weekends
fixing up the basement into a primitive party room, with tables and
chairs, shelves for our beer mugs, and a place of honour for the fraternity beer keg. We had some wild parties down there but not bad
enough to draw complaints from neighbours or a visit from the police.
A few Mac Hall girls got caught in the fraternity dorm after their cur-
few time, though, and one of them was expelled, poor soul.

I SETTLED IN TO fourth year, which looked much more interesting as
we were finally getting into "real" veterinary subjects, such as small
and large animal medicine and surgery. By late September, I knew I
had to dump the car as there was no way that I could afford to repair
it. My pals and I scouted around town and finally found a used car lot
situated conveniently at the bottom of a fairly steep hill. One Saturday
morning, someone towed me to the top of that hill and I was able, with
the help of a good push, to coast the vehicle right up to the front of the

dealer's office. The car windows were all cracked but, when we rolled them down, the cracks didn't show. I came away with $200 cash and a guilty conscience, but relieved to be liberated from my car.

At the beginning of the term I had been elected president of our fraternity, which was a great honour and privilege. At that time there were five chapters of the OTS veterinary fraternity, one in Guelph and four at US universities. Every year one of the chapters hosted a small convention, and in 1956 it was held at the University of Alabama in Auburn. George Heath borrowed a car from his sister so the five of us could drive down and back. George had promised his sister that he would do all the driving but he almost got us all killed by going through a red light. He then admitted that he was colour-blind and we figured out that this town's traffic lights had been installed upside down, reversing the colour sequence. The rest of us took over the driving.

We took a side trip to Lexington where we spent the day visiting some of Kentucky's most prominent horse farms. In Auburn, we were put up in a fraternity house and generally had a great time. It came as a shock, though, to have our meals served by a contingent of young black waiters in white jackets. The way the Alabama boys treated these fellows made us uncomfortable, with lots of references to "niggers" and a blatant we-are-better-than-them approach. It was our first experience with segregation and racism. On the way home, we stopped at a tavern for something to eat and were confronted with two entrances—one for Whites and one for Blacks. Being very stupidly righteous, we chose to enter through the Blacks' entrance and were promptly thrown out by some huge black men (which shouldn't have come as a surprise). After that, we mostly ate at roadside barbecues, and at one place, someone bought a quart of "white lightning." As its name suggests, it seemed to dissolve in your mouth before you could even swallow it. Split five ways it didn't do too much damage—we escaped with just headaches—but that one quart was enough.

THE FALL PROGRESSED AND I spent as much spare time as I could with Phyl. I was proud to introduce her to all my college friends and they teased me endlessly about being "in love" and our "upcoming nuptials." She was working her heart out as a special nurse, either in the hospital or in people's homes, for $12 a shift, and saving every penny she could. I had various jobs around the college for which I was paid the princely sum of twenty-five cents an hour. Our final exam of the fall term was scheduled for December 20; Phyl and I decided to get married in Toronto on December 21. Her brother Terry and his wife, Marilyn, had kindly offered to help us make arrangements at their church and to put on a reception for us at their home after the wedding.

In the meantime, we were looking for a place to live after we married. One of my professors, Dr. Jack Cote, had been born and raised in Guelph and told me his mother still lived in their large family home with several of his brothers and sisters, and that at one end of his mother's house there was a very small apartment. We quickly went to see it, immediately liked Mrs. Cote, and decided that we would take the apartment. Phyl gave her two old biddy landladies two weeks' notice and we moved into 302 Eramosa Road.

The place was truly tiny. The front door opened directly into the living room, which led to the kitchen, dining room, bathroom and bedroom. The double bed—once we squeezed it in there—took up the entire bedroom, so to make the bed we had to stand on it. There were no cupboards or closets at all, so we bought a used wardrobe and put it in the dining room. But it was like a palace to us, and Phyl soon made it homey. We bought an old sofa and a used Admiral TV set that was missing its buttons and needed a pair of pliers to turn it on or change channels. Phyl spent the next few weeks at her sewing machine making her own wedding dress, which I thought was simply amazing, especially as she was working at least one, sometimes two shifts a day, six or seven days a week.

As the December date drew near, Phyl went down to Toronto to stay with her brother Terry and her mum, who had come from Vancouver. Meanwhile, I studied for the eight exams that were upon us, finishing the last one just before noon on the twentieth. Coonhunter and I planned to catch the train to Toronto and find our way to a hotel where about fifteen or twenty of my classmates had rented a room for my stag party. As we settled into our seats on the train, Coonhunter produced a bottle of Drambuie.

By the time we got to Toronto, the bottle was empty and we were in pretty rough shape. We got to the hotel at about 6:00 p.m. and the guys were well into party mode. The food they had ordered quickly disappeared and we reverted to the drink of the day, rye and ginger ale. We held up until about midnight when Coonhunter and I crawled into bed. There is absolutely no doubt that I was more than plastered. The wedding was scheduled for 11:00 the next morning.

I was not feeling at all well the next morning, but struggled into my one and only suit and, with Coonhunter, took a taxi to the church. Phyl's brother Terry was to give her away and her youngest brother, Roger, was to be my best man. Because of the expense, my family and my best friend, Tom White, were unable to attend. Mrs. McLorg was there, of course, with Phyl's sister-in-law, Marilyn. A friend of the family, Marian Murphy, was Phyl's maid of honour, and a dozen or so of my classmates came along.

Phyl looked radiant in the dress she'd made and I was the happiest groom in the world. Roger, bless his heart, was somehow able to make a sound recording of the ceremony and later on presented us with a 33 rpm record. We had engaged a photographer and he took some wonderful pictures—the proofs we saw were superb. (Sadly, by the time we had saved up enough to order the photos, the photographer had vanished.)

All the guys showed up at Terry and Marilyn's house for the reception and, being a bit subdued from the previous night, they pretty much behaved themselves. Mrs. McLorg and Marilyn put on an amazing Lobster Newburg lunch and Terry sprang for champagne. As the celebration wound down, Phyl changed into a Black Watch tartan suit and we took our leave in the little green Austin that Phyl's mum had given us. The guys had put signs all over the car and a string of tin cans underneath, which trailed behind us, attracting a fair amount of attention as we drove out of Toronto. We grinned and waved at all the well-wishers, and before we hit the freeway we pulled over to dispose of the evidence.

We had $100 to spend and had decided that we would go to New York City.[9] At 6:00 p.m. we arrived at Niagara Falls, where the border official greeted us with, "Just married, eh?" I asked him how he knew and he just winked at me, with my white shirt and tie, and suit jacket

I married the love of my life, Phyllis McLorg, on December 21, 1956.

with a carnation still in the lapel. We spent our first night together in a small hotel on the US side of Niagara Falls.

It took us a couple of days to get close to New York and I was pretty nervous driving through the Lincoln Tunnel. We found our way to the bottom of Eighth Avenue and I started driving up amongst a swarm of big yellow taxis. I think our tiny car was the only non-taxi on the street and, with Ontario plates, it drew a lot of curious stares from the taxi drivers.

It took us a while to find a hotel that we could afford—we settled on $4 per night for the room and $6 per day for parking! We spent our days wandering around Lower Manhattan and eating at kiosks. *My Fair Lady* was playing and we decided to splurge on this one big performance—a chance to see Rex Harrison and Julie Andrews—so I went off at six one morning to line up for tickets. It was cold and snowing and the box office didn't open until 8:00 a.m. By 8:30, I was about third or fourth from the booth when the "sold out" sign went up—a big disappointment for us both.

We headed home, but along the way I drove the car over a curb and punctured the gas tank. Luckily, Phyl was a big fan of Wrigley's Juicy Fruit gum so, armed with a big wad of it, I crawled under the car and stuffed it into the hole. It did the job and was still there plugging the hole when we sold the car a year and a half later. We arrived back in Guelph on New Year's Eve, broke but happy.

COLLEGE WENT WELL FOR me that spring term: I had a wife, good food and a quiet place to study. My grades improved and that spring I stood twentieth out of sixty or so. Phyl had steady work and soon discovered she was pregnant. We were very excited by this event and used to spend our evenings watching and feeling the baby kick. Her mum came to stay in an apartment that she had rented not far from our place. We stayed in Guelph that summer and I was fortunate enough to get a position with the college, working on rotation through the various clinics. We were paid but not a great deal.

On the morning of September 6, Phyl proudly delivered our daughter Kathryn Ann into the world. We were the proudest parents as we brought her home, marvelling at this tiny being, especially her little hands and fingers. I bought a box of cigars and handed them out to classmates, professors—actually to anyone who put his hand out. Boy, was I proud!

Phyl had found and lined a basket, which served as a bassinet. Having an infant in the house was a huge learning curve for both of us but Phyl's mum—having raised five of her own—was a great teacher. This little being certainly changed our lives! With the apartment being so small, we used to put Kathy to sleep in the bathtub. As she grew up, I told her that she got the dimple in her chin from sleeping in the tub under a dripping tap, and for years she believed me!

Phyl's mum pitched right in to help us, taking on whatever was necessary, especially babysitting. Phyl went back to work as soon as she was able, leaving Kathy with her mum. I made a place to study in the basement although it was so humid down there that I had to hang a bag of calcium chloride from a floor joist to collect the moisture, which would drip into a bucket that I emptied periodically. But as the summer ended, life was good. We were happy, we had a beautiful, healthy little girl, and the future looked bright.

Now in my final year, I had a heavy workload as well as a weekend job at the college. I really enjoyed the coursework, though, as we were spending more time in clinics than in lecture rooms. We were divided into threesomes, so Coonhunter, Dunc Sinclair and I teamed up. We were rotated every three weeks between large animals, small animals, and the ambulatory clinic. When we were on ambulatory duty, we were expected to be there day and night to take calls. Luckily, my team let me off from time to time to go home to visit my wife and tiny daughter. Mrs. McLorg was always there to hold things together for us.

That fall, a new graduate from the UK, Tom Alexander, arrived to work in the large animal clinic. He was a great favourite with all of us and he loved to party. One day it was his job to show us how to castrate a two-year-old colt.[10] He decided to take our class out to a soccer field next to the highway and give us a real-world demonstration of how to anaesthetize and castrate a colt and, just as importantly, how to get him back on his feet without injury. Unfortunately, while Tom was trying to administer the anaesthetic, the colt broke loose and ran off down the middle of the highway dragging a long cotton rope, with Tom running frantically behind it. After about half a mile, the colt finally tired, having miraculously avoided the busy highway traffic. We all had a great laugh at Tom's expense.

Around this time, each of us began to consider our options after graduation. The majority of my classmates wanted to go into small animal practice. I was most interested in equine practice but, at that time, there were no jobs in Canada at all. Dr. Maplesden, head of the ambulatory clinic, who had a PhD from Cornell, tried to talk me into postgraduate studies at Cornell. Of course I was flattered and in retrospect it would have been the astute thing to do. But at the time, after spending the better part of five years in college, I felt that I had had enough of the academic end of veterinary medicine and was ready to sink my teeth into practice. I was also drawn like a magnet to the West, back home.

I heard that an old veterinarian in Kamloops, BC, was looking for a graduate to work in his mixed practice. The location (being in the Interior and not that far from Kelowna) and knowing that horses and beef cattle would make up a good chunk of the practice certainly appealed to me. And I knew my options were limited: at that time there was only room for one practitioner in most of the larger Interior cities. Even Penticton didn't have a vet, and Dr. Clerke in Kelowna didn't need help. So in January 1958, Phyl and I decided to go look things over during Christmas break. We left Kathy with Phyl's mum and boarded the CPR train, coach class, for Kamloops.

We started off with a big thermos of coffee, sandwiches and cookies. As we travelled west, the temperature dropped and from Winnipeg on, our coach was so cold we could see our breath as we sat and talked. Our food and coffee soon ran out and we had to make do with the terrible coach-class food, very occasionally slipping into the dining car to get something decent.

After three or four uncomfortable days, we were relieved to step off the train in Kamloops and settle into our very inexpensive room at the Princess Margaret Hotel. We spent some time with the vet and his wife at the Kamloops Veterinary Hospital. He seemed quite nice, and she had us in for coffee and sandwiches.

Phyl's mom, "Gran-Gran," with Phyl and Kathy at Kathy's first birthday party.

The hospital building was divided in half, front to back, and they lived in one half. The hospital itself was unimpressive. The pharmacy was cluttered with myriad bottles, jugs and pots; the labels on most were unfamiliar to me. The old vet had graduated from OVC in 1905, so it was understandable that things weren't exactly up to date. He offered me a salary of $500 a month and an opportunity to purchase the practice within a year or two for $40,000 (the annual gross, which was the standard way of calculating the worth of a practice then), lock, stock and barrel. I can't remember when we made the decision to take his offer, but take it we did. We didn't really have much choice.

Mom and Dad drove up from Kelowna to join us for dinner in Kamloops and then gave us a lift to Salmon Arm where we could pick up the train. It was very cold and, with no heater, we almost froze to death in Dad's old car. We boarded the train that night at 11:00 and headed back through the frigid Rockies, across the equally frozen prairies to Guelph.

WE WERE DELIGHTED TO be back in our tiny flat with our little bundle of joy. The spring term went along smoothly, punctuated by the usual fun and games with the Aggies. The Aggies still seemed to have a lot of time on their hands for partying and taking out Mac Hall girls, much to the envy of Vet students. Many of them had cars, which were parked, usually unlocked, in the residence parking lots. One winter night some Vet students took a collection of cat feces from the kennel rooms, broke into the Aggie cars and used tongue depressors to smear their collection into the heater grills. Mac Hall was about a block's drive away and by the time the Aggie owners had warmed up their vehicles and arrived there to pick up their girlfriends, the stench in the car had "bloomed" to an unbearable level. Apparently it took much painstaking effort, working in the cold with buckets and toothbrushes, to get the grills clean. The guys in our year had nothing to do with this but, nonetheless, we were worried about retaliation. Luckily for me, I was living off campus!

Another night, the Aggies took a mature Angus bull over to Mac Hall and turned him loose in the Common Room, the large living room where girls waited for their dates. Apparently the Aggies thought that the bull would be discovered in short order but, unfortunately, as the girls slept, the bull spent the entire night destroying the room. We were oblivious until the next morning, when we were all assembled (all two thousand of us) on the lawn in front of the college, and marched over to Mac Hall for a walk through the remains of the Common Room. Every student was assessed an equal amount to cover the cost of repairing the damage. The Aggie students, as can be imagined, were not popular.

On one weekend some medical students from the Western University (London) came up for an event and were allowed to eat in our dining hall. Evidently, they had been inspired by the Guelph "spirit" and had prepared themselves by scavenging in their own anatomy lab. Several Vet and Aggie students found human ears and other body parts in their jacket pockets that afternoon.

One of our favourite professors was Dr. Chuck Roe, who specialized in large animal medicine and surgery. He was the one who usually took our rotations through the large animal infirmary where we practised diagnosing and treating ailing animals brought in by local farmers. One of our classmates, Albert van der Meulen, was attempting to catheterize a Holstein cow. He was in a loose box and the two other members of his team were holding the cow. Dr. Roe was in an adjacent stall with another group when Albert called out, "How can you tell if the catheter is in the right place?" Dr. Roe, without a second thought, said, "Suck on it." According to his teammates, that's exactly what Albert did and then he knew immediately: he was indeed in the right place. Dr. Roe (and the students who were with him) had to go outside to collect themselves. Poor Albert.

Another day, when Dunc Sinclair, Coonhunter and I were on small animal duty, a prominent and wealthy family brought in a parrot that had been in their family for at least seventy-five years. It had a large growth on its head and, after a long consultation with Professor Archibald, the family decided that the parrot should be euthanized. Dunc, Coonhunter and I were dispatched with the parrot to the kennel room to do the deed and then return it to Dr. Archibald and the waiting clients.

Dunc moved the parrot from its cage into a small kennel while we prepared for its demise. When we were ready, Coonhunter volunteered to reach in and bring the parrot out onto the table. The next thing we knew there was a bloodcurdling screech. The parrot had Coonhunter by his index finger and there was blood everywhere. We got the parrot off his finger but as soon as we had Coonhunter bandaged up, he grabbed the guzzler."1 Clearly on the warpath, Coon-hunter flung open the door of the kennel, put the loop of the guzzler over the parrot's head and pulled on the handle. To our utter horror, the parrot's head flew right off and its body was bouncing around in the kennel with blood spraying all over us—what a mess! How would we return the dead parrot to its waiting owners now? How could we ever explain this? We cast around desperately for a solution and, thank God, one presented itself. The perfect box had arrived that morning with a small shipment of instruments: the parrot and his head fitted quite nicely inside. To prevent anyone from viewing the remains, we wrapped the box in several layers of adhesive tape, cleaned up Dunc as best we could and sent him out to deliver the body. We never heard a thing about it and, as a matter of fact, it seemed that Dr. Archibald was impressed with our makeshift casket.

As THE TERM WORE on and final exams approached, something else was affecting our little family. Phyl had become pregnant once again, and we were looking forward to a new addition sometime in the early fall of 1958. Graduation would take place in about mid-May, two weeks or so after exams. Dr. Milne had kindly arranged for me to go to Lexington, Kentucky, to spend those two weeks with a very famous equine practitioner, Dr. Delano Proctor, and his colleagues. They had a state-of-the-art equine hospital and treated horses from all over the world. I was very excited about this opportunity, packed and ready long before I was to leave. Sadly, the night before I was to leave, Phyl had a miscarriage, an event that was devastating to both of us and to her mum.

Of course I cancelled my Lexington plans immediately and spent the next while with her as we began preparing for our trip west. Life might have turned out quite differently for us if I'd gone, but for better or worse, who can know?

After five long years, the day that we had all been waiting for, graduation day, finally arrived. We were all decked out in our gowns and mortarboard hats and marched up to Memorial Hall for the ceremony. Fifty-eight of our original seventy-four graduated. I did well that year, standing third in the class. My good friends, Rick Miller and Dunc Sinclair, stood first and second. I won several prizes and was especially

I graduated from OVC in 1958, in high spirits after discovering that I was third in my class.

proud because Mom and Dad and my sister, Wendy, had come all the way from Kelowna to see me graduate. My Uncle Milton, Dad's brother, also came from Ohio. It was the only time I ever saw him—a large affable man, someone you immediately liked. He and Dad hadn't seen each other since Dad was six years old so they had a wonderful reunion.[12]

That spring, we bought a 1956 Chevrolet station wagon from Red Fraser, a 1954 graduate, who was one of the clinicians on ambulatory clinic. I don't know where the $1,700 came from, but it was likely from Mrs. McLorg. Phyl and I were thrilled at having an almost new and dependable vehicle that could get us home to BC. I built a primitive roof rack for it, and Rick Miller gave us a heavy canvas cover, army surplus, that had once been used to cover an airplane engine. I got our old TV set and some other items up on top of the car, covered them up and tied them down. Not having a dog at that time simplified things.

We had forged a lifelong friendship with Rick and Alex Miller, who lived only a few blocks away. As married students, we had a good deal in common, and Phyl and Alex had really hit it off. The night before we were due to leave, the Millers invited us for dinner. We took Kathy with us, which proved to be a real mistake as all four Miller children were ill with bad tummies and colds.

We left early the next morning, but by mid-afternoon, it became obvious that Kathy had picked up a real flu bug and was suffering from fever, diarrhea and cold symptoms. By the time we got to Minnesota, she was showing signs of dehydration and we started to really worry. We stopped at Duluth where, by luck, we found an older, very kindly pediatrician. It was a toss-up as to whether or not she should be hospitalized. Because Phyl was a nurse, the doctor gave us some medication and sent us on our way. I drove and Phyl sat in the back, patiently caring for our sick and cranky eight-month-old.

By the time we got to the BC border at Osoyoos, Kathy had begun to improve. The weather was unseasonably hot for that time of year (105°F when we got to Kamloops) and when we passed Falkland there was a good-sized forest fire burning beside the highway—we were lucky just to get through. At Monte Lake, we spotted my new employer's car beside the road where he was calving a heifer in a nearby corral. We waited until he was finished and he led us to our rented house on Valleyview Drive in Kamloops, where we started a new chapter in our three lives.

WHAT DOESN'T KILL YOU MAKES YOU STRONGER

IN THE SWELTERING HEAT of an unseasonably hot May day in 1958, we unpacked our few belongings in our little rented house on Valleyview Drive, finding it just as hot in the house as it was in the driveway. We were still bringing boxes in from the car when a lovely young woman appeared, bearing a cake and introducing herself as our next-door neighbour, Anne Munro. Her husband, Don, was a forester with one of the local lumber companies and, at that time, they had three children. The friendship that started that very day has endured these many years.

Anne quickly sized up our complete lack of furniture and hurried over with a card table and two chairs. We must have slept on the floor that night because it wasn't until the next morning that we bought a bed, a used refrigerator and a few other items from Dalgliesh's furniture store. We had inherited a half-acre yard that had once had been a large vegetable garden. In those last few days before starting my career as a veterinarian, with a shovel borrowed from the Munros, I prepared enough planting space to feed an army. My hands blistered and I got a good sunburn, but you could grow almost anything in Kamloops and we soon had an abundant vegetable garden.

June 1 marked the first day of my career as a veterinarian; I was proud and excited as I headed off to work. Reality hit pretty quickly, though. My most vivid memory of those first days at work is of my complete horror. The single kennel room, for starters, was nothing short of a hellhole. The temperature in the windowless kennel room must have been in the nineties, and, unbelievably, there was no run for the dogs. The kennels, instead of being lined with newspaper, were lined with dusty paper sacks from the local feed mill. I gave the lazy kennel attendant the weekend off and spent most of it scrubbing and cleaning.

Even with the kennels clean, it was distressing to see the number of sick and dying dogs that filled them. In those days, distemper in dogs was all too common, and this old vet's unique "treatment" only contributed to the mortality rate. With a rationale known only to him, he treated dogs with distemper with a double dose of live distemper vaccine: most often, the dog would die within a week. His small animal surgery usually resulted in failure or infection. It was acutely embarrassing to be associated with the small animal end of the practice.

And the large animal side wasn't much better. The doc knew a good deal about horses, but I wasn't impressed with how he handled cattle. Penicillin and several other antibiotics had only recently come into use and a very small dose of penicillin would work wonders at that time. We'd been taught to use the recommended dosage, but because these products were still quite expensive, he used just a fraction of the recommended dose. In one case, he treated a mature bull with foot rot using 5 cc's of penicillin. The dose should have been at least 30 cc's, with a repeat dose daily for three to five days.

"YOU COULD FRY AN egg on the sidewalk" was not an urban myth in Kamloops—almost every year the *Kamloops Sentinel* newspaper would feature the success of someone who enlisted the sidewalk of the main street for this purpose. Very few houses had air conditioning and it was unheard of in cars. Phyl and Kathy endured the heat by playing outside in a plastic pool and running through the sprinkler. For me, keeping drugs cool in the back of the car while I was on call required careful strategizing to ensure a regular turnover of ice packs in the cooler box. In the winter I used the same box with a hot water bottle to keep things from freezing.

As fall approached, the practice focused on beef cattle. At that time, both the provincial and federal governments were deeply involved in eradicating tuberculosis and brucellosis in cattle. Practitioners were paid $1 per head to vaccinate calves for brucellosis and $30 a day to blood-test entire cow herds, while the federal government veterinarians were responsible for TB testing. Both tests were mandatory for cattle being shipped for export. Calfhood vaccination was a big and lucrative part of the practice—about ten thousand head every year at $1 apiece. I was soon busy vaccinating calves at the stockyards, which got me out of the clinic and brought me into contact with a good many of the local ranchers and cowboys.

Later that fall the old vet presented me with a legal document setting out the details of the sale of his practice. This was a pretty big step for me. I had absolutely zero knowledge of legal and business practices—we didn't cover this at college and my poor dad, as an orphan and a schoolteacher, had little business experience to pass on. I took the document home where Phyl and I read it over together: immediately, she was suspicious. At her suggestion, we took it to Mr. Verchere, a partner in the foremost law company in Kamloops. After reading it over, he asked me if I realized that I was taking on a $40,000 mortgage as well as paying $40,000 for the practice. *My* understanding had been that I was to purchase the practice—lock, stock and barrel—for $40,000! I was stunned, angry, and not the least bit interested in this arrangement.

But the doc wasn't through with me yet. I had been getting a monthly cheque, as we'd agreed, for $500 per month. A few months into our relationship, though, I received what I thought was a cheque, endorsed it, and cashed it at the Bank of Montreal. Just before Christmas, the bank manager phoned our house asking, "When do you plan to arrange payment to cover your $500 loan?" My "cheque" had been a banknote! The old vet and I had a row over this and he finally gave me a $500 cheque to cover the note, but I was sure now that I couldn't trust him. Interestingly, a few years later, the entire concrete block wall that formed the side of his clinic collapsed into the adjoining alley, exposing the entire clinic. I was pleased that I was not the owner.

IN THE SPRING OF 1959, Phyl had been pushing Kathy around the neighbourhood in her stroller and had spotted a lot for sale. We agreed almost immediately to buy it and built our first house on it that fall. My mom and dad mortgaged their own house and provided the down payment. We arranged an NHA mortgage[1]—twenty years at 5 percent—at a repayment rate not much more than the $100 per month we were paying for rent. The exterior of the house was stucco but, to save money, I took on the painting of all the wood trim. The NHA inspector insisted that all the exterior painting, a base coat and two finishing coats, be completed before we could move in. He even had a mirror attached to a stick that he used to check that the tops of all the doors had been painted! I painted the gable ends of the house with early winter sleet running down my neck, but we moved in just in time for Christmas and were delighted with our new home.

That same month, I submitted two months' notice in favour of setting up my own practice. The only way we could swing it was to set me up in our small, unfinished basement where I could provide small animal services, and I'd spend the rest of my time doing large animal work, which was done off-site anyway. The drug and instrument companies allowed me to order what I felt was needed, offering generous credit. Mr. White, Tom's dad and a partner in the Kelowna machine shop, made me half a dozen metal dog kennels and a few smaller cat kennels. With these, I set up shop in the basement, using our old ping-pong table for examinations and surgery. Phyl whipped me up some surgical drapes and gowns on the sewing machine, and we were ready to open our door for business!

I have to admit it was scary, though, when March 1 arrived and I got my last paycheque. I felt very much alone and worried about trying to make enough money to keep us going. Luckily, it didn't take too long for people to show up in our driveway with dogs and cats, in spite of the primitive set-up in our basement.

Calving season was just beginning and I was soon called out to deliver large calves out of small heifers. Sometimes they needed Caesarean deliveries and I performed them using only local anaesthetic, with the heifer standing. The ranchers hadn't seen this done before and usually they were quite impressed. Operators of some of the larger ranches told me that they had pretty much given up on veterinarians because—especially in situations like this—the outcome had most often been the death of both the heifer and the calf, but that they'd give me

The company that built our house also built our first clinic. The Kamloops Veterinary Clinic opened in 1960.

one chance to make good. I had to be careful because so often the cowboys and ranchers left a straining animal for too long or had inflicted considerable damage while trying to deliver the cow themselves. All too often, I was presented with a suffering heifer or cow that was in shock or almost dead. In those situations, I would refuse to work on her and would bill for the call, which certainly got their attention— they soon learned to call me early and leave the vet work to a vet.

I was also fortunate to be given some testing work by the local government veterinarian. The pay was $30 a day and I had to do one hundred head to qualify for a "day." I could usually get through a hundred head in less than half a day, but if I kept working it annoyed the government vet; it made him look bad. I soon learned to use my afternoons for other work. Not only did this give me some income, but it put me in contact with more and more ranchers. It was actually quite busy that first spring, but the summer, as is usual in a beef practice, was quiet. Things picked up rapidly again in the fall. By then, we knew we would make it.

Over several months, it became increasingly difficult to do the small animal practice out of the house. We decided that the business was doing well enough that I should look for a more suitable place from which to practise. We had become good friends with our neighbours and one of them, Molly Sjoquist, was in real estate. She knew people at the company that had built our house, and suggested we have them build us a veterinary clinic. This worked for me because I was very busy with fall cattle work. Within a couple of weeks, they had identified a nice piece of property in Valleyview, about a mile from home. Phyl's mum came to our aid with the down payment, while Molly arranged a mortgage for the balance through Peter Stratton, a good friend of hers from Vancouver. After only a few months, the Kamloops Veterinary Clinic was built and equipped. In the fall of 1960, we proudly hung out our shingle and opened for business. I hired a young man, Bob Jones, as an assistant.

Business increased immediately but before long, we had a new set of issues to deal with. The clinic was located in a residential zone (we didn't know anything about zoning and the builders had overlooked this) and with kennel space for approximately forty dogs and cats, the neighbours—rightfully—began to complain about the barking. We installed air conditioning that allowed us to keep the windows closed in the kennel rooms, which helped considerably, but we were under a lot of pressure to close or move.

And we had another problem that was just as serious: an erratic water supply. With no domestic water service in the entire subdivision, we relied on water pumped from the river. The clinic had a pump in the basement and a two-hundred-foot line to an intake in the river. The sandy river bottom was prone to shifting, though, and the intake would get plugged, shutting down the whole system. I'd have to haul water from home until a plumber could get the system back in service. This happened often and was a huge problem, to say the least. I was running a mixed practice, and it was difficult enough just to juggle the large animal calls with the dog and cat portion. To accommodate both sets of clients, I did small animal surgery in the early mornings before going on calls, then opened again for evening office hours three nights a week. It all added up to a very long, seven-day week; packing water was the last thing I wanted to be doing!

MY HEART WAS ALWAYS in the large animal practice, and the time I spent on ranches, though physically demanding, was fascinating and rewarding.

Pregnancy Testing Comes to the BC Beef Industry

MY FIRST REAL BREAK came in the fall of 1959 when Dale
Cochrane, the manager of the Diamond S Ranch at Pavilion,
asked me if I thought I could pregnancy test their beef herd.
They had six or seven hundred head of cows to check; by
identifying the empty cows, they could avoid feeding them
through the winter. Most ranchers were still in the habit of
selling the cows that had not produced a calf that year, culling
the "bad mothers" and "dry cows." They didn't realize that,
in fact, most of these so-called dry cows were indeed pregnant
(having been on the range all summer) and were probably
worth keeping. Savvy cattle buyers were aware of this, bought
these cows, and re-sold them as pregnant cows at a premium
price. Dale, being from Oregon where pregnancy testing was
done routinely, wanted to use this modern procedure.

I had had a little bit of experience with pregnancy testing
on dairy cows in college and wasn't in a position to turn this
work down, but still... While testing several cows might be
normal on an Ontario dairy farm, I had no idea how I was going to manage doing several hundred! I had some arm-length
rubber gloves and some lubricant that I'd used during the
calving season and not much else. I would have to figure out
a method of doing this kind of volume, and doing it quickly.

I looked forward to working with Dale, a large, strong
man about thirty years old, who had been born and raised on
a ranch near Bend, Oregon.[2] I arrived at the ranch the night
before we were to begin. At this time, Col. Spencer's (of Spencer's Stores) son Victor owned the historic Diamond S and
was staying in the owner's quarters of the large, old ranch
house, with several of his Vancouver buddies. I was put up in
the adjoining bunkhouse with the cowboys. There was a large
kitchen between these two parts of the house, complete with

a huge iron stove and a cook. At one end of the kitchen there was a long table where everyone on the ranch ate their meals. As was common in those days, only the owner's quarters and the kitchen were heated. The bunkhouse was very cold. Cowboys were paid $40 a month plus board.

Preg-testing a whole herd takes a good team of cowboys and a decent corral and chute set-up. The cow has to be caught by the head in a squeeze that virtually immobilizes her. She tends to thrash around initially, but once she has settled down, my job was to get down into the chute behind the cow to perform the examination. An experienced vet can identify the cow's uterus through the rectal wall and feel the developing fetus from about sixty days post-conception. You can estimate when the cow will calve and, on the empty ones, check for the various abnormalities that render a cow sterile. The whole process takes only thirty to forty-five seconds, but it takes at least that long to get a cow settled in the squeeze. Of course, at the time, I was so green that I was lucky if I could even tell if a cow was pregnant! The stakes were high and I was pretty worried—costly mistakes would destroy my budding reputation.

Dale had the cows corralled the night before and had kept them off feed and water to facilitate my rectal examination. This particular corral set-up was about as good as one could expect at that time, with a pen off the main corral large enough to hold fifteen or twenty cows, leading into a chute. At the end of the chute was a squeeze with a head gate that allowed the operator to catch and hold one cow at a time while I got to know her personally. However, in order to get in behind the cow, I had to wait until each one was caught in the squeeze before climbing over the rails and down into the chute. The whole process of climbing up and down the side of a six-foot chute was slow and tiring—definitely a young vet's game— and the more tired I got, the more often I'd rip a hole in my $7 glove. But I investigated every cow. We painted the pregnant cows with a stripe across their backs, left the empties unmarked, and kept them separate until they were shipped.

To the best of my knowledge, this was the first beef herd in BC to be preg-tested. That first year, starting each morning at daybreak and working until dark with no lunch break, it took us two full days to do approximately six hundred cows.

It was the Canada Packers cattle buyer, Reg Hook, who bought the empty cows and put them into his feedlot to fatten them up before shipping to the Canada Packers plant in Vancouver. In early spring, he called in a great fury to tell me that, "these so-called empty cows are calving all over my feedlot!" I was so unsure of myself that I believed him and drove out there to apologize. But, of course, Reg was just pulling my leg, capitalizing on how inexperienced I was… Everyone had a good laugh when I got there, but my relief was palpable.

After my initial preg-testing experience at Diamond S, I quickly learned to dress in a rubber suit and have a good supply of yellow arm-length rubber gloves. I also started using liquid soap in a pail of warm water as lubricant. I had decided to charge a dollar a head for the first one hundred cows and fifty cents per head for the remainder. As preg-testing caught on, I gave smaller ranchers a break, charging a dollar for the first twenty-five and fifty cents thereafter. At some point I became known as "The Man with the Golden Arm."

There were a few cows that weren't pleased with my examination, though. Some of them would kick or thrash around, coming close to breaking my arm or dislocating my shoulder. Usually there was lots of snow within easy reach, and I'd keep a pile of snowballs by the chute. With an especially ornery cow, I'd get even by putting a snowball up her arse. She'd go flying out of the chute, snorting, with her tail standing straight up! It sure made the cowboys laugh.

I felt at home with the cowboys, ranch managers and owners, trying to help solve some of the problems they faced. The geographical remoteness, varied demands and rustic set-ups of the various ranches made the work challenging and often had me on the road at night, or away from home for days at a time. But we were young and healthy and had always expected to work hard to get established, so we pressed on.

I MET SOME COLOURFUL characters along the way, especially among the ranchers. Their wives, too, were a breed of their own. It took a special kind of woman to live on these isolated ranches with only their kids and endless work for company. Many of these operations were scratching just to make ends meet, and luxuries like extended health benefits, pension plans and life insurance were almost unheard of. This was really hard on the women, who were often left caring for a disabled husband or even widowed, with very little income. And some of the men were pretty rough around the edges.

I remember having lunch at one place where the rancher had married a "woman of ill repute" and installed her in this godforsaken, broken-down ranch house miles from nowhere. His widely broadcasted intention was to "get a raft of kids going here to help me work this place." His wife made us a hearty lunch but complained about not having anything to bake desserts with. Her point was that, without a second vehicle, she could never go to town herself to get the groceries she wanted. Her husband gestured toward her shapely bottom and said simply, "Quit yer whining and do what you like. You're the one sitting on a goddamned gold mine."

One old-timer I really loved was E.M. Hall. When I knew him he was still, at more than eighty years old, an imposing figure, well over six feet tall and well built. He loved to tell stories of his past. At one time, he had made a living playing poker in the US and had led a colourful life. For many years, one of Mr. Hall's close neighbours was Pete Cordonier. Pete had a nondescript herd of Herefords and annoyed Mr. Hall by letting his bulls wander down the road and mess with Mr. Hall's purebred cows. At some point, Mr. Hall lost patience, took his .30-30 rifle, and blew the horns off several of Pete's bulls. Pete was motivated after that to keep his fences in better shape.

Mr. Hall surprised me one day by presenting me with a pair of brand new oxford shoes, saying that he couldn't wear them because his feet were swelling up. I very much appreciated this gift; I didn't have a pair of decent dress shoes. When we opened our first clinic in Valleyview, he called in with a large, framed picture of a group of Hereford cattle in a pasture, which I proudly hung in our waiting room.

PHYL WAS ABSOLUTELY MARVELLOUS, putting in days as long as mine, looking after Kathy, doing the shopping, cooking and gardening, and washing all the clinic laundry, which most times was quite literally a bloody mess. She put up with my being away most of the time, and soon we were thrilled to find out she was pregnant again. For several months, we anticipated a new addition to our small family, but sadly, in February 1959, this pregnancy ended in a stillbirth. We were both devastated; Phyl took it especially hard. By great good fortune, however, we managed to get pregnant again and on February 5, 1960, our son came into the world. We named him Terrence for his uncle and Cameron for our good friend, Mr. Cameron of Kelowna.

We had a few good rows, though. At one point, I thought we had sufficient money in the bank for me to invest in a shotgun for hunting pheasants and ducks while I was on calls. I was a pretty good shot and had visions of free food on the table. I found just the right one, a perfect match to the beautiful .30-06 Browning rifle Phyl's mum had given me for a wedding present. Accounting was not my strong suit, however, and I was soon faced with an overdraft and a very angry, unhappy wife. Here we were at home struggling to make ends meet, and I had bought a $200 shotgun! That was the end of my involvement in the business part of the practice; Phyl took over and straightened things out right away. We hired my old school friend Tom White (who was nearby in an accounting practice in Williams Lake) to set up our books. Bob did the billing, and I was relegated to the easier, most agreeable part of the whole process—making the bank deposits.

LIFE MOVED ON FOR my school friends as well. Tom White had married Maureen Monaghan ("Mo") and was having kids at the same pace as Phyl and I were. They had four wonderful children and bought the lot next to ours at Shuswap, where they built a cabin and became

Blowing Off Steam

EVERY SPRING, THE ANNUAL Bull Show and Sale served as a great excuse for some enthusiastic celebrations at the downtown watering holes. Cowboys and ranchers would often get a bit out of hand, resulting in occasional overnight bookings in the city jail. On one memorable occasion, cattle buyer Reg Hook and a few cowboys liberated several second-storey rooms of the Plaza Hotel of their furniture, throwing mattresses, chairs and anything that would move out the windows and onto Main Street. Of course these antics were frowned upon but, given how hard these guys worked all fall and winter, it was inevitable that they'd come to town and let off steam. It's what cowboys do... and the coast loggers were known for the same kind of behaviour in Vancouver.

even more of our extended family. Tom continued to ride in all the big equestrian events. He'd always been a better rider than I was—in fact, he became one of the best jumping horse riders in Canada and was chosen to ride for Canada in the Pan-American Games in Mexico.

Sandy Boyd married Molly Rendall, who was a well-known horse-woman in her own right, and as they raised their five children, they became increasingly involved in skiing. They owned and developed a ski hill near Vernon and their son, Rob, competed in world-class skiing events. They retired to a small house they built in the mountains above the Coldstream Valley.

Alf Fletcher married Heather Dunlop and went on to a full career as an official, steward and judge at the highest levels of equine competition. He held several roles with Jump Canada,[3] including its presidency, and was named "Official of the Year" in 2009. Sadly, Alf died the same year.

Things got busier and busier, especially in the spring and fall. I got pretty worn out, so I decided it was time to hire an additional veterinarian. We were able to find a Washington State (Pullman) graduate, Wes Marshall, who came to Kamloops with his wife, who was also a

Our son, Terry, almost two years old, already absorbed with machines,
Christmas 1961.

graduate veterinarian. We hit it off, and he soon became a partner with
all the legal documents signed and sealed. As it turned out, however,
there really wasn't sufficient work for two of us year-round and we
began to fall behind financially. We were finally forced to dissolve the
partnership, so we hired Gordon Elliott, a very good accountant in
Kamloops, who worked with our lawyer to straighten things out. The
practice was appraised, and in order to keep it, I had to take a bank
loan to buy Wes out. When the dust settled, I had two choices: declare
bankruptcy or hang in there on my own and work night and day until
we were solvent again. I chose the second option and the next two to
three years were tough. However, the practice continued to grow, and
soon I was racking up at least forty thousand miles a year on calls in the
car, as well as handling the busy small animal side.

Sandy Boyd and his wife, Molly, with their children at the christening of my godson, Ian.

IN THOSE DAYS, YOU could call Kamloops a cowtown—its economy depended largely on both the cattle and the forest industries. The town really came to life twice a year: in the fall with the Provincial Fat Stock Show and in the early spring with the Bull Show and Sale. In the fall, the ranchers and 4-H clubs would bring in their prize fat steers to be shown and sold. The fat steers were auctioned off, and the competition to buy the Grand Champion steer was always exciting, with the winning bid often made by a local restaurant or hotel. The Bull Show was made up of two-year-old purebreds that were shown and then sold to ranchers from all over BC and Alberta. A Grand Champion bull was always declared and usually got the top price at the auction. I was asked to check all the young bulls for soundness and health in general.

There were many young professional couples, like ourselves, starting out in Kamloops, and we began to have a bit of a social life,

though it was often curtailed by the demands of the practice. We took
our first break in September 1961 to spend a long weekend—just the
two of us—in Spokane. What I remember most about that weekend
was getting a flat tire on the way up the Monte Creek hill. We left on
a Friday evening and just as it was getting dark, we felt the tire go. It
would have to happen on our first break! In the process of changing
the tire, I dropped the spare on the road only to have it bounce and roll
down a steep bank into a creek. Scrambling down through the brush,
scratched and dusty, I completely lost my temper—I can still remember how furious I was. But I retrieved the tire, got it on the car and we
went on our way.

The practice was growing by leaps and bounds and I now had
seventy-five to a hundred ranches on my client list. The small animal
side had grown as well, and it appeared that soon there would be more
than I could handle again.

At some point, as if I didn't have enough to do, I was elected to the
board of directors of the Royal Inland Hospital. This was an interesting
diversion and I enjoyed the company of the other directors, especially
the board chairman, Gordon Nicol. I also became a founding director of

Our second son, Steven, age 15 months, in new gear on Christmas morning.

the BC Wildlife Park, which was struggling into existence. I joined the Gyro Club and had great fun at the evening meetings as often as I could fit them in. We met in a basement room of the Plaza Hotel, and after every meeting, five or six of us would stay on to play low-stakes poker with cards we had secreted away above a ceiling tile. Phyl and I enjoyed many club dinners and dances and made some wonderful friends.

Phyl delivered a healthy and beautiful second son, Steven, on October 9, 1961. Now with three children at home, Phyl was a very busy mother, and I regret that I wasn't able to be very helpful.

THE OTHER BIG EVENT of 1961 was our purchase of a leased lot at Shuswap Lake. We got a good-sized lot with 135 feet of lake frontage and hired Eddie Miege and his partner, Gus, to put in an access road and clear a building site. We had very little money to spend on a summer cabin, but Phyl saved the day by discovering that we could buy two Pan-Abode garages and, since they were precision cut, put them together—end to end—for a total of 800 square feet of living space.

The garage kits were dumped on the beach off a low-bed truck in February 1963, and Phyl and I packed each piece up to the building site,

Our Shuswap Lake cabin under construction in 1964.

where I had put in a foundation and subfloor. I took eight days off at Easter and, with the help of a very good Italian carpenter, Louis Basso, we completed the building in the eight days. I put in some internal partitions and we added a large deck along the front. Louis bought a caselot of glass and put in the windows. I think everything was done for around $2,000.

Of course, we had no power, no running water, no fridge, no phone and, of course, no indoor plumbing. We packed water from the lake in buckets, used a wood stove for cooking, an ice chest and blocks of ice to keep food cool, and coal oil and gas lanterns for light. The summer swimming was wonderful, and the peace and quiet provided a welcome respite. By sheer good fortune, our next-door neighbours turned out to be a veterinarian from Salmon Arm, Dr. Rex Mears, and his family, and it wasn't long before we'd become one big family. It turned out to be a wonderful place for us to recharge our batteries and the kids especially loved the summer days we spent there.

AFTER TWO YEARS OF independent practice, we had recovered from the brink of bankruptcy and I decided once again to try recruiting some help. I hired a new graduate from OVC, Al Purvis, who arrived with his wife, and I was able to take some time off that summer at Shuswap. Al's wife didn't take to Kamloops, though, and when pregnancy testing started in the fall, the ranchers didn't want an inexperienced new graduate and insisted that I do the work. This made it difficult for me and uncomfortable for Al too. He spent the fall doing the small animal work and handled routine calls and we made it through until Christmas. He and his wife then took a couple of weeks off, and then, as I had anticipated, Al gave his notice. He left at the end of February to take a job as track veterinarian at Hastings Park in Vancouver.

This really left me in the lurch because the busy calving season was around the corner. I got through that hectic period by literally working day and night. I remember too many times falling asleep while driving, and that became a real problem. I tried every known remedy but nothing seemed to work. I would often wake up as I hit the gravel on the side of the highway or find myself staring into the lights of an oncoming freight truck. I still can't figure how I managed, over all those years, to avoid a serious accident.

The three cowboys: Terry, me, and Steven.

After Al left, I hired a new Washington State graduate, Phil De Bok, who had been raised in Oregon. Phil turned out to be a real character, deaf as a post, unassuming, even shy. I didn't learn until later that he had graduated top of his class—he certainly didn't tell me. He arrived in his pickup with several large and noisy coonhounds and a complete set of exercise weights. He wasn't tall but it was easy to see that he used the weights and was exceptionally strong. He often came to dinner on Sunday nights and became a great favourite of our children.

Phil was a hard worker and proved to be a good veterinarian. That winter he spent weekends hunting cougars with his dogs and the local conservation officer. Sometimes he didn't show up on Mondays as he was trying to find his dogs somewhere in the mountains. He was with us for about a year when he was drafted into the US Army Medical Corps to serve in Vietnam. Unfortunately we lost touch with him but I know that he married a girl from Thailand, stayed in the army and

It was another one of Phyl's brilliant ideas to move our Valleyview clinic—lock, stock and barrel—onto a new lot in town.

became a highly respected general. Not bad for a kid who spent his spare time chasing cats.

It was around this time that we decided to move the practice into town. We were able to purchase a corner lot adjacent to the stockyards. A clinic there would be easily accessible to cattlemen, as well as to our small animal clientele. Phyl came up with the idea of physically moving our Valleyview clinic into town to become part of a new set-up. She even found a guy who specialized in moving houses. He loaded the whole building onto a flatbed truck and drove it to the new site one night when there was minimal traffic—it was quite a sight!

Our contractor set our old clinic down onto its new foundation and added to it, doubling its size and improving the layout. We added a large pharmacy, which we stocked with drugs and supplies needed by ranchers. Since we were located next to the stockyards, ranchers soon got used to coming in to make purchases on Sale Days. We enlarged the waiting room and added a dozen boarding kennels with heated floors down one side. It proved to be an excellent, affordable move. We sold the old lot, charging extra for the "basement already in place," and the purchasers built a new house right on top.

The practice continued to grow and at one time the large animal component was spread out over an area about the size of England. This meant a lot of driving, early mornings and late nights. I remember driving out of Kamloops on a call one morning at about 3:00. I happened to catch sight of our milkman delivering milk and I thought to myself, "What a terrible job having to be out and about at this time of night." But it suddenly dawned on me: I was no better off than the milkman.

And some of those trips were pretty adventurous. The first time I went to Earlscourt Ranch, for instance, was on an emergency call at night to treat a purebred Hereford cow with a prolapsed uterus. David Spencer of Spencer's Stores in Vancouver owned the ranch.[4] It was on the other side of the Fraser River from Lytton and since the ferry didn't operate at night, I drove to Lytton. To cross the river, I had to leave the car and walk across the CP railway bridge, carrying everything I thought I might need. Crossing on foot was tricky as the bridge had no decking—I had to step from tie to tie in the dark, with no dawdling, in case a train came along. The purebred herd manager was waiting for me on the other side and drove me to the ranch about a mile away. When the work was done, Col. Spencer himself invited me in for a coffee and something to eat. He was in failing health at the time but friendly, and we passed the time eating and telling stories until I finally left at about 1:00 a.m. to pick my way back across the trestle, find my car, and make the three-hour trip home.

Another time, in mid-March, I was asked to take a look at some sick bulls at Gang Ranch. It was my busiest time of year and Gang Ranch was a nine-hour drive, so they offered to fly me out from Clinton with Baldy Boyd. Baldy was a good pilot and just a great all-around guy. The next morning, I drove to Clinton. As it was still winter, the plane was on skis. We flew out to the Gang, I did the work and by late afternoon we were heading back. A surprise awaited us there, though: there had been a chinook in Clinton and all the snow had melted off the runway, leaving huge water puddles and lots of mud. It was getting dark—too late to find anywhere else to land on skis—so Baldy decided our only option was to land in the water and mud. He was pretty sure the skis would snag and we would tip over, so we prepared anxiously for the landing. We got bounced around a little but never flipped, although when we stopped, we couldn't see through the windshield for all the mud. I was glad to get home that night.

ONE FALL DAY, OUT at the Diamond S Ranch, owner Ted Termuende showed up with old Harry Marriott. At one time, Harry had owned the OK Ranch and he and his wife, Peg, had lived in the Big Bar area for many years. He and Ted were great friends. Harry had written a fascinating book called *Cariboo Cowboy*, describing his many experiences over years of cattle ranching and I was honoured to meet him.[5]

That day at Diamond S, Harry insisted on coming down to the corrals to lend a hand with vaccinating and dehorning calves. He was at least eighty at the time and pretty frail, and he told me, "Son, at my age, you can hear Gabriel's wings flapping most nights." The ranch had stocked several cans of "dehorning blood stop powder" which was supposed to stop excess bleeding. Veterinarians knew very well that this was a myth perpetuated by the drug company that sold the product, but old Harry believed in it and insisted on smearing this powder on each calf's head after it was dehorned. This slowed everything down considerably but nobody said a word: it was only right to humour old Harry. After lunch, Harry brought the flour bin from the kitchen down to the corrals, in case he ran out of dehorning powder. Sure enough, he wound up using the flour, with his dirty old gloves on, for most of the afternoon. When we were finished, we went up to the house and Harry set about making baking powder biscuits, using flour out of the same bin. The biscuits were great but full of black spots and red and white calves' hair!

BEING A MIXED-PRACTICE VET in a rural community has its unique set of challenges. One of my least favourite requests came from would-be pet skunk owners who wanted the skunk's scent glands removed. It was usually pretty straightforward because people brought in baby skunks; very few people attempted to tame an adult skunk. But from time to time, we'd get a full-grown one, which required a much more cautious approach. Having been on the receiving end of a frightened skunk in the clinic (where even my stainless steel instruments reeked for months!), I had a policy of doing all skunk work out near the city dump.

TED TERMUENDE: A LIFETIME OF INNOVATION

ONE OF THE MOST innovative, progressive and intelligent men I ever met, someone we all respected, was Ted Termuende. Ted had been raised in Saskatchewan and had a degree in electrical engineering from the university there. In all the years I knew him, never once do I recall Ted talking about himself; everything I know about him came to me second-hand. He had a special kind of creative ingenuity that kept him ahead of the game in every business. He founded a wire rope (cable) manufacturing company (Western Rope and Cable), which was eventually bought out by Canada Wire Company. A holiday in Hawaii piqued his interest in helping pineapple growers control weeds, which led to his development of plastic mulch—large sheets of black plastic with holes in them that allowed the plants to grow through—now common practice with many growers. When he got into ranching, he applied the same innovative thinking to everything from irrigation to artificial insemination to crossbreeding to progeny testing.

To keep up with new developments in agriculture, Ted often went to one of the world's largest agricultural exhibitions, held annually in Paris. He always came back with some new idea that he was able to apply. In those days, hay was put up in bales, usually about a hundred pounds each, held together by two strands of sisal twine. The bales were stacked and, in the winter, tossed by hand off of sleighs, wagons or trucks to feed livestock. Ted was irritated that the sisal would rot, or that mice could chew through the strings—the broken strings caused a considerable waste of hay. His invention of plastic baling twine revolutionized the hay-baling process.

Ted came to a Bull Sale that fall with one of the first rolls of his twine. A bunch of us were partying in his suite on the top floor of the old Stockman's Hotel and as usual, we had all had too much to drink. Someone spied the roll of baling twine, which sparked a real debate about whether it would be as strong as sisal. Ted bet anyone in the room that they couldn't break it and nobody could. Not being satisfied with that, Gary Hook suggested that we lower somebody down from the balcony to the street below to see if the twine would hold a man's weight. I didn't volunteer but soon found myself dangling above the street on a thin plastic thread. Fortunately, it held!

Getting implement companies interested in this new twine was Ted's next mission. Ted toured plants across the US, but although they agreed that the twine was superior, he was unable to convert them—the plastic twine was too slippery for the knotting mechanism in the balers and none of them was willing to redesign the knotters. But Ted was nothing if not tenacious. He took himself off to Germany where he found a company that designed a suitable knotter: it not only tied the bale but was universally adaptable to any North American hay baler on the market.

He ordered hundreds of these knotters and initially gave them away in order to market the plastic twine. He also adapted the manufacturing process, roughing up the outside coat of the twine to give the knotters a better grip. Over just two or three years, sisal baling twine became a thing of the past. Ted sold the patents on the twine process and the business to Imperial Oil Ltd., which went on to develop plastic twine and rope of all kinds—it's now known as Poly Twine.

On his frequent trips to his factory in Saskatoon, Ted noted a huge glut of barley on the prairies. Typically used for feeding swine, barley was undervalued and the surplus caught

Ted's attention. He opened a whiskey distillery in Weyburn, Saskatchewan, using barley, and was soon producing an acceptable rye whiskey called "Number 1 Hard." It seems there was nothing that this unique man couldn't do to turn adversity into opportunity.

Over the years, Ted and I became very close friends, and there's no doubt that he was my mentor. He kept track of me after I left Kamloops and we were always in close touch, with many long phone calls and visits when we could manage them, until he died few years ago. His ranch has stayed in the family and is now operated by one of his sons, Mark. I miss him very much.

It was also my policy to have an assistant for these jobs, since at least two sets of hands were needed to manage the continuous anaesthetic on one end of the skunk and a delicate piece of surgery on the other end.

But against my better judgment and at the end of a long day, I found myself out at the dump with a skunk trapped in an old metal milk can and no assistant in sight. I decided I'd just stick the ether-soaked cloth into the milk can until the skunk was asleep, then stretch him on the ground and lay the ether-soaked cloth on his face, dissect the scent glands—a quick and dirty job—and get home in time for dinner.

I started off well, but I just didn't have enough hands to keep the ether flowing onto the cloth. The skunk woke up and before I could grab him, he was off across the dump, heading for the woods. Frustration welled up in my chest and without thinking, I picked up a rock about the size of a baseball and let 'er rip, nailing the poor old skunk— no word of a lie—right between the ears and killing him dead as a doornail. The next morning, I told the family that, in spite of my best efforts, their Mr. Skunk had not survived his operation.

Long days like that were pretty much the norm for me, at least on the large animal side. Stan Creech and Bob Rudolph, for instance, had a small place near the US border between Rock Creek and Osoyoos, so I had to leave home at 3:00 a.m. in order to be there for an 8:00 a.m.

Learning by Doing #2:

Spaying Heifers at Gang Ranch

ONE SPRING, I GOT a call from Wayne Everett at the Perry Ranch inviting me out to Gang Ranch to watch a veterinarian from Montana spay heifers. He had been flown in and would be there for three or four days. I knew nothing about this procedure; it hadn't even been mentioned at college. The idea was that I could learn how to do it and replace the Montana vet, as he really was too busy to keep coming up to do the job.

I had heard of the Gang Ranch for years and I knew it was one of the largest in Canada. I was also curious about spaying heifers. It was a busy time of the year for me but Wayne and I figured we could get out and back in two long days. We left on a Sunday morning and, after a nine-hour drive, we made it in time for dinner, and were put up in one of several guest cabins. Chert Sidwell, a wise old cattleman, managed the ranch, and his son Irwin was the foreman.

At that time, Gang Ranch was running about eight thousand cows. They were probably weaning in excess of seven thousand calves, keeping the top end for replacements, and selling a good bunch as yearlings or two-year-olds. What was left over, the bottom end, often created a problem. Many were smaller, having being born late in the calving season, or were just not good enough to make the cut. They were turned out as yearlings with the others in a separate pasture, away from any bulls. However, bulls occasionally got in with them and, if they got bred, these undersized two-year-olds were often difficult, if not impossible, to calve out. Therefore, it made good sense to spay them before they were turned out. They could then be grown out and sold in almost the same way as steers.

To the best of my knowledge, no ranches in BC were using this management practice at the time—the influx of US ranch managers into BC introduced all kinds of new methods. So Wayne and I spent the morning watching and learning the spaying procedure. The Montana vet was friendly and more than generous in giving us instructions.

My trips to Gang Ranch to spay heifers always fell at the end of March or in early April: bad timing for me, but convenient for them. The first year out I took Wayne with me; you didn't have to be a veterinarian in order to spay heifers, and I needed an extra set of hands. The Sidwells had everything set up for us: two chutes with metal squeezes that enabled us to work quickly. I got Wayne all set up on the second chute and we got started.

The cowboys clipped an area of each heifer just back of the left ribs, washed and dried the surgical site, and applied an iodine disinfectant. The heifer was then moved into the metal squeeze and the operation was completed quickly, usually in less than minutes. It took us almost three days to do about eight hundred heifers. The Sidwells were good people, easy to work with, and certainly knew what they were doing.

We left the evening of the third day and got home about 3:00 a.m. Several days later, I was home for lunch when I got a phone call from a very agitated Chert Sidwell, telling me there were dead heifers all over the place. He was a very authoritative man and I remember almost fainting. I said I would drop everything and race out to the ranch to see what I could do. I was gathering myself to leave when Wayne called. It didn't take him long to realize what a state I was in and to start laughing. He had put Chert up to making the call and, as it turned out, not even one heifer got sick or was lost. Boy, was I relieved! Since I had promised to pay Wayne $100 for his help and I had to get even with him, I went to the bank and got $100 worth of pennies. I had Bob unroll every roll and put them in a one-gallon jug, which I dropped off at the Perry Ranch a few days later.

start on their preg-testing, and didn't get home until one the next morning. Another time I was called to the famous Chilco Ranch, seventy miles from Williams Lake, to fertility test their bulls. I had to leave home in the middle of the night in order to arrive at a respectable time in the morning. It was a two-day job, and the first night I was invited to stay in the ranch house where I joined the owner, John Wade, and his girlfriend for a gourmet meal. John was an odd duck, a middle-aged man from Hawaii, who seemed out of place on this ranch in a rather remote part of BC. His girlfriend was a good deal younger and a knockout.

The funny thing is that he never went near the corrals or the cattle; his favourite pastime was cooking! That night he prepared a wonderful leg of venison cooked in red wine. The table was set like nothing I'd ever seen, with expensive china and crystal. He was dressed in a jacket and tie and she wore a very fancy evening dress. I was immediately uncomfortable in my work shirt and jeans—but the food was wonderful.

I didn't see him again until the next evening, when he wrote me a cheque for my work, and I left before dinner for the long drive home. I was very sleepy on the way out and got about fifty miles or so from the ranch, when I almost ran into a load of lumber scattered all over the road. I walked up the road in the dark and found a trucker who had lost his load on the curve. He was inside the crushed cab, badly injured. I could hear that he was still alive, in pain, and with my flashlight I found one of his hands protruding from under a pile of boards. I took his hand and within a few minutes he died. There was nothing I could do but go to the nearest ranch and phone the RCMP. I was pretty shaken up and didn't have any trouble staying awake for the rest of the trip home. I later found out that his name was Bert Buckle and that he left a wife and young family.

I BEGAN TO DO a lot of work, especially each fall and early winter, for the cattle buyers.[6] I was often called upon to pregnancy test and, for cattle tagged for export to the US, they had to be TB-tested and the heifer calves had to be vaccinated. Many were shipped to Alberta and some even as far away as Ontario.

The buyers had to be particularly vigilant when buying cattle directly from a ranch. After the bidding process was over, the procedure was to have the cattle stand overnight, off feed and water. They were then picked up the next morning by cattle liners and hauled to the nearest stockyards to be weighed. An agreed "shrink," generally 3 percent, was then deducted from the payweight. The process had to be carefully observed by the buyer, as some ranchers were known to let the cattle fill up on water and sometimes pellets. No one wants to pay for water and undigested feed!

When Phil De Bok got drafted, he recommended one of his class-mates, Dr. Don Olson, who agreed to join me in the practice. Don was the youngest of sixteen brothers and sisters and had been raised on a ranch near Grass Range, Montana. His wife, Bonnie, was a nurse whose family was also in the cattle business. The first time we met, I knew immediately that he was going to fit very well in the practice. He was a mixture of veterinarian and cowboy—just the kind of person my ranch clients would appreciate. He quickly became very popular with the cattlemen and horsemen and we were soon accepted equally when going on calls. Don was also competent with small animals and became well liked by those clients. He was a hard worker and always willing to do more than his share.

Don was as much of a practical joker as I was. One day Don and I castrated a colt in the Co-op Yards and decided to stir up the accountant there—a nice guy, but well known for his queasy stomach. We took the colt's testicles and some dill pickles and arranged them strategically on a nice lunch plate for him. We snuck back to his office and put it on his desk in time for lunch. His secretary told us later that he upchucked in his garbage can.

ONE OCTOBER DAY AT Diamond S Ranch, I had a few minutes to spare and wandered into one of the barns. To my surprise, there was a big grey stallion tied in one of the standing stalls. His name was Specula-tion and he had been imported from Ireland some years before, as a gift from Mr. Ross to Col. Spencer when they were joint owners of the Douglas Lake Cattle Company.

I was told that Speculation had a full brother, a winner of the Grand National Steeplechase. Speculation had been shipped to Halifax and by rail to Kamloops, and during the trip had almost died from a serious case of pneumonia. It had left him with severe emphysema (better known as "the heaves" by horsemen). He ended up at the Diamond S, but the

Speculation, imported from Ireland, almost died of pneumonia on the rail trip from Halifax.

manager, Dale Cochrane, admitted that the horse was a nuisance and that he simply didn't know what to do with him. Knowing that Cleveland Bays were often good jumping horses, I asked him if he would be interested in selling him to me. To my surprise, he gave him to me on the spot. So I borrowed a trailer and hauled him to Kamloops where I found a good home for him on the Indian School property. The caretakers there agreed to look after him in return for breeding their mares.

He was a sweetheart of a horse and enjoyed having his feet trimmed, being groomed, and being turned out in a large outdoor pen. I saddled him up one day and walked him for a few hundred yards. It must've been years since he'd had a rider on his back but he never made a wrong move. But his lung condition was clearly distressing. I didn't have the money or the time to get involved in any kind of a breeding program with him, but word got around that I had this marvellous old stallion and a wealthy couple from Calgary, the Grahams, came over to see him. They had a horse farm near Calgary and were interested in show jumpers. They intended to put Speculation with twenty-five or thirty good thoroughbred mares, so I gave them the old boy and their breeding program proved a success. Many good jumping horses were produced and several were sold to the Mexican International team.

Everyone thought that I should have sold the horse to the Grahams, but he was given to me and it didn't feel right. As it turned out, my

Early-morning reading time at Shuswap with Steven, Kathy and Terry.

friends R.J. and Tom often went to the Calgary horse show, where they entered the jumping events, and they knew the Grahams well. A few years later, when I was managing the Eldorado Ranch in Kelowna, I was pleasantly surprised when Tom and R.J. Bennett arrived back from Calgary with a strapping big three-year-old bay gelding, a Speculation colt, a gift to me from the Grahams. We named him Major Cameron.

Major was supposed to be halter-broken but proved to be difficult to handle, stubborn and powerful. He had a bad habit of pulling back when tied to anything, and to cure him I tied a one-inch soft cotton rope around his withers, took it up between his front legs through the halter, and tied it as high up as I could reach to a power pole that was located just inside one of our corrals. He fought for a good half-hour that evening so I decided to leave him tied up overnight. When I went down the next morning he had managed to pull the pole over to about a twenty-degree list. He never pulled back again, but everything I did with him took time and endless patience. He did, ultimately, become a pretty good jumping horse. I even used him to ride on the range when we had the Soda Creek Ranch. He came with us when we moved to Southlands in South Vancouver, but when we moved back to Williams Lake, I decided to sell him. I don't think his new owner did much with him.

LEARNING BY DOING #3:
DON'T ELIMINATE——INSEMINATE!

I WAS AT THE cattle sale one summer day in 1960 when Ted Tremuende, the new owner of the OK Ranch, and his manager, Bud Watt, approached me. They had noticed that most of their cows had not settled and that the bulls were overly active. To me it sounded like a typical case of vibriosis, a bacterial venereal disease spread throughout a herd by an infected bull. To make a positive diagnosis, one had to insert tampons into the vaginas of a sample of the cows, retrieve them after a few hours, and send them off to the veterinary laboratory. I ordered the diagnostic material from the lab, collected the samples, and within a few days we had a positive diagnosis.

This was serious: it meant a greatly reduced calf crop the following spring. The treatment was to remove the bulls from the breeding pasture and ship them for slaughter. The cows would have to be "rested" until the following year, while the infection played itself out, then they would have to be bred by artificial insemination (AI). It was daunting to imagine performing AI on a large beef herd, but the only alternative was to ship the cows for slaughter and replace the entire herd, including the bulls—something you just don't want to contemplate! Besides the massive expense of replacement, a herd needs cows that are familiar with their range and know their way home in the fall. Ted immediately made the decision to use AI, and Bud was sent down to the AI Centre in Milner (near Vancouver) for instructions.

The AI Centre was put in place to serve the BC dairy industry and had never handled a beef herd. However, Bud learned the ropes and was prepared for the next year's breeding season. Special holding pens and chutes were built in the breeding pasture and teaser bulls purchased. The young teaser bulls are usually culls that had to be sterilized, then fitted with a dye-soaked apron that went on their chests, around the front of their shoulders. When a cow came in heat she was mounted by one of these bulls and her rear end was marked with the dye. She could then be picked out by the cowboys and brought to the breeding corral. Frozen Hereford semen in dry ice canisters was shipped by bus to Clinton every few days.

It was an expensive and labour-intensive treatment but it proved to be successful. I pregnancy tested the cows that fall and we had about a 70 percent success rate. The empty cows were shipped for slaughter and the next year some new bulls were introduced. There was a great upside to this story, as Ted turned this entire trial into a very profitable venture. Crossbreeding was just being introduced in North America and Ted was the first to import Simmental semen from Switzerland. He then imported several bulls from Switzerland, which were kept at Milner Centre to supply a burgeoning market for frozen semen across Canada and the US.

THERE WAS HEARTBREAK ON the ranching side as well. One Saturday in late March, I was called by the new owner of the Sky Ranch, a spread out in the Chilcotin, at least a twelve-hour drive from Kamloops. He was losing cows at a considerable rate and was convinced that some dreadful disease had caused their deaths. Luckily, he had an airplane and had plowed out a usable runway. I promised to get there the next day and was able to hire a good pilot and plane to fly me out there.

When I arrived, it took only a few minutes to diagnose what the old ranchers referred to as "pitchfork disease"—these cattle were slowly starving to death. Almost all of the cattle wintered in the Chilcotin were fed exclusively on meadow or slough-grass hay, which is very low in protein compared to alfalfa hay. By March, when most cows are heavily pregnant and, especially if the weather is severe, this poor-quality feed simply can't sustain them. I sent a sample of this

THE ONE MINUTE THAT CHANGED OUR LIVES FOREVER

MARCH 16, 1965, MARKED the birth of our third son, Thomas Everett, named for our best friend Tom White and for my dad. During her pregnancy Phyl had read about a condition called Phenylketonuria (PKU), a genetic disease of rare incidence—about one in every ten thousand births. The joining of an autosomal recessive gene (carried by each parent) can result in mental retardation, and is more commonly seen in children with a light complexion. Knowing this, Tom's blond hair and blue eyes raised a flag with Phyl, but the nursery nurse told her that the test for PKU was no longer administered in the hospital.

We had a warm relationship with almost all the doctors who worked at the medical clinic we used, and often met socially as well as professionally. About six weeks after Tom was born, knowing that he hadn't yet been tested for PKU, Phyl dropped in to the clinic to have him checked. The test itself was very simple; it requires a drop of ferric chloride onto a freshly wet

Terry and Steven with Tom as a baby, 1965.

diaper, which results in a greyish green spot to indicate a positive result. No colour change indicates a negative result.

Although Phyl didn't have an appointment, one of the pediatricians offered to do the test. It took only a minute and, tragically, he misread the result. Phyl questioned his decision as she could see the discolouration on the diaper, but he firmly insisted that it was negative and she had little choice but to thank him and leave. That one minute in time changed our lives forever.

Phenylketonuria is the inability to metabolize one of the ten essential amino acids, phenylalanine, which is found in breast milk, dairy milk, and baby food and supplements. The result of this inability is a buildup of phenylketones to a toxic level (ketosis) that causes serious, irreversible damage to developing nerve cells in the child's brain. If the affected baby is put on a special phenylalanine-free diet, the damage can be minimized, but an early start is essential.

When Tom was about eight months old, Phyl began to suspect that something was not right. He went from being a smiling, happy baby to being extremely cranky and irritable. She took him to the clinic and the pediatricians agreed that he was not developing as he should be and sent us off to Vancouver, where we soon found out the worst.

At first Tom spent several months in Woodlands Hospital to regulate his phenylanaline level and prevent any more brain damage, and then he returned home. We tried for several years to look after him. He was on an exclusive diet of a very unpalatable powder, called Lofenolac, given by bottle. He was allowed nothing else—no milk or protein of any kind—only puréed fruit. He hated the Lofenolac and Phyl's efforts to disguise it with flavourings were rejected outright, even vomited. He was hungry, irritable and not gaining weight. To get the required amount of food into him, Phyl often was up at night, even splinting his arms and tube-feeding him.

Tom's future had been outlined to us in very pessimistic terms: his late diagnosis had caused significant, irreversible brain damage, and it wasn't likely that he would walk or be toilet trained. He was an exceptional case, having been diagnosed so late, so a PKU specialist tested him constantly at Woodlands. Sometimes he was admitted to Vancouver General Hospital for several weeks at a time and Phyl's mum would go down every afternoon to play with him. Phyl's sister Mary and her husband, Ernie (Hill), were wonderfully supportive during this time, opening their home to us on our frequent trips and always on hand to listen and help problem-solve. As well, Phyl's sister-in-law, Barbara McLorg, kindly offered to have Tom stay with her for a time—a kind offer we've never forgotten.

After several months of this, it was suggested that Tom be placed at Woodlands Hospital—an idea that we rejected outright. However, to have Tom in a more natural environ-

ment and to give Phyl a break, we began leaving him with a friend of Phyl's sister, a woman who lived on her own, close to Woodlands Hospital, and who appreciated the income. She was a loving soul and happy to take him for short breaks, and, over time, we left him with her for longer periods. It was a really difficult time for us but he was happy there. I was busy

Tom, 45 years old, a gentle and good-natured soul.

with the practice and away from home so much, and we worried that Kathy, Terry and Steven were getting shortchanged by our preoccupation and travel to Vancouver with Tom.

It continued to haunt us that there was no acknowledgement of the missed diagnosis. Without a doubt, the doctor had made a mistake, but strangely, no excuse or apology was ever offered. Even our own pediatrician remained silent. The attending pediatrician, at one point, denied having conducted the test at all.

The clinic simply closed ranks against us, to the point that we felt shunned. They refused to book appointments—not just for the children but for Phyl and me as well—so we had to move the whole family to a different clinic. It was extremely hurtful, especially for Phyl. We kept waiting for one of them to drive down our driveway: all we needed was an apology.

We felt so mistreated that upon advice from our lawyer, we decided to proceed with an action. The Examination for Discovery turned nasty, however, as the clinic brought in a high-powered lawyer from Vancouver who soon reduced Phyl to tears. We left their offices to come home for lunch and decided to drop the case.

By the time Tom was fourteen, his wonderful caregiver was aging and he was getting bigger and stronger. She asked to be relieved, and he then lived for many years with a loving family in Surrey, and is now well cared for and happy in a special home with three other men and their caregivers. Under the thoughtful, consistent care of his primary caseworker, Bridgette Brodie, he has developed excellent social skills and is productive at a sheltered workshop.

Sky Ranch feed for analysis and it turned out to be 2 percent protein, probably not as good as straw; good meadow hay can be as much as 8 percent protein. These cows couldn't possibly eat enough of this low-grade hay to keep from starving. Unfortunately, because of spring breakup, the roads were impassable and there was no way to bring in higher quality feed. There was nothing he could do but watch as he lost several hundred cows before the grass grew.

I did a lot of work for Thurman and Hally Clements at the Cherry Creek Ranch. They had a string of good quarterhorses and one day they called me up to have a look at an expensive breeding mare that had failed to foal. A rectal examination revealed a recto-vaginal fistula, a relatively rare outcome of foaling when the foal's legs are twisted and it punches a tiny, sharp hoof through the mare's vaginal wall into the rectum. The hole allows fecal material to gather in the vagina, making it impossible for the mare to conceive. I knew I needed to repair it but there was no literature on how to go about it, so I had to figure it out myself.

The surgery itself was relatively straightforward, but I was worried about scarring and adhesions, and needed a way to stabilize the incision. I decided to put a clean glass milk bottle into the vagina and sew the vagina closed, and leave it for a couple of weeks to let the internal incision heal. It worked like a charm except that I had stupidly put the milk bottle in neck first, so when I went to retrieve it, it was so slippery that I couldn't get a grip on it. It must have taken me an hour to get it out. She delivered a nice little foal the following spring—my intervention was a success. I wrote up this experience for the *Journal of the Canadian Veterinary Medicine Association*, and they printed it that summer.

THE KIDS GREW LIKE weeds in those years and kept Phyl busy with school, skating, swimming, piano lessons, Boy Scouts and Girl Guides. She sewed costumes, uniforms and dress clothes, preserved endless jars of fruit, and turned out wonderful meals on next to nothing. And the house was never without music, either from the piano or from our old Zenith record player.

My parents and Phyl's mum continued to be a big part of our lives, and the cabin at Shuswap gave us tremendous pleasure. We all took up skiing, spent as much time as we could at the cabin, and the kids were getting old enough to come on occasional calls with me.

I HAD ANOTHER REALLY interesting call in March 1968. The DeMarnis were clients who lived just outside Kamloops on the Thompson River. They owned, bred and trained racehorses, and had just purchased a beautiful racehorse, Prince Alymer, to use as a stud on their thoroughbred farm. He'd passed through the hands of several owners and had been treated for years with antibiotics for suspected bladder infections

We removed an 11-pound bladder stone from Prince Alymer. No wonder he was unsuccessful at stud!

Dad retired in 1968 at the age of 60. Phyl made all the kids' clothes for the celebration.

because he dribbled urine when he trotted. As it turned out, he was not successful at stud either.

When I went out there to take a look at him, I started with a rectal examination and bumped right into what felt like a watermelon. I knew immediately it was a huge cystic calculi—a bladder stone! It had to be removed but with equine care in its infancy, we had no proper facilities and only the most primitive equipment.

Don, Rex and I mulled it over that night and decided it would take all three of us to tackle it. The next morning, we started by wrapping thick padding onto my old set of hobble tethers, then secured them snuggly on Prince's back legs. Rex (our designated anaesthetist) gave

Prince a good dose of intravenous chloral hydrate, and, using a front-end loader, we hoisted Prince by his back feet until his bladder area was about waist-high off the ground. With gravity pulling the rest of his belly contents down and out of our way, we were ready to operate.

Don and I prepped and draped him, and I made an incision just off the mid-line. The bladder was huge and the bladder wall was about an inch thick and tough as leather because the stone had been bouncing around in there for so long. We had to hack our way into the bladder, finally managing to create a ten-inch incision. When we finally freed the stone, we were stunned by the size of it—it weighed almost eleven pounds!

We sewed up the bladder wall, repaired the peritoneum, and used suture as thick as a guitar string to close the incision. We got Prince back on his feet and gave him some antibiotics, and he healed up in no time. The operation was a success—his dribbling was cured—but poor old Prince had been rendered sterile by the long-standing inflammation and was never able to successfully breed a mare.

For the first time in my life as a vet, I finally had adequate and competent help as well as two colleagues who I really liked. I was beginning to enjoy life, had some time for the family, and the future looked very bright. What could possibly go wrong?

THE EXPERIENCE OF TOM'S illness, diagnosis, treatment and placement left Phyl and I exhausted, grieving and deeply wounded. The profound sense of loss seemed, at the time, insurmountable. The life we had been building with our kids—the predictable, fair-handed world we'd believed in—had been pulled out from under our feet. By coincidence, Dr. Red Fraser, Chief of Large Animal Veterinary Medicine at the brand new Western College of Veterinary Medicine (WCVM), had been hounding me for months to join him there. One wretched Saturday morning in April, Red got me on the phone and for the first time, his enthusiasm for the new program began to pique my interest. Believing that a fresh start might help, we sold the practice to Don Olson, left Kamloops, and moved to Saskatoon, where I went to work for the University of Saskatchewan's WCVM as an assistant professor.

RANCHES, RANCHERS, HOOLIGANS, PRANKSTERS

IT WAS WHEN I was working on the ranches side by side with the cowboys and ranchers that I was most in my element.[1] Getting established wasn't easy, though, as many were suspicious of veterinarians and skeptical about the value of new practices. And most of them didn't have much money, so it wasn't always easy to collect on the work. But they all had their stories.

The Gang Ranch was one of the most magical places I ever worked. It was founded in the 1860s by two brothers, Jerome and Thaddeus Harper, from Virginia, who had come out on horseback, responding to the lure of gold in the Cariboo, and then discovered the huge bunch-grass-covered benchlands west of the Fraser. The brothers abandoned their gold-seeking plans and secured enough land from the colonial government to start up a cattle ranch. With no bridge across the Fraser, every crossing was on horseback, and all the cattle they purchased to stock the ranch had to be swum across as well. The Harpers then bought the Perry Ranch at Cache Creek and another ranch near Kamloops that bore their name until recently; Harper Mountain still does. At over one million acres, the Gang Ranch—at least at one point—was the largest ranch in the world.

During one of those early years, since there was no ready market for their cattle in BC, they decided to drive them down to Montana to meet the railhead that would ship them to Chicago. Along the way, they heard that there was a market in San Francisco, so they re-routed and drove them all the way, crossing rivers, dealing with Natives and cattle thieves—a true wild-west cattle drive.

THE GANG RANCH CHANGED hands several times and wound up with a group of Englishmen. These wealthy owners would spend their summers at the ranch and built a two-storey mansion, with a verandah overlooking a full-sized racetrack. I was lucky to be taken through the old house; it must have been magnificent in its day. In the basement there was a room full of large batteries encased in glass that apparently provided electricity. I found an old enamel 1910 BC licence plate (number 124); years later, I gave it to my good friend Roy Eden in Kelowna for his collection. A few years after my visit, someone burned the place down, which I felt was a terrible loss.

In 1952, there was an outbreak of foot and mouth disease in Canada; the entire country was quarantined and cattle prices plummeted. Two men from Idaho bought the Gang Ranch, lock, stock and barrel, for $750,000. Shortly thereafter, the cattle embargo was lifted, cattle prices went up and they were able to sell enough heifers and steers to pay off the purchase price and still keep the cow herd and bulls. They had ended up with a wonderful piece of property that could support upwards of ten to twelve thousand head of cattle.

The new owners were from Idaho Falls: one was a rancher, Bill Stoddert, and the other was the owner/operator of the Idaho Falls Livestock Auction Market, Floyd Skelton. Floyd only had time to come up once or twice a year, but Bill used to fly up to the ranch regularly in a dilapidated old airplane and have his pilot land in a hayfield near the river. When they left, they would take off out over the river canyon to give the old plane a chance to get airborne. Not long after buying the ranch, Bill evidently decided that they needed a bulldozer and a couple of diesel engines to provide electricity, so he flew to Vancouver to make a deal with Finning Tractor. He was a very disreputable dresser and showed up there in torn, dirty jeans and a battered old hat. When he blithely wrote a cheque for a D6 Caterpillar bulldozer and two engines, the Finning people had him sit and wait while they phoned his bank in Idaho Falls. I'd love to have seen the looks on their faces when they learned that he had over $20 million in his chequing account!

Gang Ranch cowboys were a bit of a special breed. Many cowboys from all over North America were anxious to work on the ranch because of its remoteness, its size, and the fact that many of the practices were still those of yesteryear. There was even a young teenager from Malta, of all places, learning to be a cowboy.

The cooks at the Gang Ranch were Chinese and there was a lot of friction between the Chinese and the cowboys. The ranch went through a lot of beef and it was the cooks' job to do the slaughtering and the cowboys' job to deliver a fat cow to the slaughterhouse. There was a corral leading to a chute and, when the animal was secured, it was shot and was supposed to tumble into the slaughterhouse through a trapdoor. The cooks, stationed inside, took over from there. On one of these slaughtering days, the cowboys were mad at the cooks so they picked out a particularly rank old cow, got her into the chute and riled her up, shot the gun up in the air and opened the trapdoor, dumping the angry cow into the slaughterhouse. The boys had blocked the only exit and soon the cooks were hanging on meat hooks yelling like hell, trying to escape getting banged around by this very irritated cow. Luckily the boss came along, gave the cowboys what for, and made them go inside and shoot the cow.

It was a pretty rough-and-ready kind of a place. Wayne Everett and I were there preg-testing one spring, when a group of about twenty steers fell through the ice into the reservoir. It was impossible to fish them out, so for weeks afterwards, we found clumps of red and white hair floating in the tap water.

I'll always remember my times at Gang Ranch, the people there and the friends that I made with a great deal of fondness. There's something about that ranch—it gets to you—probably because of its size and its history. When you first break out onto the benches above the Fraser, you are struck by a real sense of the environment in which you are fortunate enough to live. Most ranchers that I know appreciate the value of the environment from which they take their living: they don't fight it, they live with it. City folk should realize that ranchers are there for more than just beef production—they are custodians of our collective environment.

The Gang Ranch brand is "JH" for Jerome Harper; I still treasure the JH branding iron I was given.

ANOTHER BEAUTIFUL SPREAD WAS the Empire Valley Ranch, adjacent to the Gang Ranch on the west side of the Fraser. At that time, the property belonged to an experienced rancher and real gentleman, Clarence Bryson. He had three adult children and their families, as well as several hired cowboys, working on the ranch and running twelve to fifteen hundred head of cows.

As with Gang Ranch, the Empire Valley summer range ran back fifty to seventy-five miles into the mountains. One year, they decided to put six or seven hundred head of heifers way back into some virgin country in the Spruce Lake area. They were turned out with bulls, and I was asked to pregnancy test these heifers that fall. I was to meet one of Clarence's sons, Mac, who would be waiting with horses near Gold Bridge (north of Lillooet) on the side of the road. I arrived about noon and we put my gear on a packhorse and headed up the trail following Tyaughton Creek. Just before dark we arrived at an old cabin where Mac's brother and several Native cowboys had supper waiting. After supper we settled down to a good game of poker using four-inch spikes for poker chips. We bunked on the floor, and the next morning rode on to a new set of corrals and the heifers that had been rounded up the day before. These heifers proved to be wilder than any cattle I had ever worked on; they fought us every inch of the way. It took three days to complete the job.

One afternoon, when we had run out of cattle, Mac took me over to see Zane Grey's cabin. This famous author often came to Spruce Lake for the fishing and the peace and quiet. His cabin was just an ordinary little place with a shake roof. To show me how good the fishing was, Mac produced a length of line and a bare hook, and tied the line to a willow pole that he had cut. We pushed out into the lake in a dilapidated, leaky old boat. We were only about fifty feet from shore when he dangled the bare hook in the water and immediately hooked a twelve-inch Kamloops trout. In no time at all, he'd caught half a dozen, enough for supper. I don't think there are too many lakes where you can catch trout without bait.

The unfortunate part of this whole venture for the Brysons was that about two hundred of the wild heifers disappeared into a huge canyon and could not be rounded up. They had to be left there, and no doubt perished that winter. It proved to be a very expensive experiment.

I was getting good—and fast—at preg-testing, and the last time I worked for Clarence Bryson at Empire Valley we did 1,126 cows in one long day—a personal best for me. We used only a single chute but the crew knew how to move cattle.

Not long after, Clarence sold the ranch to Bob Maytag, owner of the US-based Maytag appliance company. To show his appreciation to the people in Kamloops who had served him well over the years, Clarence brought eight dry, fat young cows to a small slaughterhouse in Kamloops and had them slaughtered, butchered, wrapped, frozen and delivered. We were given one entire beef. This came as a complete surprise to me, and it was a great honour to have been singled out.

CORRALS, CHUTES AND SQUEEZES are often what a large animal veterinarian remembers most clearly about a ranch's set-up: they can make or break your day. Conducting pregnancy testing on entire herds became a significant part of my practice—and a good way to get some of the bills paid—but, especially in the early years, it was tiring and sometimes even dangerous. One of the things that made the process so slow was the endless climbing up and over the rails to get in behind the cow. And sometimes, the next cow in line would crash into me from behind, which wasn't pleasant, especially if she had horns.

One homemade set-up I particularly remember was a squeeze made out of planks, complete with a lid. The side was supposed to open if a cow lost her footing and went down in the chute or if she went over backwards. The head gate was made out of a small, unique jackpine tree with a natural bend in it that held the cow by the neck. A lever-like pole was bolted at the bottom so that a cowboy standing on top could supposedly catch the cow as soon as she stuck her head out. This took considerable concentration and coordination! Often the cow would run right through before she could be caught, heaping blame on the unfortunate cowboy on top of the squeeze.

I nearly came to a sorry end in one of these contraptions, when a cow crashed through and ended up on top of me. She was followed by two or three more cows pushing to get out, and the guy on top wasn't able to undo the head apparatus to let us out. I had my arm up the cow in front and two cows jammed in on top of me, with others pushing from behind. I didn't say much but I was getting pretty short of breath and starting to hurt in several places. I could hear the commotion and panic outside until finally, with the help of a sledgehammer and an axe, the side of the squeeze was freed and we all tumbled out. Cows can get pretty cranky ("waspy") after being off feed overnight and into the next day, and this was no exception. Two of the freed cows took after the rancher and crew, and ran them up against the side of the corral until they scrambled over. I shook out my arms and legs, marvelled that I was still in one piece, and we all had a good laugh while we put the squeeze back together.

In another one of these haywire corral set-ups at old Dave Corbould's place near Heffley Creek, the first cow to go through the homemade head gate tore it off and ran across the field with it around her neck. Old Dave and his hired man were so dumbfounded that they didn't realize that the whole front of the chute was open and before we knew it, the entire herd—about a hundred head—had run through and escaped. I returned the following week, after repairs had been made and the herd had been rounded up. At another place, near Falkland, we were just getting started on a three-hundred-head herd, when there was a great crash as the side of the main corral gave way and the entire herd took off with their tails up, heading for the hills.

Eventually, having a significant vested interest in improving the situation, I designed a better corral layout, complete with a gate in the chute behind the squeeze that allowed me to enter and exit quickly.[2] The gate opened into the chute and was easily fastened so that cows could not crowd in on top of me. Soon these adaptations were incorporated by most of the ranchers. Some of the larger ranchers began importing metal chutes (squeezes) from the US made by the Powder River Company. These were wonderful inventions and made working with cattle easier and safer for both the cows and me.

JUST WHEN I THOUGHT I knew it all, Reg Hook decided to experiment with buffalo. On one of his trips to Alberta, Reg found a mature buffalo bull and cow, and decided to keep them through the winter in an empty feedlot pen. The first spring, Reg called me to attend to the buffalo cow that had calved several days earlier and hadn't dropped her afterbirth. When I arrived, the pair, with their beautiful little heifer calf, was in a holding corral near the chute. Reg's sons, Gary and Roger, were working on separating the cow from the bull, aiming to catch her in the metal squeeze at the front of the chute. Roger was manning the head gate and, much to his surprise, the cow ran right through the squeeze before he was able to close the head gate on her neck. Gary gave Roger hell for being asleep, and the cow was rounded up for a second try. Again she went through the chute and head gate like a freight train. That's when it dawned on us—a buffalo does not have the same build as a beef cow! Buffalo have large, wide heads attached to very short necks and wide shoulders, and their bodies taper off to narrow hips. It is almost impossible to catch a buffalo by the head in a metal squeeze: once you open the front gate wide enough to entice the animal to stick its head out, the rest of the body slips through before you know it.

While all this was going on, the bull was getting more and more restless, tearing at the ground with his front feet, snorting and pacing up and down the side of the corral beside us. The cow was finally driven into the metal chute with the head gate closed and a pole slid in behind her to keep her from backing up. From there, my job was fairly simple and we thought we had it made. I was just climbing out from behind the cow when there was a loud crash, and the bull came through the side of the corral and around the squeeze and had us all running for safety. We were up and over the side of the chute in seconds. He was in a rage and on the prod, ready to hammer anyone or anything that got in his way. Finally someone was able to release the cow, and she and the bull ran off across the field to freedom.

Over the next few weeks, the bull was on a rampage all over the property, demolishing gates, wrecking fences and, at one point, getting out onto the road. As that part of the ranch was right up against a subdivision in North Kamloops, the Hooks became concerned that the buffalo would get loose in the town and terrorize the townsfolk. An effort was put into capturing them, and the trio was shipped back to Alberta on the next available liner.

GARY HOOK AND BUD Stewart were two of my first good friends in the cattle industry. Gary was one of Reg Hook's five sons and he was responsible for running the ranch. He was a good bronc rider with a reputation on the BC rodeo circuit. At that time, Bud was working for Doug Palmer's 7-0 Ranch just north of Kamloops. Bud had come west from Alberta as a young boy—Wilfred Lulu remembers seeing him getting off the train at Ashcroft with his saddle over his shoulder. He was just a teenager, on his own and on his way to Gang Ranch for his first job as a cowboy. He worked with the Native cowboys there and soon was able to converse with them in Salish.

On days off, he went fishing for salmon and sturgeon. The Native cowboys showed him where the big fish lurked in the back eddies of the Fraser. They had a crafty set-up: they got the ranch blacksmith to modify several bale hooks so they could attach a couple of hundred feet of quarter-inch rope. They would bait a hook with a dead chicken, weight the line, and tie a good-sized balloon to the rope. When the eddy floated the baited line out to the right spot they would shoot the balloon with a .22 rifle and sink the bait. When they hooked a sturgeon, they dallied the rope to a saddle horn and dragged the fish onshore with a saddle horse.

Gary and Bud were a great pair of practical jokesters, and it wasn't long before I was on the wrong end of one of their pranks. One sweltering August day in Kamloops, Phyl and I had decided to go downtown during my noon hour to purchase a new fridge. Phyl was very pregnant with Steven and was suffering with the heat. I parked the station wagon and thoughtlessly left the keys in the ignition. Bud and Gary saw us go into the store and, when they spotted the keys in plain sight, quickly pocketed them and left a note on the dashboard. The note warned me not to leave the keys in the car and said that they could be retrieved at the police station (about four blocks away)—signed by Constable someone or other. We were desperate to get home to have our lunch where it was cooler and I had to get back to work. Furious with myself and with the policeman, I sat Phyl down in the car, and ran all the way to the police station.

By the time I got there I was dripping with sweat. I slapped the note down in front of a receptionist and demanded my keys. The look on her face was enough to tell me there was no such person on the force and that probably someone was playing a trick on me. I ran back

WILF LULU: A GOOD OLD-FASHIONED COWBOY

I FIRST MET WILFRED Lulu at Ashcroft Estates ranch (the old Cornwall ranch), where he was the manager. Wilf was an excellent cattle and horse man and had a great roping arm. He'd been mauled by a grizzly bear when he worked up north, but when he talked about it, he laughed and shrugged it off, saying, "Jeez, the thing I remember most is that big old bear on top of me, breathing on me with his terrible breath!"

It took me years to figure out what some of these Native guys had been through, but from time to time, Wilf gave me a glimpse of his sad and painful past. Like so many Native children, he had been treated very badly as a youngster, taken away from his parents and placed in the Indian Residential School in Kamloops. He told me that the priests whipped them if they were caught speaking their native tongue, and that they were always hungry. The boys were called upon to dig and sack the potato crop on the school farm, and he said that sometimes they were so hungry they would hide a few potatoes in their pockets to eat raw at night in the residence. If caught doing this, they were severely whipped.

As with many Native people of that era, Wilf lived with some pretty tough memories, but he was a kind and gentle soul, a hard-working cowboy and a good friend.

to the car and, sure enough, there were Bud and Gary with the keys, apologizing to Phyl for keeping her out in the heat. They had never imagined that I would tear off before they could come clean.

I waited a long time to get even with Gary Hook for the trick he had played with my car keys. In 1961, Gary's father, Reg, was killed in a tragic traffic accident. It was a great loss, particularly to cattlemen all over Western Canada. Besides owning the ranch in North Kamloops, Reg had been the BC cattle buyer for Canada Packers. Gary inherited the responsibility of operating the ranch and, along with his mother,

raising his three brothers and four sisters. He was immediately confronted with the problem of having to come up with a large amount of
cash to pay succession duties, or death taxes. Knowing his whole operation was in jeopardy, he took the bull by the horns, so to speak, and
enlarged the feedlot operation, buying cattle to fill it at the Kamloops
sale until he had completely exhausted his line of credit at the bank.

I knew how worried Gary was about his debt load, but a prank was
definitely in order, so I bought several dozen "For Sale" signs and stapled
them to fence posts all over the Hooks' various properties. Poor Gary
immediately assumed that the bank had foreclosed on him! I let him suffer for a few hours and then called him, posing as a potential buyer. Of
course, the truth soon came out and—for the time being—we were even.

Bud went to auctioneering school in Kansas and became a first-
class cattle auctioneer and popular rodeo announcer. He was always a
great one for playing practical jokes and we had a lot of laughs. On one
of those sweltering Kamloops summer afternoons, it was even hotter
inside the clinic than it was outside. Work was hectic and, although I
didn't have time to go on a call, I was looking forward to getting on the
road with the car windows rolled down. Bud, however, had snuck into
our small lot and had sabotaged my car by smearing pitch on the insides
of all the door handles. I spent a good half-hour in the blazing sun cleaning each handle with alcohol and getting the pitch off my hands. I hope I
got him back for that one, but I can't remember. At some point, Bud and
Gary moved to Washington State, where Bud still sells cattle and Gary
operates various ventures, as well as owning a string of racehorses.

CATTLE BUYERS WERE AN interesting lot, each one of them having
remarkable histories, and I enjoyed working for them. They worked long
hours, especially during the fall run when large numbers of calves and
yearlings were sold either at the BC Livestock Co-op sales or directly
off the ranch. Starting in September every year, Co-op sales were held
on Mondays in Okanagan Falls, Tuesdays in Kamloops, Wednesdays in
Merritt and Thursdays in Williams Lake. They also had to accommodate those ranchers who preferred to sell straight off the ranch.

All this resulted in little sleep and long hours of driving, usually at
night. Cattle buyers often travelled two or three to a car—provided
they were getting along with each other. They lived on coffee, ham-

burgers, whiskey and an occasional splurge, usually in a Chinese restaurant. They were always impatient to be served, especially Slim Dorin, who would harass the Chinese waiters and cooks to the point that a fight would often ensue. Slim had been raised in cow camps at Douglas Lake and had become quite a famous saddle bronc rider, and later became Douglas Lake's cow boss. He was a big, imposing man, with a bad scar on one side of his face caused by a gas lamp explosion. Things came to a head one night in Kamloops when Slim and Gary took on the staff of the Rose Garden café and a waiter was thrown through the plate glass window onto the street. Another waiter was mistakenly stabbed in the hand by the cook coming to his rescue. It took Slim and Gary some months to pay off the damages inflicted upon the Rose Garden and staff. I was often invited to these late-night suppers, but was usually too busy or too tired to attend—actually a blessing in disguise.

Cattle buyer Lew Williams was well liked and good at his job. In the off-season, he and Dale Miller scoured the country for old and crippled horses. They would have them delivered to the old CP stockyards across the street from our clinic. Each had his own holding pen and they often called in for coffee in the morning after feeding their horses. Dale was a big strong guy with a great sense of humour, renowned for his ability to judge an animal's weight. Once he was known to have stopped a sale, demanding that the scales be balanced. This was done and, sure enough, the scales proved to be thirty-five pounds over because of an accumulation of manure.

One morning when Dale came down to feed his horses, he noticed that one of the large work mares had aborted a foal, close to term. Rather than carry the dead foal out to his truck, he figured the easiest solution was to drag it over into Lew's pen. He used a bundle of hay to whisk out the drag marks, and came over to the clinic to tell us what he had done. Don and I joined Dale in the waiting room to watch for Lew and, before long, Lew drove up in his big pink Chrysler carrying that morning's feed—two or three bales of hay—in the trunk. He immediately spied the dead foal. Lew was a Welshman, not very tall, and you could see that he was perturbed. He took off his hat, scratched his head, and started walking around his pen, stooping to look up at the udders of each mare to see which one had foaled. He finally gave up and began dragging the dead foal, which weighed almost as much as he did, to the gate and then to the back of his car. We thought he'd come over for coffee and ask for a hand, but instead he stubbornly pushed, pulled and levered this dead foal until it finally fell into the trunk, then drove away and was never any the wiser.

LIFETIME FRIENDS THURMAN CLEMENTS and his wife, Hally, came into my life as the owners of the Cherry Creek Ranch. Thurman was (and still is) a real character and Hally, well educated and as sharp as two tacks, was very wealthy and is one of the 100 First Ladies of Texas. Thurman's father had been in the oil business and Thurman had served as a pilot in the Pacific. Somewhere along the line, he had developed an alcohol problem and Hally decided to make the move to Canada in hopes of straightening him out.

Kamloops hadn't ever experienced anyone like Thurman. He was funny, could tell wonderful jokes, wore his pants tucked into almost knee-high cowboy boots and chewed and spat tobacco everywhere he went. He used to pack a Navy Colt .45 revolver under his jacket, until the RCMP told him it wasn't legal to carry a gun in Canada.

The Clementses had purchased a very rundown but historic property that ran about three hundred cows. Immediately they set about renovating the ranch house, putting in a swimming pool, adding a bunkhouse and a cookhouse, and painting the large old barn CPR red. The entire deeded property was re-fenced and new corrals were built. All this activity (and expenditure!) raised the eyebrows of the locals and, after a couple of social events in Kamloops, Thurman's conduct became the talk of the town. The move to Canada hadn't much curbed his drinking (he was a Cutty Sark man) but Hally always managed to get him home somehow and, amazingly, forgave him his trespasses. Years later, I can see why she was so patient because, beneath it all, he really was very special.

Thurman was just starting out in the cattle business and relied heavily on his hired help, who weren't always knowledgeable either. Therefore, I was often called out to diagnose and treat things that most ranchers would handle on their own. I thoroughly enjoyed these calls, as Thurman was a gifted storyteller and would regale us with stories of his goings-on in the war and in Texas. It wasn't too long before he hired my friend Bud Stewart as his foreman. Bud had a good practical knowledge of the business and they got on well, as they were both

Thurman and Hally Clements owned the Cherry Creek Ranch.

such good storytellers. Bud also had a knack for imitating people, which really tickled Thurman.

Thurman always ate lunch in the cookhouse with the crew and one day after lunch, early on, he said, "Y'all go to the back where you were yestiday and finish fixin' the fence you were working on." In his mind, he was talking to just one of the boys but, to his surprise, they *all* jumped into the pickup truck and took off in a cloud of dust. They soon got used to his Texas drawl.

Thurman wasn't too impressed with any of the horses on the ranch or, for that matter, anywhere around, so he decided that he and Bud should drive to Texas to bring back some quarterhorses. They took off in the ranch cattle truck and about three weeks later returned with ten registered quarterhorse mares and a black stallion called King Motion. These were some of the first quarterhorses to arrive in BC.

Cutting horse events were becoming popular in the rodeos and horse shows in Alberta, and Thurman decided that he and Bud should turn King Motion into a cutting horse. No one had seen cutting horses in action in the Kamloops area, so Gary Hook and I decided to put on a cutting horse show at the old rodeo grounds east of the stockyards. There was a grandstand and a good set of pens in the arena, Thurman supplied the cattle, and we had a contingent of Albertans come over to show us how it was done. We scraped up some prize money and the event was a great success. The ability of these horses to work out a specific animal from the herd was almost unbelievable. Some were able to do it without a bridle on. And, thank God, King Motion did quite well. We had such a great time that Thurman decided that what his ranch needed was a good indoor arena. One of the men who worked on the ranch, Bill Patterson, was a real handyman so he and Thurman decided that they would build this arena on their own. It's still in use to this day.

Thurman wasn't content with running commercial cows, so he decided to get into the purebred business. Typically for Thurman, he got into it in a big way by buying a complete herd of purebred polled Herefords in Virginia—cows, calves and the herd sire. He contracted a special train to transport the herd from Virginia to Kamloops and they arrived in good shape and with much fanfare. This was another real eye-opener for the locals. I came out to the ranch for a look and was especially impressed by the herd sire, which carried the unheard-of amount of $100,000 worth of insurance.

One summer evening several months later, I was at home in the middle of dinner when I received a frantic call from Hally asking me to get out to the ranch as quickly as possible because the bull was bloating. Bloat in cattle is very serious, usually caused by eating green alfalfa or other legumes. The grossly inflated rumen exerts such pressure on the diaphragm that the animal cannot breathe; and it will often die very quickly unless attended to. I got there within twenty minutes, but the bull was already down and in severe distress. I was able to get a stomach tube down but this bull had frothy bloat, which is far more difficult to treat than the ordinary gaseous form, especially at that stage.

Within a few minutes, the bull was dead. We were all in turmoil and finally Thurman instructed one of the boys to hook onto the bull with a tractor and drag him up to a gravel pit about half a mile away where I could perform a postmortem examination for the insurance. Thurman got in my station wagon with me and on the way to the gravel pit told me that the renewal for the bull's insurance had come up about a week before, and that he and Hally had decided to drop the insured amount from $100,000 to $10,000; they had just lost $90,000. That would be the equivalent of about a million dollars today. I completed my examination and was cleaning up when suddenly Thurman said, "Son, you cut me a big steak off that dead sonofabitch so I can show Hally what a $100,000 steak looks like." He stomped back toward the house and spat a great stream of tobacco juice in disgust.

The following spring, at about two o'clock in the morning, in the middle of Bull Sale week, I got another call from Hally asking me to get out there as quickly as I could because one of their good quarter-horse mares had gotten out onto the highway and had been hit by a car or a truck. It was extremely cold for March, about twenty below zero. By the time I got there, they had the mare in the barn in a loose box and had already hooked up a good set of lights. The mare had a great gash in her side, just behind her shoulder, and a bloody froth was coming out of the hole, so obviously she had a punctured lung. I clipped away the hair from around the wound, cleaned it up as best I could and disinfected the area prior to suturing.

Thurman was sitting on a box next to me, watching, and we both got miserably cold. My hands were shaking and stiffening up, so Thurman sent one of the boys up to the house for a bottle of Cutty Sark. He took a long pull and handed me the bottle. It was my first experience with Scotch but several big swallows warmed me up almost immediately. It went down so well that when he offered it again, I couldn't turn it down! He gave the boys each a good swallow and sent for another bottle.

The suturing went faster and easier after that and, by the time I was finished, we had killed the second bottle between the four of us. I threw my stuff in the car, said goodnight, and headed for home to get some sleep—I was supposed to be on deck at the Bull Sale at 7:00 a.m. I was only a mile down the highway when I started having trouble seeing the road. I pulled off, slept for an hour or so until the cold woke me up, and found my way home by following the white line. I finally got into our driveway about 5:00, staggered into the house, and climbed into the warm bed beside Phyl. But almost as soon as I lay down, the bed took off spinning—boy, was I drunk! Not long after I was sick as a dog and, when Phyl tried to wake me in the morning, I wasn't even able to get out of bed.

I stayed in bed that whole day and couldn't eat anything until the following morning. Calving and other calls came in constantly and I didn't know what was happening at the Bull Sale. Phyl and Bob were doing their best to cover for me but things were right out of control. Finally, at noon on the second day, I left for a call to Hughie Robertson's place at Pritchard to attend to a heifer with a huge calf stuck in her. I was sick again even before I got there and would have given anything just to stay in the car. Somehow I got going and, after some difficult manoeuvring, was able to deliver the calf alive. That entire episode was a nightmare that I'll never forget and, to this day, I can't even look at the yellow label on a Cutty Sark bottle. Later on, when I told Thurman what had happened, he slapped me on the back and had a good laugh. He said that the same thing had happened to him many, many times. The mare, thank goodness, healed up and foaled in the spring.

One fall Thurman sold his calves to a buyer in Washington State and, of course, they had to be tested for export. Given his exceptional state-of-the-art, flood-lit corrals and since I was very booked up at the time, we decided I would do the work in the evenings. It was a nippy November evening and Thurman was pacing the catwalk over the chute, supervising, as he liked to do. He had on a big coat with deep pockets and I could tell he was getting cold—Texans really don't stand the cold all that well—and it wasn't long before he dragged a bottle of Cutty Sark out of one of his pockets. He cracked the top and before long the bottle was empty. He passed it around and found some takers among the boys but I had learned my lesson. Before long, he sent up to the house for another bottle and got well into that one when suddenly there was a great crash: he had passed out, fallen off the catwalk, and landed on his back in the mud. The boys loaded him in the back of the pickup and took him up to the house where they helped Hally get him cleaned up and into bed. We were almost done, so I decided to quit for the night and start again at first light. When I arrived the next morning, the boys were standing around, looking down at the ground... There in the mud was a perfect impression of Thurman, six inches deep, frozen for the duration of the winter.

I HAD WANTED TO work at Douglas Lake Ranch since I was a kid, when I had ridden from Kelowna through the ranch from Westwold to Pennask Lake. Like the Gang Ranch, Douglas Lake Ranch was huge, had an equally fascinating history, and the same magical quality. Col. Spencer and Frank Ross (who was to become the Lieutenant-Governor of BC) had recently sold the ranch to C.N. Woodward, owner of the Woodward's chain of department stores. The previous manager, Brian Chance, had not required the use of a veterinarian except for vaccinating their heifer calves—as with many ranches, it wasn't worthwhile to use a veterinarian except for herd problems—and Mr. Chance had always used a North Kamloops vet, Geordie Clark, who was about the same vintage as my old employer. I must admit that I had envied this arrangement, as I certainly could have used this lucrative work.

Mr. Chance hired a young man named Neil Woolliams to become his understudy. Neil became a very close and lifelong friend, not only to Phyl and me, but also to our children. When Mr. Chance retired, Neil became ranch manager and it wasn't long before he proved he was up to the job. He had several very competent farm managers and a legendary cow boss, Mike Ferguson (son of Harry Ferguson). Mike was a World War II veteran who had seen action in the Italian campaign. He had been in charge of a string of pack mules used to carry supplies to Canadian soldiers fighting in isolated and difficult mountain terrain. Mike was held in high regard, even revered, by everyone who knew him, and especially by his cowboys.

Mr. Woodward, or "Chunky" as he preferred to be known, had spent much of his early life on the Alkali Lake Ranch owned by his maternal grandfather, Wynn Johnson. He had a good knowledge of cattle and horses, and at some point became very interested in cutting horses. It wasn't long before he had a large indoor arena constructed, complete with stalls and pens, and set about purchasing several top cutting horses as well as a number of quarterhorse mares, fillies, colts and a stallion. He hired a well-known BC horse trainer, Jimmy McDonnell, to work with the horses and the ranch was soon in the horse business in a big way. Several aspiring young horse trainers were hired to help Jimmy, including Art Graves and Dave Batty.

Early on, some of the more promising fillies and colts were sent to Texas to be trained by the world-famous Matlock Rose. After a few years, Jimmy and Art moved on, but Dave stayed to become a renowned cutting horse trainer. The Douglas Lake Cattle Company, already famous in its own right, made a real name for itself through the quality of the horses it produced, including several world champions. I became the veterinarian on call to treat and care for these valuable animals—a role that I enjoyed tremendously—and I developed lasting friendships with Dave, Jimmy, Art and, especially, Chunky.

The reputation of the ranch drew the attention of the Duke of Edinburgh, who was interested in cattle ranching and these specially trained cutting horses. He accepted an invitation from Chunky to visit the ranch for a week and spent a great deal of time at the cutting horse

arena, appearing early in the morning to hang out with Jimmy and
Mike and watch Dave and Art in the training sessions. One morning
during his stay, I got a call and was within a few miles of the ranch
when I ran into the first of two RCMP roadblocks. When I finally
arrived at the barn, I was unloading equipment from my car when I
saw an unassuming figure dressed in jodhpurs approaching. It was the
Duke—all by himself—and I had five minutes or so with him, explaining what I was proposing to do. He became very popular with everyone on the ranch. Later, the Canadian Cutting Association had one of
Douglas Lake's best quarterhorse fillies flown to England as a gift. She
became one of the Duke's favourite polo ponies.

I didn't do a great deal on the cattle side of things at Douglas Lake
but, from my point of view, there was no ranch in my entire practice
that had more competent management, better cowboys or handling
facilities. Under Neil and Mike's direction things always went very
smoothly and on time. The cowboys working under Mike had to measure up to his high standard or they simply didn't last long.

There were quite a few black bears on the ranch and, if they were
unfortunate enough to be spotted, they were immediately pursued.
Being well mounted on good steady horses, a couple of experienced
cowboys could rope a bear, and they'd kill it if they caught it, given
the number of calves that got mauled and often killed. It was a dangerous sport—if you could call it that—but these cowboys couldn't be
deterred. In those days, cowboys were really cowboys.

In the mid-sixties, the ranch received an order from Chile for eight
hundred two-year-old heifers. They were to be trucked to Vancouver
and loaded onto a specially designed cattle boat, accompanied by Neil
to ensure they were well looked after. I was to inject them with long-
acting penicillin just prior to their trip to Vancouver, to lessen the risk
of "shipping fever," which is often brought on by stress. There were
about two hundred in the first lot and eight or ten at a time would be
loaded in the chute. All I had to do was walk along the catwalk and inject
each one in the hip with my automatic gun syringe—what could be sim-
pler? But after we had done the first hundred or so, someone noticed that
about half of them were lying down, some flat out. It turned out that they
had had a severe reaction to the penicillin! Luckily, it was short-lived and

they all recovered, but it was quite a scare. We stopped injecting them and for the next load, I found another formulation that worked perfectly.

Once under way, Neil's trips went smoothly, with no losses and one pregnant heifer safely giving birth during the twenty-one-day trip. I had supplied Neil with a considerable stock of drugs (Chloromycetin, PenStrep, and others) in case he had problems on the trip. The drugs came in very handy with the customs officials in Valparaiso, who lined up to receive "gifts" of cigarettes, boxes of T-shirts, alcohol, and modern drugs not available at that time in Chile.

When we announced our decision to leave Kamloops in 1968, Chunky Woodward threw a great going-away party at the ranch for Phyl and me. Many of our good rancher friends and ranch staff were invited and we had a wonderful time. The highlight of the evening was when Chunky presented us with a beautiful lamp, the base of which was one of his most prized possessions: his World Champion Cutting Horse Competition trophy, which he had won with his mare Stardust Desire in Texas the previous year. The trophy itself was a sculpture of a cutting horse by a very famous artist, one of a kind and very expensive. I remember being completely overwhelmed by such generosity. The BC Cattlemen's Association also had a party for us, and I was presented with a personalized briefcase, which I still have.

BC CATTLE COMPANY WAS another ranch, owned and operated by Jack Koster, where I did a fair amount of work. Jack and his brother Henry had been raised on the Empire Valley Ranch just downriver from Gang Ranch. When Empire Valley was sold, Jack wound up ranching and Henry became a cattle buyer and, later, a real estate agent specializing in the sale of ranches. Jack's ranch at Canoe Creek was a fair size, probably running eight hundred to a thousand cows. I was called there only once or twice a year, usually to vaccinate heifer calves for Bangs (brucellosis). With each call, before I left town, Jack always asked me to run around and pick up parts for tractors, trucks and other machinery. This was a bit inconvenient since I liked to get away early and invariably came back late, outside of regular business hours, but it was pretty hard to say no to Jack.

Because the ranch was such a long way from Kamloops, I often stayed for meals and Jack loved to tell stories. When I told him the story about the Native cowboys and the Chinese cooks in the slaughterhouse at Gang Ranch, Jack—who was half Native himself and employed all Native cowboys from the reserve next door—said he had encountered similar situations. In the '60s, most ranches were still using Chinese irrigators who came up every summer season from Chinatown in Vancouver to flood irrigate the hay fields. No one could hold a candle to these amazing men—they were so good at handling water that it was said they could even make it run uphill.

The creek that brought the Natives their drinking water ran through the reserve, and Jack's ranch had hay fields straddling the reserve. The Chinese were working upstream of the reserve, spreading the water evenly over the hayfields with only a shovel and their innate knowledge of how water moves. They lived rough while doing the work, and to rig up a temporary toilet, they put poles across some of the main ditches that they would sit on when the need arose. This set the Natives off and, to solve the problem, they went out one night and carefully cut the poles with a saw almost through from the underside so that the cuts wouldn't show. A day or so later when the irrigators went to do their business, the poles collapsed and at least one of the Chinese guys got dunked in the cold water. They got the message.

When Jack and his family went to Calgary for a break at Christmastime, the Native cowboys were left in charge. There was a cookhouse with a Chinese cook who lived in a room at the back. All the cowboys, even though they lived nearby, ate their meals at the cookhouse. Evidently the cook got very drunk on Christmas Eve and the next morning when they came for breakfast there was not the least sign of life, not even smoke coming from the chimney. They banged on the door, even the walls, but couldn't rouse the cook. Somehow they were convinced that he was awake but just didn't want to work on Christmas Day. As they didn't want to break anything, they went up to the powderhouse and got a roll of dynamite fuse. They lit the end, stuffed it through the keyhole, and kept feeding it in. Fuse really smokes and they were finally able to smoke out the cook and get their breakfast.

I never could understand why so many calls seemed to come on Sundays. I got a call from Jack one Sunday morning, telling me that he had at least thirty dead cows not far from the ranch house. I left right away and arrived at the site about five hours later. Jack was on his D6 Cat digging a large trench in which to bury the dead cows. Tears were streaming down his face, somewhat surprising me as he was a big tough man and had been through no end of hardship during his life. Anyway, he told me that he always put the cow herd down on the big river benches just south of Crows Bar after weaning, and would leave them there, on good bunchgrass, until late November or early December, depending on the weather. The boys had rounded them up the day before and brought them up to an old stackyard for the night before moving them onto the winter feeding grounds.

I could see the remains of a good stand of lamb's quarters weeds where the old haystacks had been. Lamb's quarters, at certain times of the year, is often laced with nitrates and many of the cows, being hungry after the drive, had filled up on it. A diagnosis of nitrate poisoning was pretty obvious, although I did send off some samples to the lab for verification. Luckily, many of the cows recovered after being moved, but over fifty succumbed. A big loss on any ranch.

BUD WATT, CHARLIE BAKER and Loy Finley[3] were three real characters, always up to something. They all belonged to the Clinton Cattlemen's Association, which held one or two meetings a year, usually in the old Clinton hotel. Real estate agent Gordon Abbey owned the hotel. Gordon and Henry Koster formed a company (A and K Cattle Limited) and, from time to time, traded a few cattle. In Gordon's eyes, this made him a cowboy and gave him the privilege of wearing a large white cowboy hat, shiny boots, a fancy snap shirt, Levi's and often even a kerchief around his neck. He liked to sit in with the boys during their Association meetings.

The fall meeting usually signalled that the year's work was pretty much done, and that called for a celebration. Gordon provided good food and, towards the end of the meetings, the booze always flowed freely. Some of the guys, bothered that Gordon dressed like such a dude, cooked up an excuse to adjourn to the woodshed behind the hotel. In the middle of the shed was a good-sized chopping block with a sharp axe stuck in it. They all stood around with their drinks in hand, including Gordon, sporting the big white cowboy hat of which he was so proud.

As the conversation got rowdier, Charlie Baker suggested to Gordon that he couldn't sink the axe into that big chopping block, blindfolded. The idea sparked a wager and soon a collection was taken and Gordon agreed on a bet of $25. Someone produced a big hotel towel to serve as a blindfold, which of course could only be secured once the big hat had been removed. Once Gordon was blindfolded, the hat was carefully placed in the middle of the chopping block and, at the count of three, down came the axe, squarely in the middle of the hat. When the blindfold was removed, Gordon saw his hat on the chopping block, the axe stuck through the crown of it, and the penny dropped. He was never seen in a cowboy hat again.

OF ALL MY CLIENTS, the Pozzobon brothers—Sammy, Marino and Friede—had the most wicked sense of humour and the greatest love for practical jokes. In this regard, no one could top them. Their reputation preceded them long before I met them—they had pulled a number of stunts that people still talk about. Harvey Heathfield got on the wrong end of one of their pranks. Harvey was a big, happy-go-lucky guy and the area dealer for International Truck and Implements. He had just built a new showroom on the main street in Kamloops. Sammy and Marino thought they had an axe to grind with Harvey, so early one morning they loaded a really cranky cow with a good set of horns into the back of their rattletrap old truck. They arrived at the showroom just as the place was opening for business, backed the truck up to the main door, and dumped this miserable cow. They just sat back to watch, laughing, as this mean old cow chased everyone out into the street. That was their idea of a good prank.

Sammy was one of those people who made you feel good just being around him. He delighted in sneaking up behind me, no matter where I was, and giving me a great rib-crushing bear hug. As I got to know them, and went on calls to their ranch, I was also subjected to the Pozzobons' wacky sense of humour. They would steal my car keys, hide my equipment, siphon gas out of my car, and so on. I happened to be up at their place one day to vaccinate calves while they were sorting out some cows they had rounded up—some were theirs and some belonged to Brigadier Bostock.[4] Brigadier, along with his two spinster sisters, had inherited the ranch at Monte Creek.[5] It wasn't a big place, probably running two hundred cows, so his cattle ran on common range along with those of several other ranchers, including the Pozzobons. The Brigadier was a nice old guy, prim and proper as the son of an English gentleman would be. His service in the Army added to his serious demeanour. The Pozzobons, whenever they got a chance, delighted in pulling his leg and generally teasing him. You could tell that it was difficult for him to tolerate these characters.

When I arrived at the corral, they had the cattle sorted and were taking turns loading them, when suddenly Sammy said to the Brigadier, "I'll bet you a bottle of good Scotch that I can get our cattle unloaded faster than you can unload yours." The Brigadier had a very good truck with an excellent tailgate that made for easy loading. The Pozzobons, on the other hand, had a wreck of an old truck with a piece of plywood across the back secured with a length of rope. The Brigadier's eyes lit up and I could tell he was thinking, "Now, at last, I have a chance to get even with these rascals."

I had a watch with a sweep second hand so I was elected to be timekeeper, and I couldn't see how "the Brig" could lose. The rules were clear and simple: the truck had to be backed up to the loading chute and timing began when the driver got out of the truck and ended when the last cow was out. They generously let the Brig go first and he got his truck unloaded in jig time. He had a great wide smile on his face as he pulled his truck away to let Sammy take his turn. Sammy jumped into their truck and backed it up to the chute. He tumbled out holding a chainsaw and, to our utter amazement, cranked it up. Before we could blink he'd cut a huge, rough hole in the side of his truck. Cattle poured out one after another in record time and ran off across the field. Sammy and Marino were practically rolling on the ground, killing themselves laughing, while the Brigadier claimed foul—but to no avail. There had been no rule saying the cattle had to end up in the corral, and these guys would stop at nothing to have some fun.

Sammy and his wife lived on a somewhat isolated piece of property on the north side of the river across from the Pritchard Store. They struggled to get their children to the school bus, especially in the winter. Sammy got fed up with this and bought a property east of

Pritchard on the Trans-Canada Highway. He couldn't afford to build a new house there, so he and Marino decided to simply move the old house. They rigged up one of Friede's logging trucks with a low-bed trailer, jacked up the house, got it on the trailer and pulled it out to the main road. Without a permit, they headed downhill, through a gully, to the river and the bridge. To negotiate the gully, the road makes several sharp turns, and they got stuck on the first one. Luckily it wasn't a busy road, so they walked back to the ranch, got their D6 Cat, and pulled the truck and trailer back up the hill, without the house falling off.

But it was still a long way down to the bridge. The clay cliffs that started out steep just got steeper. However, they found the beginning of a gap in the cliffs and bulldozed a channel wide enough to let the truck and the house through. They parked it pointing downhill and surveyed the flat and the riverbank far below. According to Marino, Sammy took a great pinch of Copenhagen, pulled down his black hat, jumped in the truck, put it into its lowest gear and took off down the precipice. It was soon evident that, no matter what Sammy did, he couldn't hold the truck and its load. Marino, recounting all this to me, said, "Christ, man, I thought Sammy was a goner. There was a great cloud of dust and he was going like hell when he hit the flat. Somehow the house stayed on and he got the damn thing stopped with just a few feet to spare, right at the riverbank. I ran down the cliff to the truck and Sammy was just sitting there behind the wheel. He was white as a sheet and all shaky." They never told me how they got the house that last couple of miles, across the bridge and up the Trans-Canada to its new location. But it all worked out in the end, and you can see the house beside the highway to this day.

It wasn't too long after this that Barbara Spencer decided to sell the Greenacres Ranch, a very picturesque place on the north side of the Thompson River, about six miles upstream from Pritchard. Sammy and Marino were somehow able to scrape up enough money for a down payment and bought the place, which, to many of us, was quite a surprise. I was called out there one day to look at a lame horse and found Sammy and Marino recovering from a nearly tragic mishap.

They had decided to run a fence down a steep hill to the buildings and corrals below, directly under a long stretch of high-tension power line. Once all the posts were in, they'd strung a roll of barbed wire down the hill under the power line, and had been looking for a way to tighten the wire before stapling it to each post. They had the wire solidly attached to the top post and had decided to use the tractor at the other end to pull it tight. Marino, on the tractor, was to very carefully and gently stretch the wire while Sammy hammered in the staples. But just before I'd arrived, something had gone terribly wrong and the tractor got a bit out of control. The barbed wire had snapped up and hit the power line. I found them standing beside the tractor, both looking pretty shaken up. The tractor was smoking and you could smell burning rubber. When I asked what had happened, Sammy summed it up for me: "Christ, man, you never saw anything like it. When the wire hit the power line, there was one big blue flash and then another when it hit the tractor. It blew Marino right off the tractor seat and onto the ground. I thought it killed him." Marino had some burns on his hands but otherwise seemed okay, and they both started laughing. The tractor's electrical system was destroyed, which seemed to upset them more than anything.

The Pozzobons didn't take kindly to being messed with. Don Olson told me a story about a neighbour who lived in a small house down the road from their place and who was suspected of cutting their fences. To send a clear message to this unfortunate offender, Sammy and Marino took a roll of barbed wire to his house one night and quietly wrapped the entire roll around and around the house. With the windows and doors barricaded, it must have been quite a chore for the family to hack their way out with wire cutters.

I saw Sammy a few years ago at a meeting when I was working for the BC Cattlemen. As usual he got behind me and gave me his customary bear hug. We had a few good laughs after the meeting and not long afterwards I heard that he had died.

A BRIEF FLIRTATION WITH ACADEMIA

MY OFFICIAL TERM WITH the University of Saskatchewan was to commence June 1, 1968, but I had arranged to work the month of May and return to Kamloops for the month of June to facilitate our move to Saskatoon at the end of the kids' school year. So on May 1, after ten years of practice in Kamloops, leaving behind my dear wife and children and many, many good friends, I left early in the morning for Saskatoon. I remember feeling very, very sad and lonely on that trip, tears welling up in my eyes until I was well past Revelstoke. The ordeal and pain that Phyl and I had suffered regarding our son Tom, as well as the strain of selling the practice to Don Olson, left me feeling very vulnerable, filled with remorse and self-recrimination. In truth, I think I was burned out. I kept trying to answer the question, "What have I done?" It didn't help that it was snowing.

I recall nothing of the actual trip other than the fact that, once I got east of Calgary, I was again taken aback by how flat the surrounding country became. To one who had been raised in mountains and valleys, it was a peculiar, uncomfortable feeling.

The building for the Western College of Veterinary Medicine in Saskatoon was still being completed and in my eyes it was a magnificent facility. The fourth-year, or 1969, graduating class would be the first group to be trained in the new clinics. When I arrived, the ambulatory service was already up and running. The university had purchased several local practices, so the college was responsible for providing the bulk of both large and small animal services in and around Saskatoon.

The college dean was the highly respected Dr. Larry Smith, who had been on the faculty at OVC during my student days. My immediate boss was Dr. Red Fraser, who had been one of the clinicians on ambulatory service at OVC and who had sold me his car just before we left Guelph. He was a good friend and mentor, and helped me get organized. Above the large animal clinic was a suite of rooms plus a kitchen, normally used by professors and students on night duty. I took a room there for the month of May.

A serious face for a serious job: assistant professor at the new College of Veterinary Medicine, University of Saskatchewan.

I was joining the staff as Director of Large Animal Clinics, an assistant professor with tenure. I would be working with three skilled clinicians: Dr. Larry Kramer, a Cornell graduate and the large animal surgeon; Dr. Otto Radostits, my "friend" from our student days at OVC; and Dr. Bill Cates from the US, who was head of animal reproduction. I was responsible for the hiring of the lay staff, procurement of feed and drugs, and for the operation of the large animal and ambulatory clinics. I hadn't been there for long when it became evident that there was a lot of animosity and rivalry amongst the clinical staff, and also with the head of the small animal clinic, Dr. Len Hurov. I was soon introduced to academic politics and spent a considerable amount of time refereeing vitriolic differences between my colleagues, which left me feeling naïve and alone in my efforts to represent the interests of the students.

I was kept very busy that month but spent what little time I had to myself missing Phyl and the kids a great deal, and wishing I were back in my Kamloops practice.

Larry Kramer and I soon became good friends, our interest in horses giving us an immediate bond. He was an equine specialist first and foremost, a first-class teacher and an excellent surgeon. His concern about the lack of a suitable equine facility was already well known to our colleagues, and he found a ready ally in me.[1] The large animal surgery, designed for cattle, was completely inadequate for horses. There was a poor recovery facility, and the tilt table was unpadded and dangerous for equine surgeries. Larry had tried to operate on several valuable horses shipped over from Calgary and one had actually battered itself to death as it recovered from anaesthetic. At that time, equine practice in Canada was in its infancy, and Larry and I appeared to be the only advocates for a separate facility to handle horses. It was terribly frustrating for us to be constantly outvoted, even ridiculed, when it came to spending money on upgrading our facilities. Of course now all veterinary colleges in North America are well set up to handle equine patients.

As a single man, Larry also had a room in the apartments above the clinic. On weekend mornings, one of the students, Ed Weibe, delighted in waking up Larry, knowing how he loved his sleep-ins. The apartment had a door that opened onto the flat tar-and-gravel roof looking over the unloading area. Farmers would bring their animals in at all hours, pushing a button by the door that set off a loud buzzer in our apartment to alert us. One Sunday morning around 6:00, I heard Ed leave the apartment and go downstairs. A minute or two later, the buzzer sounded, waking up Larry from a dead sleep—that rat Ed! I walked out onto the roof in my pajamas and looked down and sure enough, there was someone with black hair, in a western shirt and jeans and boots, leaning on the buzzer. It was Ed for sure. I reached down and scooped up a generous handful of gravel off the roof and dropped it on his head. I was mortified when an unfamiliar, bewildered face stared up at me from down below! I quickly got dressed and rushed down to help the poor man unload his ailing cow. I apologized profusely and, when I explained what had happened, he was generous enough to share a good laugh with me. Larry teased me about it for months, bless his heart.

Phyl and I had decided that she should come to Saskatoon at the end of May and spend a few days with me looking for a house we could buy

Mentor and Dear Friend, Dr. Frank Loew

ONE OF MY GREAT friends from that era was Dr. Frank Loew, Professor of Comparative Animal Medicine. He was a native of New York State and a graduate of Cornell's veterinary school. He was an absolutely delightful person, very bright, with a great sense of humour and loaded with personality. He was very highly regarded at the college and was a great friend

of Larry Kramer, who was also a Cornell graduate. Frank loved horses, and the three of us ramped up our advocacy for better equine facilities. At one time Frank had been an accomplished rider, until he was badly injured in a fall. His horse had landed on top of him, and a severe hip fracture resulted in a permanent limp and chronic pain. This was

before replacement surgery, although years later Frank did have his hip replaced successfully.

Frank became a great favourite with Phyl and our children. He completely enthralled the kids with his tricks and stories. He amazed them by passing a coin into one ear and out the other. He had an empty goldfish bowl on his desk and convinced the kids that he had several invisible goldfish. He also convinced Steven that he had a boa constrictor in his coat closet and would open the door a crack, jump back and slam it. Steven's eyes would practically pop out of his head. Several years later Frank left Saskatoon and took a similar job at Tufts' veterinary school in Boston. From there, he became Dean of the Veterinary College at Cornell and, later, President of Becker College in Worcester, Massachusetts.

Frank was very popular with faculty and students alike. He was a gifted public speaker, a real charmer who took fundraising seriously, raising millions of dollars for Becker College. Over the years, Phyl and I kept in close contact with Frank and visited him in Boston while he was at Tufts. During his time at Saskatoon, Frank researched and wrote a book on the life of the first veterinarian to join the RCMP in the late 1800s, who did the veterinary work on the police force's horses.

Unfortunately, during his tenure at Becker, Frank contracted a very rare type of cancer, untreatable and fatal. We received a written account of his funeral, which was attended by the student body, faculty, politicians and friends from all over the US. He had over five hundred people in his email address book. He was an outstanding individual, one of a kind, and it was a privilege for us to be counted among his friends. We still miss him dearly.

or rent. She took the train from Kamloops and I was so anxious to see her that I caught a train to Lloydminster and met up with her there. We found a place to rent on Phillips Crescent in a neighbourhood with good schools, quite near the college.

I WENT HOME IN June to help Phyl pack up our lives in Kamloops and bring the family to Saskatoon. We loaded Phyl's small car with as much as we could fit in it, including our budgie in his cage and a washtub full of toads that Steven had collected. We hitched it on behind the station wagon, and set off with the three kids and our two dogs, Max and Tara. We stopped overnight at Shuswap (where Steven and Sarah Mears managed to collect *more* toads), and then again in a campground near the Calgary Stampede grounds, where we met up with R.J. and Lois Bennett and Tom and Mo White. R.J. said we looked like something out of *Grapes of Wrath*.

We settled in to our Saskatoon house and, as usual, Phyl had things well in hand. We enrolled the children in school and they adapted

Phyl, Kathy and I attended the Western College of Veterinary Medicine's first convocation and met former Prime Minister John Diefenbaker, who presented the certificates.

quickly. Our rental agreement stated that we could not have the dogs in the house or the basement, so I fenced off part of the yard and built sleeping quarters for them under the back porch. They were good enough to not cause us any trouble by barking. There really wasn't much to do on days off except to drive around the city, and occasionally we ventured out into the countryside. These drives soon became quite boring, as everything was flat and uninteresting. Before long, to my detriment, I began pining for hills and valleys and friends in BC.

I soon had my first encounter with the union at the university. I had four men responsible for cleaning stalls and feeding animal patients. Unfortunately, one of them left a pitchfork in a stall with a valuable racehorse. Kramer was livid and insisted I fire the man and, since I agreed with him, I did. The next morning, the local union rep contacted me and explained that I couldn't fire someone without going through a lengthy process involving a series of grievances and a hearing that would decide if the complaints were deemed serious enough to take this action. I had little time for union nonsense (my time on the pipeline, paying useless dues, had really left a bad taste in my mouth) so I responded by having this person sit on a chair outside one of the stalls from 8:00 a.m. to 5:00 p.m., with time off for coffee, bathroom breaks and lunch. He lasted about two days and quit, thereby solving my problem but making me most unpopular with the union leaders.

IT BEGAN TO GET quite chilly in September, and winter arrived in late October. It got colder and colder until forty below zero was quite a common occurrence. I remember getting up one morning and noticing frost on the ceiling in the kitchen where the vent led from above the stove to the outside. The only way to be sure your car would start was to plug it in, both at home and at work. Downtown, it was common practice to leave your car running after you parked it. At work, we took extra care to keep the professor and students on ambulatory calls in close contact via radio. Each car was supplied with survival suits in case they ran into a blizzard or went off the road.

The kids were busy with school and activities and Phyl took up curling, which she very much enjoyed. As a family, we enjoyed my more regular hours and weekends off. I came home for lunch every day and gained ten pounds that year.

With the approach of Christmas 1968, we found ourselves missing friends and family and dreading the prospect of the long, cold Saskatchewan winter that still remained after the holidays. Feeling a bit flush on my regular paycheque, we decided to splurge on a colour TV set—they were all the rage then and we'd been using a pair of pliers to change the channels on our second-hand black and white set for ten years! On an impulse, we bought two more, one for Phyl's sister Mary, who'd been tragically widowed that year and left with five children; and one for our dear friend Tom White, who had so patiently done our complicated accounting for so many years. Wanting to really surprise them, we had them delivered with a card that read "With love, Roy Gbiv."[2] They puzzled over the identity of their mystery "Santa" until we finally let the secret out of the bag.

In January, quite out of the blue, I received a call from my friend R.J. Bennett telling me that he and his brother Bill had bought the famous ACT Ranch (or Eldorado Ranch) from Austin C. Taylor, a well-known Vancouver businessman and thoroughbred breeder.[3] R.J. and Bill had become developers and had built the first strip mall in Kelowna, and their plan was to build a three-thousand-home subdivision on the bottomland surrounding the ranch headquarters.

At that time, the federal Liberal government had in place a program that gave generous grants and tax considerations to any industry that wished to locate in western Canada. Hiram Walker distillery had bought a two-hundred-acre parcel from Bill and R.J. for the construction of a distillery. Distilleries produce a by-product of water and used corn, which can be placed in huge dehydration towers and turned into valuable animal feed. This is an expensive process, however, and rarely breaks even. But in Kentucky, to avoid the expense of dehydration, the fluid waste is fed directly to cattle in feedlots. Hiram Walker had approached the Bennetts about pumping the by-product over to the main ranch to be used in such a feedlot. The question put to me was whether I'd be interested in setting up and managing such an operation.

They offered to fly me to Walkerville, Ontario, to visit the Hiram Walker plant, then on to Kentucky to see first-hand some of the feedlots that utilized liquid distillery waste. I was able to arrange some time off and, after spending a day in Walkerville, was off to Louisville with a very experienced distillery executive. What we saw was, to me, nothing short of appalling. Tanker loads of liquid distillery waste, about

3 percent solid, were delivered to a system of troughs and the only way the cattle could get nourishment was by drinking it. The liquid went right through them and the feedlots were at least knee-deep in liquid manure. Wherever there was a sufficient grade, the liquid was run off into adjacent creeks. I remember several dead animals were lying partly submerged in the mess in one lot. They may have drowned! The fellow I was with had seen this before and certainly didn't like it, but was not fazed by it. I was horrified.

When I got back to Saskatoon I made my report to the Bennetts and put the idea to rest. The size of the distillery that Hiram Walker had proposed was many times larger than the average one in Kentucky. In order to handle this much waste, one would need a huge feedlot and sufficient dry feed to mix with the liquid coming from the distillery to make things work properly and humanely. It seemed completely impractical to me, and I put aside my thoughts of returning to my roots and my beloved, warm Okanagan.

Back at the university, however, I became more and more disillusioned. I got into a real row about the building of a hayshed. I had been asked to include the construction of a hayshed in my budget and, envisioning a simple pole-and-steel-roof structure (that had worked perfectly well for my Kamloops ranch clients), I budgeted $50,000. The university's building and grounds staff, on the other hand, decided that a concrete structure was needed and insisted that I budget $500,000! I refused, of course, but it made me unpopular.[4]

In the meantime, I had a small personal project underway. I had always been interested in antique items and had been given some old veterinary instruments when I worked for Pat Talbot. It struck me that a collection of old instruments would be an interesting addition to the college, so I contacted the four western provincial veterinary associations and asked them if they would be kind enough to include a small notice in their publications. To my surprise, within only a few weeks, I was literally inundated with shipments large and small from all over Western Canada. Kramer and I sorted and labelled them, but it took months of begging and pleading to get a $200 cabinet built to house some of the more interesting pieces. When we completed it, it was a huge success as a teaching tool, and I understand that there are now several glass display cabinets! But the struggle to get support for the building of the cabinet, following the hayshed budget debacle, just added to my disenchantment with the university system.

Easter came along and we were pining for our cabin at Shuswap, so we loaded the kids and dogs in the car and took off at about 2:00 p.m. on Good Friday. It was dark by the time we got to Drumheller but it was a clear night and we could almost taste being there, so we decided to drive straight through, seven or eight hundred more miles. We arrived at about 3:00 a.m. and there was a foot and a half of snow in the driveway, so we bundled the kids up and lit a fire. It was wonderful to be back in BC, and I was regretting ever having left.

I WAS BECOMING MORE and more restless and unhappy. Things culminated on the May 24th weekend when I mowed the lawn, put the lawnmower away, and then watched it snow three inches. As far as I was concerned, that was it. I didn't want to spend the rest of my life in the university system or living in a refrigerator. I wrote a letter of resignation that day and mailed it off. At the same time, Dr. Begg, university vice-president, had written to me, offering a promotion from Assistant to Associate Professor. Our letters crossed in the mail.

In the meantime, I knew that R.J. and Bill still wanted me to come to the ranch in Kelowna to help set up a feedlot operation so I decided, quite unilaterally, to take them up on their offer, starting July 1, 1969. What I hadn't considered was that Phyl and the kids were happy in Saskatoon. We'd had a taste of normal family life, unlike the terrible hours and days endured in a busy veterinary practice. In retrospect, I really didn't give Phyl any option other than to leave Saskatoon and I realize now that I shouldn't have ever left Kamloops; neither should I have left Saskatoon. One mistake after another.

Our trip to Kelowna was uneventful and we arrived at our new home, a large house by the highway that had been built as a hunting lodge for Mr. Taylor. R.J. had never been inside to look around and we arrived to find it almost uninhabitable, dirty and dark. Not a good start.

FROM THE FRYING PAN TO THE FIRE

I HAD ALWAYS ADMIRED the old Eldorado Ranch.[1] With its good-looking buildings and rolling alfalfa fields, it was a picturesque property—at least from the highway. I had known the ranch manager, Hugh Stewart, for years. But as soon as we arrived, I could tell that Hugh resented the new ownership and all the changes in the works. He'd had a pretty settled life working for Mr. Taylor, whose only interest in the ranch had been the occasional pheasant-hunting trip, but the prospect of a feedlot operation changed just about everything on this traditional, low-maintenance ranch. Hughie had already been instructed to replace about half of the hayfields and put in silage corn.

We'd been there only about a week when Hugh quit, without any notice, so I took over running the ranch as well as handling the feedlot proposal. Oddly enough, Hiram Walker decided to install dehydration towers but, with so much corn already planted, we were stuck using corn silage for the first year in any case, so R.J. and Bill decided I should still go ahead and organize a feedlot.

What I found out during that first week was quite disheartening—everything was in a terrible state of disrepair. The first time I opened the gate into the main corral, six or eight panels collapsed right before my eyes. Miles of fences were down, and most of the equipment, except for a new Ford tractor and a corn harvester, was old and almost useless.

Steven on Smokey. It was great watching all the kids learn to ride.

Most of the adjacent pasture land had been mismanaged and was choked with knapweed. The manager's house and two smaller houses for ranch hands were in rough shape. In addition, perhaps in a vindictive state of mind, Hugh had turned out the six hundred cows and calves without branding, dehorning or castrating them.

I knew immediately that I was out of my depth. I could handle the cattle end of ranching but not the farming. I needed good people around me and was lucky to have the right contacts. I hired a good cowboy—my friend from Ashcroft, Wilfred Lulu—and Nobby Clark from Kamloops as a farmer. We had hayfields to irrigate (most of which needed re-seeding) and, of course, the corn crop to look after.

There was no sprinkler system, so the corn had to be irrigated using gravity-fed ditches and water that came from Beaver Creek about three miles away. Water flowed through an open dirt ditch that leaked badly and was overgrown with large cottonwood trees—the whole thing was probably 50 percent efficient. Problems everywhere.

Nobby, Wilf and I sunk our teeth into the work, repairing the ditches, the corral system and some of the fences. We bought a second-hand jeep with a post pounder on the front and ordered a truckload of treated six-foot posts. We tried to stop the leaks in the ditch by using several loads of bentonite, which helped a bit.

But none of this was cheap. Luckily, there was a good deal of standing timber on the ranch, so Bill and R.J. had it logged off and milled several miles from the ranch. This gave us a steady source of planks for the feedlot corrals.

With the corn crop only weeks away from maturing, we had to organize harvesting and storage. We had an old dump truck that was still running and R.J. bought us another one, pretty much an antique, and there was a silage wagon that could be pulled behind a tractor. Someone had purchased a two-row corn chopper that attached to the new Ford tractor. That covered harvesting, but where to put the silage? There was an old alfalfa silage pit, but with a bumper crop coming on, we weren't sure it would be big enough. R.J. had purchased a D6 Cat bulldozer for the logging operation above the ranch, so we used it on weekends to enlarge the silage pit. As it turned out, I had miscalculated and made the pit almost twice as large as it needed to be, which was embarrassing. The upside was that we salvaged the clay soil from the pit to build some decent roads. That helped.

We needed a smaller bulldozer to spread the silage around in the pit as we dumped it so R.J. arranged to borrow a bulldozer from an old friend of ours, Jimmy Pollard, who lived up the Chute Lake Road. I set off to Jimmy's place in the dump truck, to haul it over. I hadn't gone very far on the highway when all of a sudden the steering wheel came loose in my hands and I had no control at all! Luckily, in spite of crossing the busy highway and jumping the ditch, the truck came to a stop without causing serious damage. I hitchhiked back to the ranch and Nobby returned to the scene with the Ford to pull the truck out and tow it home. We got it repaired and I was more successful on the second try.

We had the kitchen renovated, but Phyl was having a terrible time trying to make the best of things. We had no social life whatsoever, as

Behaving ourselves (for a moment) at Neil Woolliams' wedding: L–R: Me, John Cuthbert, Neil, Sandy Boyd and Neil's brother David.

I was working day and night in an attempt to get the ranch back on its feet. The kids did well, though. They walked along the railway tracks every morning to the school bus stop, the boys joined the Cub Scouts, and Steven fell in love with his teacher, who was young and beautiful, and wore short skirts. They all learned to ride and helped out when they could. With my mom and dad back from their two years in Australia, we were all back in the same town again. When my work slowed a bit in winter, we were able to start skiing as a family, which we all loved. We spent many weekends driving between home and Silver Star or Sandy Boyd's Tillicum Valley Ski Hill, singing along to our eight-track tape player. And, of course, it was wonderful to be closer to Shuswap—we did our best to spend every spare moment there.

AFTER MANY YEARS AS an eligible bachelor, our good friend Neil Woolliams decided to get married. His friend Guy Rose hosted a stag party for him, to be held at Guy's ranch and in the famous old Quilchena Hotel. On the afternoon of the party, I picked up Sandy Boyd in Vernon and we drove over to Nicola. When we arrived, things were in full swing and I think almost everyone Neil knew was there. Most were feeling little pain. There were businessmen from Kamloops, cowboys from all over the Nicola area and ranchers from everywhere. At one point, Neil was grabbed and chained to the banister in the hotel lobby, a big logging chain around his leg.

When Sandy and I left at 2:00 a.m., Neil was still in captivity. We were both pretty drunk; I took the wheel and got us as far as Kamloops. Sandy took over and I crawled into the back seat and promptly fell asleep. Not long afterwards, I was suddenly awakened by a bump and loud noises. I looked out the window of my station wagon and saw that we were off the road and in the trees on Monte Creek Hill. Sandy had gone to sleep but woke up just in time to steer the car back onto the road with minimal damage. We stayed very much awake for the rest of the way home.

The next night, a second stag party was held for Neil in Penticton, and many of those who attended were friends going back to Neil's younger days at school in Summerland and Penticton. Sandy and I were there again, as we didn't want to miss anything but, after what had happened the night before, Neil was pretty gun-shy. He had arrived in his car but during the evening someone flattened all his tires. Neil was anxious and suspicious all evening, and around midnight he felt pretty certain that something was going to happen to him. So he dashed out, jumped in his car and headed for his parents' home in Summerland. He somehow made it the entire ten or twelve miles, driving the last stretch on the rims.

The wedding was held in the lovely stone Anglican Church in upper Summerland, which was filled to overflowing. Their tasteful, carefully orchestrated ceremony unfolded smoothly until Neil and his bride, Nina, had to kneel before the priest at the altar. Neil was wearing new shoes and someone had marked the sole of the left shoe with a large capital HE and the right one with LP. Everyone in the church (except the priest and the wedding party) could see this and immediately there was a wave of giggling. The happy couple was unsuspecting but the priest was none too amused.

The reception was held at Neil's parents' beautiful lakeshore property and things went off uneventfully until Neil and Nina were to leave. Mr. Woodward (who owned Woodward's Stores as well as the Douglas Lake Ranch) had brought up several cases of puffed wheat cereal and had filled up Neil's going-away car with breakfast cereal. I remember Neil's new brother-in-law waterskiing in his tuxedo and Sandy's two boys, Ian and Rob, up an apricot tree throwing overripe apricots at the wedding guests. The newlyweds spent their honeymoon at our cabin on Shuswap Lake.

BACK AT THE RANCH, it had been decided that the feedlot should operate as a separate entity under the direction of four equal partners (R.J., Bill, a friend of theirs from Vancouver and me). I purchased several hundred head of yearling steers and heifers and put them in our makeshift feedlot. Harvesting the corn was a real nightmare as the old equipment continued to break down. We brought in several truckloads of barley from the Prairies and mixed it with the corn silage we had produced to improve its nutrient value.

At about this time, the cattle began to come down from the summer range and I was rudely awakened one morning by a very irate orchardist complaining that our cows were in his orchard eating apples out of his harvesting bins. We had missed checking the fence in that area, so the whole family was dragged out of bed and enlisted to chase about fifty cows and calves out of the orchard. We spent the day putting in a new fence.

We had no idea how many cows and bulls had been turned out in the spring. R.J. and Bill thought there had been about six hundred head included with the purchase of the ranch but, when we gathered what we could at the end of October, we had about five hundred cows and four hundred calves. Unbranded calves are easy to steal on the open range. More cows kept drifting in, and in the end, I think we had about five hundred and fifty.

The calves, now much larger and stronger than they'd been in the spring, had to be branded, dehorned and the males castrated. It was tough work and we spent considerable time cursing Hughie Stewart. We finished up the calves, and I moved on to pregnancy test the cow herd. We sold off the empties along with the calves. Having been left uncut, many of the bull calves were exhibiting masculine traits, which made them less valuable at the sale.

On a trip to Kamloops to observe the sale of our cattle, I had noticed that the CPR was renewing railroad ties along the highway. I contacted the Kamloops maintenance supervisor and he was happy to let me have the used ties. I hired a large flatbed truck and all of us went up to Kamloops and loaded up about five hundred ties, which were great for rebuilding corrals, feeders, and other things.

We knew early on that we were going to be terribly short of winter hay for the cattle. There was an apple juice plant in Kelowna and I was able to get the pulp from the juiced apples delivered for three dollars a load. This product has little or no protein but is about 15 percent carbohydrate. I purchased a large feed mixer from Calgary for mixing apple pulp and urea (for protein) to supplement the hay. This meant we had to put in a feed trough about a third of a mile long, using planks from the sawmill. It was a lot of labour, but it worked, and we were able to bring the herd through the winter in pretty good condition for calving.

PHYL HAD ALWAYS BEEN interested in the stock market, an interest inherited, at least in part, from her mother. She had met a local broker who agreed to supervise her taking the Securities course. She worked hard and passed with flying colours. This was the first step in her career as an accomplished stockbroker, and her astute investments have served us both well over many years.

The ranch, however, was not nearly as successful. The next summer was a repeat of the first, but we had a terrible time in the feedlot trying to get the cattle fat enough for sale. We were able to get a few loads out but it was obvious we were losing money. We had been shipping to a new slaughterhouse in Armstrong but they went broke, forcing us to ship all the way to Vancouver. I finally had to suggest that we eat some crow and phase out the feedlot.

We continued to have no end of problems with the ranch in general and I had done everything I could think of to keep it on its feet. I was feeling pretty discouraged about the whole situation, and R.J. and Bill, who really wanted to subdivide the place, were also fed up. We were at home on a gloomy February evening when my old friend Tom

White called from Williams Lake to say that John Kelly's ranch at Soda Creek was for sale. Phyl and I drove to Williams Lake that weekend and immediately fell in love with the place. I felt it had great potential because the soil was excellent and anything would grow as long as you had water. With Phyl and Tom both convinced that we could swing the deal, we bought the ranch. I gave my notice, and in March we left the Eldorado.

WE HAD A RANCH AT SODA CREEK...

WE MOVED TO WILLIAMS Lake in March 1971, rented a house and enrolled the kids in school. I went to work for Gordon McKenzie, who'd been in practice there for just over two years. His practice was much like mine had been in Kamloops and was a great asset to the community, especially the ranchers of the area. That spring I mainly handled calving cases and as things slowed down I started spending more and more time at the ranch.

We'd invested every dime we had in the property: twenty-two hundred acres of deeded land, three thousand acres of leased land, and a three-hundred-head range permit. It was situated on a large flat bench across the Fraser River from the historic old town of Soda Creek. The ranch had been quite isolated until just a few months before we bought it, about a two-hour trip from Williams Lake by either the Sheep Creek Bridge or the Alexandria Ferry. Luckily, by the time we arrived, our neighbour Rudy Johnson had put in a bridge across the river about four miles from our place and about twenty minutes from town. Rudy and his wife, Helen, and their children lived on the next place over, the Buckskin Ranch.

The previous owner of our property, John Kelly, had put together a herd of three hundred nondescript beef cows and bulls. There was a barn, several logging-camp bunkhouses on skids, and the house.

It was a proud day for Phyl and me when we hung the sign on the gate to our own ranch.

Ranch hand Art Hunter feeding the cattle.

ONE MAN'S VISION: THE RUDY JOHNSON BRIDGE

RUDY HAD ONLY A Grade 3 education but he was very practical, intelligent and good with equipment. He had discovered a derelict bridge in Alaska, left standing over a dry riverbed after the Alaska earthquake rerouted the river. He bought it from the Alaska government for $40,000, dismantled the steel structure and hauled it in several flatbed trucks down to its new site on the Fraser. He and his sons built large cement abutments on either side of the river below his ranch, and constructed roads to the site on either side of the river.

He started by burying two loads of logs on either side of the river to act as anchors. The river was narrow enough that the boys could shoot an arrow across with a string attached; then they used the string to pull a rope across. He bought a donkey engine and used it to pull a three-inch cable across the river, anchoring it on either side to the buried loads of logs. Finally, with a large pulley attached to the cable, they started bolting the bridge back together, one section at a time.

Photo courtesy Thomas Betsill.

Each section had to be attached to the pulley and pulled out over the river with the donkey engine. The sections were about thirty feet long, and as Rudy bolted the pieces together, one by one, the entire structure became suspended over the river on the cable. He had cemented large bolts to each abutment and had carefully measured the precise distance the bridge had to span, in order that it could be anchored to these bolts. By the time he was ready to attach the bridge, word had gotten out about the novel method he was using. Dominion Bridge sent a couple of representatives to Williams Lake to witness the process and to see if it would work.

The final day came and the fit was perfect. I wish I'd been there. No one had ever built a bridge using this method before but it has since become quite a common practice. Rudy and the boys decked the bridge and immediately he was able to charge a toll to the logging trucks headed to the mills in Williams Lake. The bridge reduced hauling time by about three hours, so it was win-win for everyone. Our friend and accountant Tom White was also Rudy's accountant. He had advised us to invest $10,000 in the bridge but he didn't put the money into Rudy's account until the bridge was attached to the abutments. It turned out to be a great investment for us, and the bridge certainly increased the value of the properties on our side of the river. After several years, the provincial government purchased the bridge from Rudy.

There was no power so we used propane for lights and the stove, and wood for heat. No telephone either, so in emergencies we used the radio telephone at the Buckskin Ranch.

We inherited a ranch hand, Art Hunter, a war veteran who had worked for many years for John Kelly. Art was severely lame in one hip, having spent several years packing railway ties out of the bush on his back.[1] He was a little slow and kind of spooky-looking, frightening

Phyl and the kids at first, but turned out to be a real jewel and quickly became part of the family.

We turned out the cows, calves and bulls onto the open range on June 1, and got ready for haying. Most of the equipment, except for a new baler, was old and in poor shape. I traded in a large Case tractor on a new Massey 1080. I also traded in a pull-type swather for a New Holland self-propelled one. We began haying in June and, literally, as soon as we had the hay down, it began to rain. It was three weeks before we could get it baled and, by then, it was more like straw than feed. Rudy was kind enough to send over his son Randy with their self-propelled bale stacker to stack it for us.

There were about 150 acres in hay, irrigated by a fairly makeshift system that John Kelly had put in. The water came from Yorston Lake above the ranch and a diesel pump brought it over a rise into another four- or five-acre dam. There was a controlled outlet (the head gate) that released it into a creek that ran down to the ranch. John had then trapped the water in an old ten-inch pipeline that ran into another lake below the house and fed the sprinkler system. The sprinklers were all old-fashioned hand lines, and changing them twice a day kept Art and me, along with the kids, busy.

The ranch house at Soda Creek had no power or modern conveniences, but it was home.

Our own brand, so simple
and with an "L"—what could be
more fitting?

Phyl did laundry in the basement
using a generator-powered agitator.
Clothes were rinsed in a
Coleman cooler.

We moved into the house on the ranch in April, and Phyl tried to make the best of a house with no power or modern conveniences. She drove the kids across the river to the bus stop every morning and picked them up every afternoon. She cooked great meals, making everything from scratch, including two large batches of bread every week. She put in a massive garden and canned dozens of jars of fruit, and made the trek to town once a week for huge loads of groceries. She did laundry in the dank, spider-filled basement, using a wringer washing machine that ran off a noisy generator and rinsing the clothes in the biggest container we had—a Coleman cooler—that sat on a rickety wooden bench. Like me, she grew tanned and lean, but it was a lonely, isolated existence.

We had some wonderful family time, though. The kids all worked as much as they could, collecting eggs from our chicken coop, weeding the garden, moving sprinkler lines and—when I wasn't looking—poking our poor old sow in the arse with a cattle prod. They all had their own horses and on rainy days when it was pointless to tackle any other work, the five of us would ride up onto the range to check the cattle. Mr. Woodward had given Phyl a nice, old gentle quarterhorse called Kootenay Spider that had campaigned in reining competitions in the US and Canada. He was perfect for her and they became good friends.

In mid-July, disaster struck. We decided to take three days off to go down to our cabin on Shuswap Lake. I had brought Nobby Clark with me from Kelowna, so he and Art were left in charge. We had a much-needed break but arrived home to our worst nightmare. Art had pulled the head gate out of the water system up above and couldn't get it back in, so we lost pretty much all of that year's remaining water supply. A torrent had come down the hill and washed out a great gouge near the house and down through the vegetable garden, covering it in rocks and gravel. We went on to harvest as much hay as we could but the lack of water really cost us. The yield was poor, and I knew that winter feed was going to be a problem.

We were extremely lucky to have a great bank manager. Simon Kouwenhoven, manager at the Bank of Montreal in Williams Lake, turned out to be the best banker anyone could wish for. He was extremely helpful to us and arranged a generous line of credit. He went on to become the Bank of Montreal's Regional Director for the Maritimes. He was very special.

THE COWS BEGAN TO come down from the range in September and October and, as we pregnancy tested them, we culled about 150 head for sale along with the bulls and the calves. I tried to repay Rudy for his generous help by spending a long day pregnancy testing his cow herd. I purchased replacement bulls and cows through a top cattle buyer from Kamloops, Dale Miller, who bought us ten very good, uniform Hereford bulls from a breeder in Alberta. I was able to get rid of the off-coloured and empty cows and replace them with pregnant Herefords: I knew that if we were going to sell calves, they had to be as uniform as possible.

Nobby's wife was very unhappy on the ranch and they headed back to her home at Deadman's Creek that fall. Art and I handled things that first winter and as spring approached, as expected, we began to run low on feed. At the north end of the ranch there were several acres of small poplar trees. Art and I cut most of them down and the cows ate the budding branches, which are high in protein, to supplement the hay that was left. This worked well and we got through the winter to calving season.

That spring, I hired a strong and hard-working young man, Fred Rosk, a nephew of Rudy's wife, Helen. He and his father, Carl, owned and operated a small equipment and chainsaw repair business in Williams Lake. Fred was willing to tackle anything. He boarded with the Johnsons, and soon became very popular with all of us. Everything he did, including driving, was done at full speed. Fred would appear early every morning—we could see him coming for miles, his old truck racing along the bumpy dirt road in front of a great plume of dust. The kids used to watch from the kitchen window as he came over the hill below the house, taking bets on whether he would get all four wheels off the ground. He was a great help and a good mechanic.

It wasn't long after we got the first crop of hay in that the indispensable diesel pump on Yorston Lake packed it in. It was relatively new and its breakdown came as a real blow. It had to be disconnected, crated up and hauled out of the bush and into town, where it was shipped by freight to Perkins Diesel in Vancouver. It turned out to have a broken camshaft. It was three weeks in a hot July before we got it back. In the meantime, with no irrigation, our second crop began to wither. We harvested the remains of what should have been a very good crop and, once again, we were in a tough spot for winter feed.

THAT WINTER, PHYL AND I decided that we couldn't endure our terrible ranch house much longer and we decided to build a house in town so that, amongst other things, the kids could benefit from after-school activities. We bought a lot on Western Avenue, had some plans drawn up and had a very nice two-storey house built. We wanted a shake roof and, as shakes were expensive and winter was downtime on the ranch, I decided to cut my own. So every morning after feeding the cows, I drove about ninety miles out past Horsefly where I had a Forestry permit to cut down large cedar trees. It took the best part of a month, off and on, to fell the trees, cut the blocks or bolts, pack them out of the bush and load them in my pickup. I was on my own, miles from nowhere, in the middle of winter, and the trees were large, four or five feet through and rotten in the middle. Some of them fell backwards and I scared myself a couple of times, so I had to pay attention.

I got enough blocks home to make twenty-four squares of shakes for the house, but the roofer complained about the pitch of the roof and the snow on it, so I wound up doing most of the roofing myself as well. We were finally able to move into the house in March and it was

Despite my busy schedule, I still managed to get some riding in. This is Major at the PNE in 1972.

a relief for all of us to have power, reliable heat and a telephone. The house turned out to be more attractive than we had expected and some people say it is still the best-looking house in the neighbourhood.

One morning, Fred missed a turn in the road on his way to work and went over a bank, totalling his old truck. Luckily he wasn't injured, but it made it difficult for him to get to work so he decided to go back to working with his father. When he left, I hired a married couple with three children, Jerry and Muriel Dodge. They moved into the ranch house, and Phyl and I rented a good-sized trailer from Tim Bayliff to stay in for the summer when we had to be there overnight. Jerry was an ex-employee of the BC Railroad—strong, hard-working and stubborn. Muriel was a warm and friendly woman who kept busy feeding her family and Art.

Having Jerry on the ranch allowed us to take a bit more holiday time, and also to make some friends in town. I could never resist a good practical joke. I pieced together a wonderful outfit—an old bamboo coolie hat, a walking stick, an old dressing gown and a flowing black tree-moss mustache that made me look (at least from a distance) like a lost disciple of Confucius. It got even better when my Williams Lake dentist, Alistair Menzies, made me a set of buckteeth dentures. That year at Shuswap, I got myself dressed and wandered along the beach in front of the neighbouring cabins. Tom White and his wife Mo had built a cabin next to ours, and I waved at them as they sat eating their breakfast. They had no idea who I was and talked about it for months!

I had a knack for accents and loved making prank phonecalls to friends. Posing as an official at the Chinese Embassy, I got a huge kick out of harassing Tom about his visa application just days before leaving for China. Several other friends found themselves on the receiving end of phone calls from Chinese restaurants confirming their "orders." Of course, having not ordered any food, people were drawn into explanations, which ended in threats of charging for "food arready made" and "derivery boy on his way." This doesn't work so well anymore now that people have call display on their phones.

Alistair Menzies and another Williams Lake friend, Grant Dickie, were even more dedicated pranksters than I was. During a sailing trip in the Caribbean, Grant surreptitiously took a photo of Alistair taking a shower off the back of their sailboat. When they returned to Williams Lake, Grant had the photo blown up into a poster, snuck into Alistair's dental office, and mounted it on the ceiling above the dental chair. Alistair's first client that Monday, a well-known old battleaxe, let out a real shriek when Alistair tipped her chair back. When Alistair looked up, he found himself face to face with an almost life-sized shot of himself in the nude! He spent much of the morning explaining himself to his outraged client.

Grant had no end of ideas for making Alistair's life "interesting." Alistair and his wife, Maggie, had built a beautiful home on the lake, with a board fence around it that ran along the highway. Grant commissioned a huge "Bed and Breakfast—Vacancy" sign and, the night before the Williams Lake Stampede started, had it mounted on their fence with an arrow pointing down to the house. Accommodation during the Stampede was always at a premium and, in no time flat, there was a string of cars and hot, weary travellers lining their driveway and banging on their door.

BACK AT THE RANCH, in an effort to increase our hay production capability, I obtained a government land-clearing grant and hired Mike Priddy from Horsefly with his D8 Cat bulldozer to clear about one hundred acres of land adjacent to the present hayfields. He cleared the worst of the trees and rocks, and all of us spent our spare time removing the smaller rocks, roots and sticks, preparing the land for seeding. We were able to put the new land into good varieties of alfalfa, which made a real difference to our feed supply. I distinctly remember what a wonderful feeling it was that spring, when the new crop began to turn that bare brown field a beautiful shade of green.

We also kept busy that year building a new corral system, of which we were all very proud. It was almost a pleasure to work the cattle in strong, well-planned pens and chutes. Our cattle had responded to the severe culling and the good-quality bulls used on the cows. That fall, we did very well with the calves, sending them over to Alberta to the Fort Macleod auction market where my friend Ken Hurlburt was the owner.

Before getting in the first crop of hay that year, I purchased a machine called the Hesston Stack-Hand that, when attached to our large Massey tractor, was able to pick up the hay left by the swather and compact it into small three-ton stacks, which could then be hauled to the stackyard and unloaded. This really sped up the process, as we no longer had to bale or rely on our good neighbours to help us bale and stack.

During this time I also got tangled up with the BC Livestock Exports Limited (see next chapter), which really didn't help things on

I was very proud of our new corral system, and it sure made life easier!

the ranch. We seemed to go from one crisis to another—but I suppose that's just ranching. Problems with the water system continued to plague us. The ten-inch pipe that John had used for the mainline had been salvaged from an old gold mine out near Likely. It was rusty and probably had been lying on the ground for the better part of a hundred years, but John had hauled it home and, being a very good welder, had been able to tie it together. It was paper-thin in places and, being under considerable pressure, it would often rupture, sending huge geysers of water fifty feet or so up into the air. The entire system then had to be shut down and a homemade patch (made of inner tubes or whatever I could find) bolted over the rupture. Some of these splits were three feet long. It was a tiresome process and made life miserable.

Knowing that water was the most serious threat to our survival, we hired a well-known, experienced hydrological engineer from Vancouver to locate potential sites for a well. He spent three days on the ranch and identified three promising locations. We also brought in a water-witcher—recommended to us by friends—who provided a convincing concurrence on the potential sites. We hired a drilling company from the Lower Mainland and they began drilling the first well. They went down two hundred feet with no luck then tried a second hole with the same result. We had soon run through $10,000, were out

The well-witcher we hired concurred with the hydrological engineer on potential drilling sites.

of money and had to abandon the drilling. This was a severe blow, as we could see that if we kept drawing water from Yorston Lake, as we had been, there was no doubt that it would dry up.

Meanwhile, the cattle on the range had to be continually checked to make certain that bears weren't bothering them or that they weren't getting stuck in the bog holes around the edges of many small lakes and ponds. We tried to do this on rainy days, but often had to drop everything to respond to emergencies relayed to us by Rudy, who had an airplane and flew over the range every other day or so.

That summer, I had a chance to buy two hundred acres from Bob Muncie right on the river two miles upstream from our place for $40,000. This would have given us the additional irrigated acres we needed to be successful, but by then we were too far in debt to buy the property. The noose was beginning to tighten. One bright spot turned out to be the quality and uniformity of our calf crop that last fall. We sold them through the BC Livestock Co-op Auction in October and received the fourth-highest price for any shipment of calves sold that year.

WE WERE NOW ENTERING our fourth winter. The BC Livestock Exports venture had failed, leaving me with a $40,000 debt and this, along with our ever-expanding operating loan, started to weigh heavily on my mind. Luckily, Phyl had done a remarkable job of supplementing our income with a new, growing granola business and I had received a part-time contract with the Ministry of Agriculture, giving day-long courses on nutrition, animal husbandry and veterinary tips to ranchers. This actually proved very successful for all concerned and added a few dollars to our shrinking income.

One of my courses was to be held in the forestry building at Tatla Lake, about a hundred miles west of Williams Lake. It was in February and, after working all day at the ranch, I left to drive out into the Chilcotin in order to be ready for the next morning's class. I was pretty sleepy by the time I got about halfway and that was almost my undoing. I collided with another pickup, driven by a logger hauling a diesel engine to town for repairs. We met head on, on a corner, and demolished both pickups. Afterwards he admitted to me that he had fallen asleep, as I guess I had. I had a sore knee and he had bruised his ribs but otherwise we were okay. What really annoyed me was breaking the

GREENAWAY GRANOLA—AS TOLD BY PHYL

BETWEEN THE GARDEN, THE fresh milk and eggs, the "free" meat and the constant stream of baking that Kathy and I did, we were pretty self-sufficient for food on the ranch. We were highly motivated to avoid the stores because the trip to town took at least a half-hour one way, life was busy and store-bought food was expensive. That might be why it irritated me so much to buy breakfast cereal. Feeding not only the family but also the ranch hands, we went through an inordinate amount of over-priced boxed cereal!

I was a faithful CBC Radio fan and never missed Peter Gzowski's *This Country in the Morning* show. One morning, he described a homemade breakfast cereal that he and his wife had made—a baked concoction of oatmeal, raisins and honey. I requested the recipe and, when I received it, made my first batch of "granola." It was delicious, nutritious and everyone loved it. There was a real movement at that time toward health food and natural products, and granola seemed to be exactly what we had been looking for. By coincidence, *Time* magazine then did a feature on a California man, Layton Gentry, who was manufacturing a new product called Crunchy Granola. The article showed a full-page photo of an empty grocery shelf with a "sold out" sign and mentioned that Mr. Gentry was looking for ways to expand into the Canadian market. It seemed that granola was on my radar and, suddenly, the convergence of all these signs just couldn't be ignored.

I wrote to Layton Gentry but didn't hear back for the longest time. Six or eight months went by before he called one evening, out of the blue, to invite me to tour his plant in California. I flew down and he met my plane, whisked me away in his convertible and installed me at a reasonable motel. I was a bit leery of this slightly racy, divorced, older man, but he was a perfect gentleman. The next day, we toured the plant

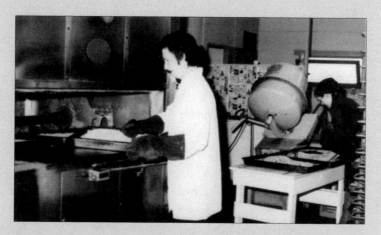

and I took photos of every part of the operation. It was not highly mechanized, as I'd imagined, but more like a professional kitchen with a pizza oven, cooling racks, large weighing scales and four or five women in hairnets. It all looked very do-able but, at the end of the day, I was puzzled and irritated that I still didn't have the actual recipe.

Layton took me out for a nice dinner and a movie, and the next morning we went for a highway drive along Big Sur. I finally had to ask him outright for the recipe, which he recited as he drove while I wrote as carefully as I could on the back of an old grocery list I found in my purse. He mentioned starting a franchise operation in order to provide employment for draft dodgers who'd settled in Canada but, with no formal plan, it was left on a very casual basis. I got back on the plane and was hugely relieved when I arrived home safely.

I realized that my highest priority was to secure a market, so I wrote to our good friend Chunky Woodward, owner of the Woodward's Stores grocery chain. I cooked up a demonstration batch for Chunky and his grocery chain manager, Cyril Keech, and without even tasting it, they placed an initial order for thirty thousand pounds. This really gave me the impetus I needed. I leased a building in Williams Lake and had Belkins Packaging design the box. I ordered stainless steel baking pans, cooling racks, flippers, scales, funnels and a brand new cement mixer that would blend the oats and oil properly. The gas-burning pizza oven was a big investment and I had a Vancouver firm professionally install it. I priced out all the ingredients: the rolled oats came in by the boxcar via the Pacific Great Eastern Railway[2] from the Saskatch-

ewan Wheat Pool, and Rogers Sugar delivered the brown sugar. Almonds, soya bean oil and sunflower seeds came in from wholesalers. Simon Kouwenhoven at the Bank of Montreal was impressed with the Woodward's order and organized a loan, using the commodities as collateral.

Thus Greenaway Granola became the first granola company in Canada. I hired Muriel Dodge as the mainstay of the production line but staffing levels otherwise fluctuated according to the number of orders. Over the weekends, Kathy and Terry often continued the mixing, bagging, sealing, boxing and labelling, while Steven was helping Lorne at the ranch, and our horses ate the sweepings. I secured listings with Safeway, Super-Valu and Overwaitea with the aid of my sales agent, and I went to the Okanagan and other parts of the Interior on my own, just to show various store managers what the product looked like. The sales accelerated. Our prime competitor in those days was Alpen, but it didn't take long for other granola-type products to hit the shelves.

When we moved to Vancouver, I re-located the whole operation to the foot of Fraser Street, and hung up my sign. Within six months, I got an unsolicited offer from the CEO at Flexo Varathane and decided it was the right time to sell.

Hundreds of sandhill cranes arrived at the pond each spring. The sound they made was unforgettable.

handle of the brand new shovel that was in the back of my pickup. The RCMP officer told us to shake hands and contact our respective insurance companies. The trucks were hauled to town and someone drove me the rest of the way to Tatla Lake.

There are many good memories associated with our brief experience cattle ranching. I had a tremendous sense of pride about the sale of our calves and about the ownership of such a beautiful piece of property. There was a steep rim of rock towering about five hundred feet above the home ranch and I remember sitting on my horse one day, looking down on the place. I don't think that I have ever experienced such a feeling before or since.

The ranch house looked out on a shallow lake, probably about forty acres in size, and spring was always heralded by the arrival of numerous species of water birds. Especially exciting was the arrival of hundreds of sandhill cranes. The sound they made in the air and on the ground was unforgettable. Another sound I particularly remember was that of the government snowplow, coming up our private road to plow us out in the middle of one terribly cold January night. We had been snowed in for a week.

The kids were happy and it was nice to have time with them and watch them grow. The first fall, I had given them each a heifer calf, branded on the left ribs with our brand, the Bar L. Kathy helped her mom after school but also had time on weekends to ride her horse, Taffy. Terry was interested in machinery and all things mechanical. Art had an old Datsun pickup and he generously allowed Terry, sometimes accompanied by Steven, to drive around the ranch property. It was quite a sight: Terry doing his best to see over the steering wheel with Steven beside him, only his hat showing. Terry loved to drive the big tractor, which caused me considerable worry, but we never had any accidents on the ranch. Steven was good on a horse and interested in the cattle end of things, and spent hours in front of the house roping fence posts with his lariat. He had a pet crow, Carl, which he'd raised on bread and milk. Carl lived in a large chicken-wire cage and had at least a half-dozen words in his vocabulary. He played endlessly with our little Yorkshire terrier, Hamlet, sneaking up behind him and pulling his hair with his beak. Hamlet would jump on Carl and the two of them would tumble end over end until one of them got tired out. Carl was with us for several years, first in Williams Lake and then in Vancouver.

We had a lot of fun taking the cattle up to the range in spring and gathering them in the fall. When we were up riding we often came across old deserted cabins, which we enjoyed exploring. The entire experience was a learning one for all of us, and we certainly learned to be practical and to appreciate the beauty and power of nature.

Phyl was a brick, especially considering our primitive and isolated situation. She juggled raising three kids and the successful start-up of a new business while still keeping her hand in at the ranch.

IT WAS IN DECEMBER 1973 that real estate agent Wayne Gardner came out to the ranch and asked us if we would be willing to sell the place. He had a buyer from Victoria, Bob Henson, who had a large excavating business. He was tired of the rain, had driven by the ranch while on a hunting trip, and was ready to buy us out for cash. We arranged a lock, stock and barrel deal with him, including the cows. The herd was valued by an independent cattle buyer, Bjorn Nielsen from Ashcroft. We did well in the end, setting a price that allowed us to pay off all our debts with some cash left over. So with many regrets, some tears and remorse, but also some relief, we sold out in February 1974 and moved to town.

PHYL'S $40,000 NECKLACE

BY THE FALL OF 1972, we had been on the ranch at Soda Creek for more than a year. It had been a tough year. I was in the middle of getting in our second crop of hay when, out of the blue, my old friend Neil Woolliams contacted me with an enticing proposition. He recounted quite an elaborate history that had started the previous fall when some of our mutual friends had been celebrating in a bar in Kamloops after a cattle sale. Chewing the fat, they began casting around for a way to tap into the lucrative overseas market. Their discussion eventually led to the formation of a company to sell BC cattle overseas.

Now, almost a year later, their idea was really starting to take shape. This was a savvy group of cattlemen,¹ well connected, and very aware that other Canadian producers were already into this game—so how hard could it be? In the interest of securing a market, they had given Ron Pilling, executive secretary/manager of the BC Cattlemen's Association, a mandate to find potential clients for BC cattle—beef and/or dairy. Under pressure to produce results, Ron had taken himself off to Greece to investigate prospects there. Precipitously and without any consultation with the group, he had signed a two-year contract with a large Greek agricultural society to deliver twenty thousand young Holstein bull calves to Greece. The delivered price was to be $200 per head, and Ron had agreed to a $200,000 performance bond for failure to deliver!

The members of this fledgling company were completely dumb-founded by this development but as daunting as it first seemed, the scheme had merit. In those years, it was common practice to destroy dairy bull calves at birth and keep only the heifers. We appeared to have an endless supply of cheap bull calves from Quebec, Ontario and BC. The idea was to ship these calves by air to Greece where the Greek Farmers' Union (called the Central Union) would disburse them for a reasonable price to its members. The Greek farmers were to grow out the calves to about 800 kilograms and then sell them for beef. With a serious countrywide beef shortage, the calves from Canada were touted as part of the Greek government's solution.

Having presented the background, Neil arrived at the purpose of his call: to invite me to the next meeting of what was now called BC Livestock Exports Limited. After discussing it with Phyl, and with some trepidation, I drove to Kamloops for the meeting. Although I was pretty leery of the whole plan, I had been getting lonely on the ranch and missed some of my good friends, especially Neil, Wayne and Gordon. Days spent sitting on a swather had become pretty tedious and I was ready for something a bit more stimulating. I had no idea then how "stimulating" the coming year would be!

By the time I arrived at the Stockman's Hotel in Kamloops, the meeting was already in full swing around a big table in the corner of the bar. Ron Pilling was in full command, confidently and effectively dispensing with a barrage of questions, wielding a gadget that turned out to be the first handheld calculator most of us had ever seen! In response to "What if we have to pay more to buy these calves?" and "What if the cost of shipping goes up?" and other questions, Ron would calculate the answers in a flash and it always turned out that we would make a good profit, no matter what.

And there was no escaping the bottom line: Ron had signed a con-tract on the group's behalf, which was (according to a Kamloops law-yer) binding—the group was in, hook, line and sinker. Because I was a veterinarian, the guys had me tagged not only to help select the calves but also to oversee their transportation and delivery to Greece. At that point I had never been off the continent so this was pretty heady stuff.

I agreed[2] and, as it turned out, the first load was to leave from

Vancouver about three weeks later. Harry Bailey had organized the delivery of the calves to the South Terminal of the Vancouver Airport and Ron had contracted a Pacific Western Airlines (PWA) Boeing 727 cargo plane to take the first load. It was a beautiful fall day when I arrived in Vancouver and watched as the calves were loaded. Everyone, including PWA, was pretty inexperienced when it came to shipping the small calves: the practice of shipping cattle by air was just in its infancy. We assumed, for instance, that they had to be crated, and decided on lots of ten calves per crate. Of course, this took up a lot of room and limited our load to about one hundred head.

It was dusk when the calves were finally loaded and I took my seat behind the navigator for the nonstop flight to Salonika. After an uneventful flight, we landed and began unloading. In the dark, with only the lights of the pickup trucks on the runway, the calves looked pretty fragile as they wobbled down the chute, but they all made it. Some Central Union officials were on hand to oversee the process. At first I was worried that something had gone terribly wrong—I was not accustomed to such high levels of shouting and arm-waving—but their broad smiles and backslapping were reassuring. The unloading went smoothly and soon the plane took off to pick up a load of tomatoes from the Canary Islands. I spent a couple of days getting to know our Greek partners before catching a commercial flight back.

Ron had obviously done a great job of setting up our Greek connection, a group of businessmen and politicians operating as Group 30 Ltd. Two members, Lee Bouboulis and Alec Tsaconas, were charged with handling our business on behalf of Group 30. They became our agents and to my great good fortune, my very good friends. They were both well connected politically; in fact, Alec later became the Governor of Crete.

I arrived back in Vancouver feeling exhausted, relieved, and generally pleased to report that the first trip had gone smoothly. But my optimism was short-lived: we now faced two serious problems. First, and very sadly, we learned that "our" plane and crew had crashed. They'd picked up a load of yearling dairy heifers from Ontario, destined for Korea, and had planned to stop in Edmonton for a crew change and refuelling. As they were approaching the Edmonton airport, they encountered severe turbulence, the nose of the plane dropped, the cattle shifted and slid forward, and they never recovered equilibrium. All aboard were killed. This was a tragedy for these men and their families. And from our perspective, it was a real setback because we now had no air freighter to handle our calves. Additionally, our first load, being so small, had resulted in a loss. Of course, hanging over our heads was the tight delivery schedule and the $200,000 performance bond. Pilling's magic calculator seemed to disappear and the pressure was on...

In our search for new transport we located an air freight company, Intercontinental Freight, headquartered in Oakland, California. They flew stretch DC-8s and evidently knew a good deal about hauling cattle. They agreed to fly to any airport in Canada on very short notice whenever we had a load ready to go. Since our contract called for calves no heavier than forty kilograms, Intercontinental Freight informed us that they could haul up to seven hundred head per load.

Since the BC dairy industry could not supply the numbers we needed, our next task was to secure a larger, steady source of calves, which compelled us to look to Ontario and Quebec. Luckily, Quebec's dairy industry was able to supply us with a load every two weeks! A few weeks later, I arrived at Dorval Airport in Montreal to find our export business operating on an entirely new scale. The plane was huge and crewed by a pilot, a co-pilot/navigator, and a loadmaster, each of whom really knew his business. They had just flown in from San Francisco, having delivered cargo from Tokyo, and had come directly to Dorval. Evidently, they ate airline food, took turns sleeping on foam mattresses behind the cockpit, and basically kept going on whiskey.

The floor of the plane had been lined with four-by-eight sheets of donnacona ("sound" or fibre board). A series of quick-assembly aluminum gates was carried in the belly of the plane and they had crews ready at every stop to put things together, take things apart and clean the plane. I think it cost something like $20,000 to fly a load from Dorval to Athens. Our agreement gave us three hours to unload and a penalty of $1,000 an hour for additional time.

Things went very well on that first trip and we landed with approximately four hundred calves. During the flight it was my job to make

LEE'S STORY

LEE BOUBOULIS HAD A fascinating history. Before becoming the executive secretary of Group 30, Lee had been the personal secretary to Archbishop Makarios (head of the Greek government in Cyprus). His grandmother several generations back had been an admiral in the Greek navy, credited with leading the navy to a decisive victory that resulted in the overthrow of the oppressive Turk occupation.

Lee's father had been the minister of defense in the Greek government during World War II. At the war's end, when the Communists attempted to take over Greece, they temporarily gained control of Athens and ordered government ministers shot. Lee's father and his colleagues were put against the wall in Constitution Square and machine-gunned in front of their families. Lee had tears in his eyes as he recounted how the gunners were ordered to shoot them from the ankles up, slowly.

A graduate of the London School of Economics, Lee had not only excelled academically but had been the first foreign student to serve as president of the student body. Upon graduation he went to work for the Niarchos Shipping Line and soon became a confidante of Mr. Niarchos. Niarchos was in competition with another tough and ruthless shipping baron, Aristotle Onassis. Onassis had founded Olympic Airlines and hired his son Alexander as a pilot. Bringing a load of calves into Athens one day, we could see part of the airport was barricaded off. Alexander had been testing a new plane when it crashed at the airport, and he was killed. Lee said that Onassis was never the same after that.

sure that none of the calves went down and got trampled. The plane had been rigged with a track in the roof and a sling-like hammock that allowed me to pull myself back and forth and drop into a pen when necessary. I was busy the whole flight, checking all the pens every thirty minutes. We lost only three calves on that first trip.

When we landed, the plane had to be very quickly connected to an air-conditioning system to prevent the calves from suffocating. Lee and Alec had arranged for a dozen small trucks to haul the calves to a depot near the airport. Unloading went smoothly, the cleaning crew soon had things shipshape, and off the plane went to pick up some cargo in Italy. I was put up in a rather inexpensive hotel in Athens and provided with a car and driver. I spent a couple of days making sure that the calves were okay before heading home.

WHILE THE DELIVERY END was taking shape nicely, we were learning some hard (and expensive) lessons on the receiving end about the care of motherless calves. Since there had never been any kind of market for these newborn bull calves, Canadian farmers had no interest whatsoever in keeping them alive or even ensuring that they had an initial

This Greek farmhouse was in better condition than most.

suck from their mothers. Thus it fell to us to devise some kind of milk substitute and to make sure that they had one meal before boarding the plane. The only solution was to rent a facility near Montreal to hold the calves and make sure they were fed until a sufficient number could be put together for a load. We bought milk powder and hired help to bottle-feed the calves. Of course, we had the same problem *after* they were unloaded in Greece, where we had to make sure that they were fed as soon as possible upon arrival, before their pickup by Greek farmers.

On the next trip out of Montreal, we put together a full double-decker load of seven hundred calves. The shipment went smoothly until we were unloading. We had gotten about one third of the animals off and were waiting for the return of the trucks. After almost two hours, Lee went to find out what was causing the delay. It transpired that the Greek truckers knew that they had us over a barrel—they were also

The goats in Greece climbed trees because there was so little to eat on the ground.

waiting, parked outside the airport, demanding double payment to offload the balance of the cattle. We had no choice but to meet their demands, and Lee paid them off with cash on the spot. Another lesson learned.

I accompanied a few more uneventful loads before Christmas that year, while Phyl continued to hold the fort at home. On one of my trips, just after our plane came into Montreal from somewhere in the US, a fellow got off the plane and was introduced to me as someone hitching a ride to Spain. He and I quickly struck up a friendship and we chatted almost all the way to Athens. His name was John Anderson, and he looked to be around thirty or thirty-five years old, but he never did tell me much about himself or what he did for a living. I learned later that he was a CIA agent and that our plane held a shipment of guns and munitions destined for some country in Africa. This cargo had to be unloaded in Spain and that was as much as our aircrew knew about it. Sadly, on my next trip out, the loadmaster told me that John had been murdered before leaving Spain. I can still remember very clearly what he looked like.

At one point, Alec and I flew to Alexandropolis (in northern Greece) to look at a large piece of agricultural property that Group 30 proposed using to create a North American-style feedlot. We were accompanied by a friend of Lee's, who lived in a small village near Alexandropolis. This fellow had purchased a black and white television set in Athens and, when we arrived at his home, he and Alec set it up in his living room and got it working. We got a kick out of observing the villagers trooping in, in twos and threes, to see this miracle. After this, we had a huge meal that seemed to go on for hours before returning to our hotel in Alexandropolis. The next day, we surveyed the property, which turned out to be rocky and covered with scrub oak. Without much ado, the feedlot idea was shelved.

BACK HOME, MY ABSENCE was being felt. The ranch certainly suffered with me being away, and it was also really hard on Phyl and the kids. With no end in sight to these separations, we considered moving to Greece as a family for a year or two. Lee arranged for Phyl to fly to Greece, where she was put up in the famous Grand Bretagne Hotel in downtown Athens. Of course, our prime concern was for the schooling of Kathy, Terry and Steve, so Lee set up an appointment for us with the headmaster of the international school in Athens. We were quite impressed and thought it might be a good experience for the children. Tempted as we were, we decided against it, which turned out to be for the best.

During my time in Greece, I had at my disposal a car and a driver named George. George was a very distinguished-looking gentleman, about sixty years old. He had been very active in the Greek Resistance and, after the war, had received the country's highest decoration from the King of Greece. He was a tough old coot who couldn't speak much English, but we understood one another and he was very good to me.

At one point, I asked George to drive me around to various farms to see how our calves were doing. He drove an old Mercedes sedan and always had a five-gallon carboy of Retsina rolling around in the trunk. Close to lunchtime, George decided that we should stop for something to eat. He pulled over beside a field of cabbages, hopped the fence, and with the large clasp knife he always carried, cut us a couple of cabbages. We drove on until we were close to a small village and pulled over near a deserted farmhouse. George hailed a young boy standing near the road, gave him some drachmas and told him to go to the village to buy us a loaf of bread. He then drove off the road, right up to the house and, with the carboy in one hand and cabbages in the other, pushed the door open and in we went.

We walked into the living room to find two or three broken chairs and a fireplace with a few dirty old glasses on the mantle. George picked up two of them, ran his finger around the inside to clean them and filled them up with Retsina. The boy returned with the bread, George thanked him with a few more drachmas and sent him on his way. He then stuck the end of the loaf under his chin, like a violin, to saw off several pieces with his dirty old clasp knife, and lunch was served: Retsina, cabbage and bread.

Visiting the small Greek farms was a huge eye-opener. I had spent very little time in the countryside and thought that, because Greece was such an ancient civilization, the agricultural industry would be pretty much up to date. Nothing could have been further from the truth. Most of these farms consisted of a few rocky acres with a farmhouse, a few chickens, and goats everywhere. The goats kept the grass down to ground level and even climbed up in the trees to eat leaves and twigs. It soon became apparent that many of the Greek farmers had no knowledge or even interest in raising beef.

At our first stop, we found six or eight of our calves tethered by the neck with rope to trees around the yard. The poor things were in terrible condition—they were only three or four weeks old and should have still been on a milk supplement and perhaps some good-quality pellets. Instead, they were being fed straw waste (which adult goats usually ate). Another place we visited that day had half a dozen calves in the basement of the house. It was pitch dark down there, and when George and I went in with a flashlight, you can imagine what we found. This was very discouraging.

To make matters worse, we had apparently agreed to go fifty-fifty with the Central Union in providing insurance to cover animal losses in the first sixty days. It turned out that many of the farmers were slaughtering these small calves, selling the carcasses *and* claiming the insurance. Because there were minimal claims investigations, the insurance scheme defeated the whole purpose of the enterprise. When the government found out, the Central Union was made the scapegoat, and the insurance contract was cancelled, but no additional support was put in place to protect the calves or the business of raising them for beef. Luckily, some of the farmers were much more progressive and did a good job of looking after the animals.

GEORGE WAS FAMILIAR WITH all of the villages we visited and had many stories to tell me about the activities of the Resistance movement during the war. Even then, in 1972, we still saw donkeys laden with great packs of onions, turnips, potatoes and other things, being led along the roads, including in Athens. George told me that the favourite way of transporting munitions to various Resistance cells had been by hiding them under the vegetable packs on the donkeys. He said the Germans never did figure it out.

Another war story was triggered by our visit to a small village that had a large old tree in the central square. The tree had a big limb that hung over the communal well, propped up to keep it out of the way. George recounted how he and some of his men happened to be in that village when several enemy tanks came in and parked in the square. It was a beautiful sunny day, around noon, and the Germans had the villagers bring them food and wine. The tank crews climbed out on this big old limb and dangled their legs over the well, leaving their weapons below. George and his men had used their Sten guns to pick the Germans off the branch "like roosting turkeys." He was one tough character!

BACK IN KAMLOOPS, THINGS were heating up. At a meeting of the members of our company, we decided to terminate our relationship with Ron Pilling. Stan Towers agreed to take his place and started running the business from his room in the Stockmen's Hotel in Kamloops. Expenses were mounting and procurement of calves was getting more difficult. In Quebec, we were buying up all the day-old bull calves we could get our hands on, and farmers there soon realized that these animals were worth something and began raising their prices. A group in Montreal was showing interest in exporting calves to Italy and there were rumours that a Chicago branch of the Mafia was going to provide the plane. Not good news for us.

We were now in the middle of winter in Canada, struggling to put together every load of calves. In early February, I was scheduled to go out of Dorval with the next load and Gordon Parke decided to come along. Our plane and an exhausted crew arrived, and while they rested for a few hours at a hotel, Gordon and I waited for the calves to arrive, watching the weather deteriorate from a heavy snowfall to an ice storm. The trucks finally arrived at about 6:00 p.m. and we began to load. In the cold, dark and chaos, the loadmaster didn't realize that our Montreal supplier had failed to find a sufficient number of calves of the right weight. Without much thought, they had substituted larger animals, some as heavy as sixty kilograms. Gordon and I noticed, but we knew we needed the numbers for the load. By the time we were loaded, the plane was frozen in. It took until midnight to chop the wheels out of the ice and de-ice the entire plane.

I was used to flying up front by now, familiar with the little alarm bell that provides a warning when you have reached the point of no return on the runway and have to continue with the takeoff. But this time was different. The pilot remarked that the plane felt heavy, opening the throttle further as the bell continued to ring. Finally, just as we reached the end of the tarmac, the plane became airborne. We cleared the fence at the end of the runway with just feet to spare, only to face several houses and apartment blocks dead ahead. The pilot was using every swear word I had ever heard as he guided the plane through a bit of a gap between two apartment blocks. I remember looking out the side window right into the well-lit window of an apartment where a family sat watching television.

We were over Newfoundland before we reached our desired altitude. The pilots still hadn't figured out that we were overloaded, but once the loadmaster started questioning Gordon and me, he soon figured out that our cargo was "way overweight." When we reached the far coast of Italy, several hundred miles from Athens, the fuel gauges began to hover near the empty mark, and the pilot and co-pilot began to discuss their options for ditching. By now, with everyone sweating profusely, the pilot radioed ahead to the Athens control tower, telling them about our problem and requesting a straight-in landing with all the bells and whistles, i.e. fire trucks and all. We landed at the Athens Airport on just fumes. One engine had stopped completely. Gordon and I were roundly cursed out by the entire flight crew.

THINGS GOT TOUGHER AND tougher with every trip thereafter and almost every shipment brought a loss. I went on only a couple more trips and since it was getting close to calving season at our ranch, I decided to take a break. Wayne and Gordon went with a load or two. On one trip, there was a foul-up, as our friends in Greece had forgotten to pay for landing clearance, so as the plane approached, it was waved off and told to land elsewhere. This was very problematic for two reasons: first, they had to find somewhere to land in Europe before they ran out of fuel, and second, once the plane touched down in Europe, it couldn't return to Canada because of the foot-and-mouth embargo on European cattle.

At the eleventh hour, Orly Airport near Paris allowed the plane to land. There the load sat, and, after some hours, several French farm trucks began to appear, lining up near the freight entrance gate. These entrepreneurs had discovered our predicament and figured that they could get the calves for nothing—doing us a big favour. The pilot was in our corner, however, and with the fuel tanks filled and the Athens landing clearance finally secured, he radioed the tower for takeoff permission. Much to his surprise, it was denied, probably because air traffic control was in cahoots with the farmers. Bless his heart, he cranked up the plane, taxied to the end of the nearest runway and took off

Getting the calves off the plane was even harder than getting them onto it.

When the tally was in, this necklace was all we had to show for $40,000.

without permission, or a flight plan, probably almost causing an international incident.

BY NOW, THE COMPANY was in serious difficulty, with our loan at the Royal Bank increasing in size like a snowball rolling downhill. Several cattlemen who had declined to join our group were going around smirking and predicting our demise. We had retained a prominent Vancouver lawyer, Harry Bell-Irving, to try to negotiate our way out of the agreement with the Central Union. Mr. Bell-Irving, accompanied by Neil and Stan, flew to Athens and, along with Lee and Alec, was successful in getting us out of the contract. I don't remember if we compensated the Union, but I do know the government was not happy. Export Company members were declared *persona non grata* and warned not to go to Greece as we would likely be arrested. It was several years before I returned to Greece, but by then the heat was off.

That was the end of BC Livestock Exports Ltd. When the smoke cleared, each of us owed the Royal Bank $30,000, except for Gordon and me, who owed $40,000 each (and that's *another* story!). Some were well enough off to retire their debt immediately. Most of us went on a payment schedule negotiated by Neil. The bank was very sympathetic to our plight and provided us with low interest rates and prolonged payments. It took Phyl and me years to square things up and this debacle was certainly one of the things that precipitated the sale of our ranch at Soda Creek.

Phyl's $40,000 necklace? On one of my last trips, I bought a relatively inexpensive moonstone necklace and earrings set for Phyl. Besides the experience I gained and all the good friends I made in Greece, the jewellery was all we had to show for a lot of money, stress and hard work.

BITTEN BY THE POLITICAL BUG

AFTER SELLING THE RANCH in January 1974, and moving to our house in town, I was rather at loose ends. For a couple of months, I caught up on things around the house and helped Phyl when I was needed at the granola plant, but I was really looking for something to get my teeth into, and at a complete loss as to what it could possibly be!

One icy, crystal-clear February day, I bumped into my friend Ted Cornwall, the district agriculturalist. We had been chatting for a few minutes when he planted the first seed of an idea that would eventually take my life in a whole new direction. He asked, "Are you at all interested in politics?"

"Not in any serious way," I replied, "though Phyl and I helped Davie Fulton in Kamloops on several of his campaigns."

"In that case," he said, "you must be a Conservative." I told him that I'd never belonged to a political party but I knew who I didn't like: Pierre Trudeau. "Well," he said, "You'd better come along to the Conservative constituency meeting and find out what's going on."

So a couple of nights later, I went to the meeting; only a handful of people showed up. Ted ran the meeting, focusing on the need to choose a candidate for the upcoming election. The election call was anticipated within weeks, and a Vancouver immigration lawyer, John Taylor,[1] had already announced that he was going to seek the nomination. He owned property at Whistler, and hoped—through being elected—to bring the Winter Olympics to Whistler and make a killing on his property. I was both baffled and outraged at the idea that someone living in Vancouver could possibly represent our part of the world. And that's how I got bitten. Phyl, who hadn't even known where I had gone that evening, remembers me coming home late, storming into the kitchen and slamming my fist on the counter, saying, "Some goddamned immigration lawyer from Vancouver is going to steal this riding!" As I filled her in, she became just as incensed as me.

Shortly after that, Phyl and I were in Vancouver on Greenaway Granola business and, when we called in at Service Packaging, we met the owner, Ron Huntington. Ron was the MP for West Vancouver–Capilano, a wonderful person and an outstanding politician, who soon became our mentor. He described to us what it meant to be a Member of Parliament and how complicated life could become. He did, however, encourage me to do it. I fussed around for a few days before I decided to throw my hat in the ring for the nomination.

I knew absolutely nothing about party politics, constituency politics, nominations or memberships. It was a huge shock to discover that there were only six paid-up members in the entire riding. The past president, a Williams Lake lawyer, was very ill, and was hospitalized. All of the constituency records, including old membership lists, were unavailable. I soon figured out that my life depended on selling party memberships, as many as possible, and then getting the paid-up members to the nomination meeting where they would vote for me. I armed myself with membership booklets and headed out with good intentions, but soon realized that my salesmanship efforts were a lost cause: I was completely useless at selling anything of any kind to anyone. My ever-supportive partner, Phyl—and her good friends Muriel Garland, Ann Devlin and Bernice Armstrong—therefore came to my rescue, selling several hundred memberships in no time flat.

On May 8, 1974, my birthday, Prime Minister Trudeau called the election. The clock was running and we still didn't have a candidate. The nomination meeting was scheduled for May 24 at the Chilcotin Hotel. I knew that John Taylor was going to run and there was a rumour that Rocky Sorenson, a sawmill operator from the Chilcotin, was also interested. Phyl's team of women continued to sell memberships. I worked on my speech, watched the news and read as many newspapers as I could.

The evening of the twenty-fourth arrived. We had an early dinner and I changed into a new suit. As I was changing, our good friend Brian Garland called with the news that John Taylor and one hundred or so young people from Whistler had just arrived at the airport in a PWA jet. It later surfaced that Taylor's "UIC Ski Team" had been promised a free weekend at a local guest ranch in exchange for their votes. Taylor had also chartered two other DC-3 jets to fly more people to Powell River, where there was to be a second ballot box.

The meeting, scheduled to start at 7:00 p.m., did not actually get underway until 9:30. There was no rule covering the cut-off date for party memberships and all kinds of people showed up at the door, which caused a great delay. John Taylor's people, under the instruction of Al Eton, the public relations director of the Vancouver Lions, were told to empty out the beer parlours and bring the people to the meeting by taxi. One of his supporters greeted them there with a huge wad of $100 bills in hand to pay for their memberships, ten at a time.

Some of these people were inebriated and the situation soon degenerated into chaos. Nearly a hundred people were backed up down the hallway and it didn't take long for fights to break out. One chap was thrown through a wall in the hallway,[2] and a couple of them ended up in hospital. In the meeting room, there weren't enough seats so John Taylor's noisy, dishevelled crowd was sprawled on the floor at the front. Meanwhile, Joe Clark had come over from his riding in Alberta (by plane to Kamloops and then in a rental car for the drive to Williams Lake) to be the guest speaker. He should have been on his way back to Kamloops to catch his return flight by about the time the meeting started.

When asked how much he paid for the chartered 737 jet, Taylor says, "We didn't charter it. If PWA wants to donate a plane to help an out-of-town nomination meeting, is that so bad?" PWA disagrees. General Manager William Harris says, "If he doesn't think it was a charter, he will when he gets the bill." He couldn't give a figure, but CP Air estimates the cost at $7,000.

—Excerpt from Alan Fotheringham's column
Vancouver Sun,
Friday, June 21, 1974

The meeting finally got underway and each candidate gave a formal speech. I was pretty nervous but I'd memorized mine and thought it went fairly well. As the first ballot began, the crowd (by then about five hundred strong) became unruly and impatient. It took a long time to announce the results: John Taylor was in first place, I was a close second and Rocky was third. Rocky, bless his heart, urged his supporters to vote for me on the second ballot.

It was decided to let Joe Clark speak while counting took place. There was so much commotion that I don't think anyone heard what Joe had to say. I had parked myself beside an elderly gentleman who turned out to be Cyclone Taylor. He told me a number of great old hockey stories and kept me entertained during what could have been a stressful half-hour.

The second ballot went in my favour and I was declared the candidate. By that time it was almost midnight, and someone drove Joe Clark to Kamloops. John Taylor's crowd disappeared, herded back onto the plane—no dude ranch weekend for the losing team. But the rest of Williams Lake celebrated long into the night and, although Phyl and I were exhausted, we were exhilarated by the win and looked forward to a new chapter in our lives. As our futures unfolded, Joe and I always had a good laugh about that night; he said it was the wildest meeting he'd ever attended.

There was certainly no rest for the wicked. As it turned out, there was a candidates' briefing scheduled for 1:00 p.m. the next day in Vancouver. At around 5:00 that morning, Brian Garland (now my campaign manager) and I headed for Vancouver in my old pickup truck. I don't remember much about the meeting except that I was given an armload of policy papers and booklets. One of the sitting MPs introduced himself to me. I asked him if he had some advice for a first-time candidate and I'll never forget what he said: "Promise the buggers anything—we've got to get elected." I knew he was just being practical, but it didn't sit very well with me and I was wondering if the entire system worked that way. If it did, I wasn't going to last long.

OUR RIDING WAS CALLED Coast Chilcotin, one of Canada's largest, covering 43,000 square miles. It ran from Ocean Falls on the coast up past Bella Coola, then inland from Quesnel, taking in all of the Chilcotin, over to Bridge Lake, down to Ashcroft and Lytton and over to Pemberton, Whistler and Squamish. I didn't know the coastal part of the riding at all, nor did I know a soul who lived there except for a few people in Bella Coola. I had, however, read about Pat Brennan, the outspoken and colourful mayor of Squamish. On a tour of the riding, I asked the waitress at breakfast where I could find him and soon found myself at his office.

Before long I was ushered into his office, where I introduced myself as the Progressive Conservative candidate, just nominated, and asked him if he knew of any Conservatives in the area. He gave a great shout of laughter, clapped me on the back, and told me he was a well-known Liberal. Needless to say, I was mortally embarrassed and he was probably heartened to know that the Conservatives were so disorganized. But, bless his heart, he grabbed me by the arm, and said, "I'll take you downtown and introduce you to everyone we meet." And that's what he did.

Over coffee, Pat generously gave me a little history lesson on that part of the world. He told me the NDP incumbent was from Powell River, where he had worked for many years at the pulp mill and, of course, was strongly supported by unions all over the riding. I was soon to learn what unions were all about! He told me that, prior to the present NDP MP, the riding had been represented by Liberal Paul St. Pierre, who was well known province-wide for his popular column in the *Vancouver Sun* and well regarded in the area. Pat described how Paul had become Parliamentary Secretary to the External Affairs Minister and had become so caught up that he hadn't been seen much in the riding. When the 1972 election was called, he didn't feel he had to campaign rigorously—he thought he'd win almost by default. Pat and others had taken exception to this and I remember Pat saying, "We sure showed him." They had, all right, electing an NDP member, which had come as a complete shock to everyone, especially Paul. It was my first lesson in how important it is to stay in close touch with the people you have been elected to represent.

Pat went on to tell me that the Liberal candidate, Jack Pearsall, had been the returning officer in the riding for several elections and was well known by those who had run the polling stations and done the counts.

I thanked Pat for his generosity and headed to Gibson's Landing. I drove up the Sunshine Coast to Sechelt where once again, I sidled up to people who looked approachable, asking them if they knew any Conservatives. I was finally directed to a drugstore on the main street, whose owner and his wife turned out, thankfully, to be staunch Conservatives. They advised me to head up to Powell River as it was a larger centre. By this time, I was beginning to feel pretty insignificant and any confidence I might have had was rapidly evaporating. But I had no choice but to persevere, so I caught yet another ferry to Powell River. I drove around a bit to orient myself, and met a delightful couple who invited me to stay with them overnight. They introduced me to several other Conservatives and I spent the better part of the next day chatting up complete strangers on the street. I was met with mostly cool receptions.

It was in Powell River that I first ran into the negativity generated by Conservative party leader Robert Stanfield's Wage and Price Control policy. I didn't know much about it—and what I did know I wasn't very happy with—but nonetheless promoted it as best I could, never missing a chance to compare Mr. Stanfield's rock-solid reputation to that of the socialistic dilettante Trudeau. And I had to be silent about the fact that, when I introduced myself in restaurants, I would be immediately presented with the unpaid tabs of the 1972 Conservative candidate—they had never been paid! In order to preserve the good name of the party, I forked over what was owed. No wonder it was difficult to elect a Conservative in Coast Chilcotin!

When I returned to Williams Lake, the campaign committee met. None of us was experienced in campaigning and we were learning completely by trial and error. Under Brian Garland's leadership, several men (Ron Harder, Wayne Reeves, Bob Stobie, Bob Patterson, Dave Worthy and Doug Belsher) plastered campaign signs in every strategic location. Tom White took the role as the campaign's Official Agent. Muriel Garland organized and staffed the campaign office in a trailer in downtown Williams Lake. The combined wisdom of the group concluded that I should attend coffee parties wherever they could be arranged, speak wherever I could get invited, run radio ads where applicable, have signs printed and post them wherever we could, invite Stanfield to come to Williams Lake, and see if some debates could be arranged.

While all this was going on, Phyl kept Greenaway Granola operating, looked after the kids and showed up at the campaign office when-

I had enormous respect for Bob Stanfield, a true gentleman and the best prime minister we never had.

ever she could. As time went on, she became an absolutely wonderful campaigner and a tremendous asset.

Mr. and Mrs. Stanfield did come to Williams Lake and I met them for the first time. He was a real gentleman, a true Canadian, and he and I hit it off immediately. The crowd was impressed with them and Phyl took special care of Mrs. Stanfield. Mr. Stanfield was presented with a very good cowboy hat and cowboy boots. Unfortunately, there were a fair number of media types in attendance and one of them asked Mr. Stanfield to tuck his trousers into his boots so that his boots could be seen. In our part of the world, people never tuck their pants into their boots, and of course, the media had a heyday painting Mr. Stanfield as "a real dude." He gave a wonderful speech and explained, in no uncertain terms, the situation Canada was in: large deficits, overspending, high inflation and the consequences of a left-leaning government. He explained his Price and Wage Control plan to get inflation under control. He made a good impression on the five hundred or so of us who attended this outdoor event.

The media continued to hound him on that trip. One of the journalists had a football and, while we were on the tarmac waiting for the campaign plane to pick up the Stanfields, journalists were tossing it around. Someone threw it—badly—at Mr. Stanfield. It hit the tarmac and bounced into his hands. Several photographers captured him just as he caught it and, unfortunately, it looked as if he just "dropped the ball" which, of course, made the headlines. The media was clearly on the Trudeau Liberal side throughout the whole election.

Not long after that, I was invited to a televised debate in Vancouver with a Liberal candidate, Simma Holt, and an NDP candidate. Throughout the half-hour session, it was clear that the moderator was on the Liberal side: I couldn't get a word in edgewise. I was immediately and consistently attacked over the Price and Wage Control policy and had difficulty, as could well be imagined, defending it. The whole effort was both a disaster and a waste of time, as far as I was concerned.

At about this time, Prime Minister Trudeau made a visit to Powell River and, predictably, caught the attention of a large rally by ridiculing the Conservatives with his famous "Zap, your wages are frozen" comment. Of course, we all remember that shortly after winning the 1974 election, Trudeau's Liberal government brought in their own version of price and wage controls.

THE SIZE OF THE riding was a huge challenge and getting around was a logistical nightmare. At one point, I was campaigning in the Lytton/ Lillooet part of the riding and was expected next in Pemberton/ Whistler/Squamish. The sure way of getting there was via Vancouver but, through the grapevine, I had heard about "the high line," a route used by BC Hydro crews to check and repair the power line that ran through to the coast. I was warned that it was pretty rough but I figured I knew what rough was, so I decided to give it a try. The road was horrendous beyond my imagination, just a trail in some parts, and I was only driving our old pickup—no four-wheel-drive—so I spent the best part of the day driving thirty miles, crawling over deeply rutted, bone-jarring road, getting stuck and unstuck. I arrived that evening in Pemberton grateful and exhausted. Some shortcut.

On that same trip I got suckered into going to an all-candidates' debate in Powell River, held at the Union Hall. The NDP incumbent and the Liberal candidate were both diehard union members and on home turf. It was a real debacle for me—a boisterous crowd of nearly

seven hundred people who made
a racket every time I opened my
mouth. The only thing that saved
me from utter despair was the
Independent candidate, a hard-
drinking Irish veterinarian. He
was even more unpopular than
I was, with the locals as well as
with the Veterinary Association.
I had the fleeting joy of putting
him in his place and got a good
round of applause.

Election day came and, knowing we'd worked hard, we were
feeling optimistic. But when the
dust cleared, I had lost the elec-
tion to the Liberals by about three hundred votes. I suppose it wasn't
too bad a showing, considering I was two weeks late getting started
and knew nothing about campaigning. Nevertheless, I was shocked to
have lost; I really thought I was going to win.

Strangely enough, several months after the election, we found
out that a large logging company owner had offered the use of a float
plane to fly me in and out of the logging camps and small communities
between Powell River and Bella Coola. The offer, made to a volunteer in
Powell River, was never passed along to me. Taking up that offer could
have changed the outcome: there were several hundred voters in those
small settlements and I would have been the only candidate to approach
them. It really grated on me to have lost by such a narrow margin.

I suddenly found myself cast in the role of a loser and that didn't
sit very well with me.

So I FOUND MYSELF out of work, again. I couldn't go back to Kamloops
because when I'd sold the practice there, I had signed an agreement
with Don Olson that prevented me from practising within two hundred miles for a ten-year period. Evidently these agreements can easily
be broken, but to me that was not an option. So Phyl and I had to make
an important decision about our future.

Several days after the election, I received a phone call from Tom Willis, a senior bureaucrat with the Canadian International Development Agency (CIDA) in Ottawa. I had known Tom in Kamloops when he was director of the Federal Experimental Range Station. He wanted Phyl and me to come to Ottawa to discuss an opportunity to go to Africa on a CIDA-funded beef cattle project. We expressed our interest and he sent us two return tickets. They had a two-year contract in Lesotho in mind, where I was to organize the feeding and preparation of cattle for export to other African countries. It was hoped that fattening cattle might provide the government some foreign exchange. We were told that Lesotho was a very beautiful and peaceful country, I would be paid a good salary and our children would be sent to a private school in Durban. On the surface, this sounded very interesting, but as we began to discuss the nuts and bolts of the operation, I instinctively knew that the project had little chance of success. So I thanked them and returned to Williams Lake. It turned out that a 1956 OVC graduate, Norm Stanger, jumped at the chance. I saw him years later, and he said that he and his wife had had a wonderful two-year holiday in a beautiful country—the project had been a complete failure.

A BIG CITY INTERLUDE

A MOVE TO VANCOUVER seemed to be the best option after losing the election. I would be able to practise there and, with a number of large brokerage firms, Phyl would be able to get her teeth into being a stock-broker. We hoped it would work for the kids—Kathy, who had been boarding at Crofton House, would be able to complete high school as a day student and we could enroll the boys at St. George's. Phyl and the kids were excited about our move to the big city and, although I dreaded the idea of running a small animal practice, I thought I would adapt if I gave it a chance.

We rented a house for the first year, while we built a very nice two-storey house on a one-acre lot in the Southlands area of Vancou-ver, near the University of British Columbia. It felt very rural there in those days—many of our neighbours kept horses—and it was like an oasis amid the cityscape and traffic. That first summer, Dad and Uncle Herb built us a six-stall barn with a hayloft, and I put up the fence. Tom brought down our two horses, Major and Sky, along with our jumps, and Steven and I spent as much time riding as we could.

We always had great pets. Our little Yorkshire terrier, Hamlet, had a personality "way out of proportion" to his size. He was completely fearless and used to harass the horses, especially Major, jumping up and grabbing Major's tail. Major would charge around the paddock,

kicking, with Hamlet swinging back and forth from his tail like a pen-
dulum gone wild. When Hamlet would finally let go, Major would
wheel around and chase him out of the paddock. Hamlet would high-
tail it out of there but stop when he was just out of reach, with a cocky
look on his face. As soon as Major went back to minding his own business, Hamlet would start the game all over again.

Our dogs, Shayna and Sam, made quite a pair, running loose in
the neighbourhood as dogs seemed to do in those days. They returned
from their daily forays with no end of loot that they'd lifted from
the neighbours: bridles, boots, horse brushes and, on one occasion,
a child's orthodontic retainer. We spent many evenings trawling the
neighbourhood, trying to return things to their rightful owners. Luckily, the dogs didn't chew and the items were undamaged, but it got to
be quite a nuisance for people.

Almost everyone living in Southlands belonged to the Ratepayers'
Association and, before I knew it, I was elected president. We dealt
with everything from barking dogs to sewage to keeping stallions on
our properties. People were friendly and co-operative, so my time as
president felt constructive and enjoyable.

I'D BEEN OUT OF small animal practice for quite a few years, so Rex
Mears (who was by then practising in the Dunbar area) offered to let
me work alongside him for a few months. He helped me get up to date.
I had consulted with Rex and a few other veterinarians to identify the
most promising place to set up a small animal practice and had settled
on Steveston, where I renovated a space in a small shopping centre. It
didn't take long before I had all the business I could handle. I hired and
trained a couple of hard-working and fun-loving women—Shannon
Hay as an assistant and Sharon Piper as a receptionist. We joked and
teased each other through a lot of long days. Being indoors all day was
difficult and the practice side was pretty predictable, but the clients
were generally appreciative and we were able to provide good service.

Without much thought, I offered pensioners a 30 percent discount
and before long we had pensioners bringing their dogs and cats from
all over the Lower Mainland. I had to rethink this offer when Tom,
still our accountant, reminded me that my profit margin was only

20 percent (when we were lucky) so I was losing money on this deal! I had to scale it back but still they came.

I had some great clients and I was constantly reminded of how much these pets meant to their owners. I've never forgotten one elderly woman whose sole companion was a fourteen-year-old Doberman. The dog was clearly going downhill, with several large tumours, incontinence and joint stiffness, but the dog and its owner were obviously fond of each other. I held the old dog together for several months; a neighbour drove them in for regular check-ups and prescription refills. One day, the owner appeared for their appointment beautifully dressed, wearing makeup, jewellery and a hat, and asked me to put the old dog to sleep. She asked me to have the dog cremated and to keep the ashes for her. I went to some effort to organize an individual cremation (not so commonly done for dogs in those days) and kept the ashes on the shelf in my office. Oddly, however, she never reappeared to collect them. About six months later, her neighbour came in with his dog and when I asked after the old lady, he was surprised that I hadn't heard: after he dropped her at her house that afternoon, she'd gone inside, lain down on her bed and swallowed a bottle of sleeping pills. And that was that.

One winter day, Sharon got a frantic call from a woman whose cat had been sleeping under the hood of her car, on top of the engine, which cats often did to stay warm. She had started the car and moved it out of their garage when she heard the cat yowling from under the hood. When I got there, I could see the cat had one foot caught in the fan belt and was thrashing around, meowing pitifully. I loaded a syringe with Nembutal, took a tourniquet and crawled under the car. Surprisingly, the cat settled right down when I started to pet it and, luckily, I was good at finding veins so I was able to anaesthetize it. I turned the belt until the cat fell loose and took it to the clinic to patch it up—it was good as new within a couple of days.

WE WERE ALL LEADING busy lives. Phyl had sold Greenaway Granola and had accepted a position at Canada Permanent Trust as a portfolio investment manager and, subsequently, was then offered a position with James Richardson and Sons. Kathy graduated from Crofton and started the nursing program at UBC, and the boys were both doing

well at St. George's. I found a good veterinarian to do locums and we
were finally able to take proper holidays at Shuswap in the summers.
We even travelled a bit, taking the kids to Hawaii, England and Greece,
and were able to take advantage of life in the city. Every Christmas, we
had wonderful celebrations and games of charades with our long-time
friends the Mears.

Several years went by and we followed politics closely. There is no
doubt that I had been bitten by the political bug, and so had Phyl. We
went to Ottawa as a family for the 1976 leadership convention when
Joe Clark was elected leader. Kathy and Steve got involved in the
Young Progressive Conservatives, which kept them busy. Terry was
happier at home in the barn, tinkering with his 1971 MGB.

I WAS GETTING RESTLESS again when, in 1977, my old friend and professor Dr. Chris Bigland¹ approached me. He had left the Western College
of Veterinary Medicine to launch an independent research facility on
the University of Saskatchewan campus. Chris had a vision of a state-
of-the-art laboratory that would develop practical solutions for everyday problems that were costing the livestock industry millions of dollars
annually. Chris was very sincere and persuasive, and had been successful in raising sufficient start-up capital from the Devonian Group of
Charitable Foundations of Calgary, the Saskatchewan government, and
the Government of Canada. The lab, the Veterinary Infectious Disease Organization (VIDO), had been built and equipped and Chris had
assembled an excellent team of qualified researchers and support staff.

What Chris faced now was lack of operating capital. His funders
wanted a cost-sharing arrangement with the private sector and had
offered to match every dollar raised from the various branches of the
livestock industry. Chris thought I would be the perfect VIDO travelling salesman, speaking to all the annual meetings of the various livestock and poultry associations in Western Canada. They had prepared
an audio-visual presentation that I would use as a basis for explaining
what we were trying to do and how it would work. In between trips, I
would work from home, preparing monthly bulletins. It would mean
travelling quite a bit but the salary was attractive.

It was an appealing offer. I was pretty bored with practice and also had an eye on the next election, expected within two years. I had never been a good public speaker and I thought that this job—if nothing else—would give me some good experience. So in the fall of 1977, I leased my Steveston practice to Dr. Bob Galloway, one of the country's best veterinary surgeons. With the practice in good hands, I set off to work for VIDO.

It turned out to be an interesting job and I made many good contacts and acquaintances across Western Canada. I also came to know the executives of many national associations. It was a lonely time, however, and I missed Phyl and the family, and quickly got fed up with eating in restaurants and staying in hotels. By the six-month mark, I had raised $1 million from producer groups, which—with the promised matching grants—translated into $4 million for VIDO, and the initiative became a true Canadian success story.[2] Now called VIDO-InterVac, the facilities include modern virology, immunology, bacteriology and clinical research labs and a 160-acre research station.

LIFE IN THE FAST LANE

WITH A FEDERAL ELECTION in the offing, the executive of the Cariboo–Chilcotin PC Constituency Association scheduled a nomination meeting for late March 1978 in Williams Lake. I announced my candidacy but I wasn't alone in the running. Dr. Hugh Atwood, a well-known general practitioner who had served the people of the Cariboo well for many years, also threw his hat in the ring. Hugh was a lifelong Conservative and had a particularly capable woman, Nova Dickie, managing his campaign. Luckily, I had many loyal supporters from the last election and after a very civilized evening (compared to the one in 1974) I was declared the winner.

My candidacy meant we would have to move back to Williams Lake well ahead of the general election (slated to be held by the end of 1979). The whole family, especially Phyl, had some difficult decisions to make. Kathy was at UBC, and Terry and Steven were at St. George's. Phyl really enjoyed her job with James Richardson and Sons. Dr. Bob Galloway was still operating my Steveston veterinary practice under the lease agreement, so I needed to terminate the lease and put the practice up for sale. We were fortunate to have our house in Williams Lake, but had to give notice to our tenants, sell our Southlands home, and organize our move. And I was still working for VIDO out of Saskatoon.

Our good friend Neil Woolliams, now manager of the Douglas
Lake Cattle Company, offered to
put the boys to work on the ranch,
a once-in-a-lifetime summer "holiday" of which they still speak. Phyl
continued to work at Richardson's
but we took a few weeks off in the
summer at Shuswap. A Vancouver lawyer had expressed interest
in buying our Southlands house
and had agreed to our price. However, when it came time to make

*Phyl became a star campaigner
during the 1979 federal election.*

the payment, he reneged, and it took several months to get that
straightened out.

In the fall of 1978, we moved back to Williams Lake with misgivings
and regrets. It was terribly hard on Phyl to leave the children, her family, a job she loved, the city she knew, and many, many friends. The
prospect of living on her own for the winter—without our children,
and with me away a good deal of the time—was completely unappeal-
ing. I knew that I was asking a great deal of the family and taking a
serious gamble with our future.

To allow the kids to continue their studies, we rented a house on
Manitoba Street in Vancouver. The three kids and Kathy's best friend,
Alison Muth, shared the house and learned to fend for themselves:
Kathy in Nursing at UBC, Terry in his first year there, and Steven
in his final year at St. George's. And so, suddenly, before we were
really prepared for it, our family was split asunder—an all too common occurrence, as I was soon to discover, for those engaged in federal
politics. I have often wondered what drove me, in the prime of my life,
to act as I did. I know that I had serious misgivings about the direction
in which our country seemed to be moving. However, I have to admit
that I was still stinging from the loss of the 1974 election. Simply put,
I had never lost anything in my life and felt strongly that I had to put
things right.

Ron Harder loaned us his motorhome to serve as our campaign office.

When I looked at the big picture, however, the stars were lining up in our favour. The Trudeau government was becoming less and less popular, and the Conservatives, under Joe Clark's leadership, were gaining strength. The riding boundaries had been adjusted, stripping away the entire coast portion, making campaigning somewhat less difficult. However, the constituency was still massive and had been renamed Cariboo–Chilcotin.

Finally, and perhaps most importantly, we were all much better prepared. Unlike the 1974 campaign, when I was nominated two weeks after the election had been called, and had very little help and no instructions on how to campaign, this time was different. I had attended a campaign "school," had been given all kinds of policy papers to review, and had help all over the riding. I had a real stroke of luck when Nova Dickie agreed to be my campaign manager. Everyone knew and loved Nova; she had a truly remarkable way with people.

The writ was dropped in April for a May 22 election and we were off and running. Ron Harder loaned us his motorhome and had it decked out with the appropriate signs. Phyl and Nova arranged to have a loudspeaker mounted on top of the vehicle and Phyl had a tape made of the music from, amongst others, the popular TV show *Bonanza*, which we played as we rolled into the many towns that we visited, as well as the theme from the movie *Rocky*.

I still had vivid memories of the 1974 campaign, going from place to place trying to find Conservatives or fumbling around in an attempt to arrange coffee parties. Of course, this had been a terrible waste of time and the best way to campaign, at least in our riding, was to go door-to-door or business-to-business on each town's main streets. We did this with a vengeance, and our best guess was that we had knocked on at least five thousand doors by the end of the campaign. We found that many people had never been contacted personally in this way and it certainly worked for us.

From day one, I had always been a very reluctant campaigner. Being shy by nature, it took a lot of urging from Phyl to get me to approach people on the street and put my hand out. Phyl, on the other hand, was a natural campaigner. We usually parked at the end of a street; she took one side and I took the other. When I was ready to quit for the day, she would convince me to carry on, bribing me with home-cooked meals from our motorhome kitchen in exchange for my doing one more block of door knocking.

As we were outside in the sun so much, we became as brown as two berries. We could hardly recognize ourselves in the pictures that were taken. Phyl figured that the pale complexions of our opponents showed that they were not doing any door knocking, and she was right. What a jewel she was—campaigner, cook, sounding board, wardrobe consultant, clipping service, memory-prompter, savvy strategist and constant companion. In retrospect, there is no doubt in my mind that my political endeavours would have been short-lived without the determination and constant support of my wife and partner.

An incredible team of volunteers did everything from putting up signs to stuffing envelopes to, finally, making sure all our committed voters got to the polling stations. Nova Dickie put together a strong, experienced team: Tom White served again as Official Agent; Doug Belsher was in charge of finances; Muriel Garland was a very capable assistant campaign manager; Bob Patterson looked after all the advertising; and Dick Ford managed my very hectic schedule.

Kathy joined us in the Williams Lake office as soon as her exams were over at UBC, skipping her graduation ceremony to work on the last few weeks of the campaign. Nova did a great job of coordinating our efforts, and never once was there any dissension. This is remarkable in the context of politics and election fever, and it allowed me such a free hand.

We returned to Williams Lake the day of the election and, that evening, along with our campaign workers, we gathered at the Bil-Nor Restaurant to await the results. Terry and Steven came up from Vancouver to be with us. A large blackboard and a TV set had been set up, and the mood was optimistic. The polls closed at 8:00 p.m. and within minutes I was declared the winner by the media. A great celebration ensued and we partied until well after midnight. We kept one eye on the TV as the votes came in on the other BC ridings, laughing every time I was referred to as the "veteran" Lorne Greenaway, instead of veterinarian!

My mom and dad, and my Uncle Melvin from Bella Coola, were there and I remember how excited and proud I felt. It was a long trip for them to have made, and I certainly appreciated them being there.

Mom and Dad made the trip to Williams Lake to be with us on election night.

L–R: Ron Harder, Dave Worthy, Don Stobbe and Doug Belsher, campaign stalwarts and good friends.

So, the next morning, I awoke as the optimistic, inexperienced Member of Parliament for Cariboo–Chilcotin. A few days later, after writing my thank-you letters, helping to dismantle the campaign office, and taking down signs, I was summoned to Ottawa. I was allotted an office in the West Block of the Parliament Buildings, and attended my first caucus meeting, presided over by Prime Minister Joe Clark. I took a walk around the Hill and was suitably awed, if not intimidated. I remember feeling very insignificant and very much alone in this totally unfamiliar environment. I was sworn in by the Clerk of the House, making things official.

I hired a staff of three women, and the most senior, Irene Bourne, who had worked on the Hill for twenty-five years, became my executive assistant and valued advisor.

Everything was new to me and there seemed to be one surprise after another. I was amazed at the number of perks one received as a Member: fifty-two flights a year to one's riding and six to anywhere in Canada; free railroad travel; free mailing privileges; even free haircuts; and on and on. Interestingly, however, the salary at that time wasn't great and that first year we dipped into our savings to the tune of about $8,000 to make ends meet.

On the third morning in my office, I was sitting at my desk reading over the Progressive Conservative policy manual, with no idea what to do with myself and fretting that I wasn't doing something useful. Mid-morning, an older, rather imposing man stopped by and introduced himself as Eldon Woolliams, a lawyer and long-time MP from Calgary North. His office was next to mine and he was related to my good friend, Neil. He asked me what I was up to and if there was anything he could help me with. I replied that I was reviewing our policy manual and as I gaped at him in surprise he reached across my desk, picked up the manual, and tossed it in the wastepaper basket, saying, "You won't need that anymore. Now that the election is over, it's of no use at all." I remember being shocked, but time proved that, basically, he was right.

All of us first-timers attended a familiarization meeting presided over by the venerable George Hees. George was his usual entertaining self and imparted a good many words of wisdom to the neophytes. Otherwise it was pretty quiet until Joe Clark selected his Cabinet. His

Outside our mobile constituency office with son Steve.

decision to sideline some of the old guard, some of whom had been cabinet ministers in the Diefenbaker government, caused a rift within the caucus. People like George Hees, Walter Dinsdale, Eldon Woolliams, Alvin Hamilton and many others had been waiting for years to get back in government and were most upset at being left out. They sincerely believed that their experience would have been useful to a young, inexperienced prime minister. I remember telling Joe that, at the very least, he should meet with this group once or twice a month over lunch or dinner, using them as a sounding board and reassuring them that they still had much to offer. I'm not sure that he did, though.

Before long, we were told to go home for the summer and to prepare ourselves for the convening of the House in the fall. On my return to Williams Lake, my first priority was to secure a constituency secretary, and to lease and furnish an office. To my everlasting gratitude, Nova agreed to take on the difficult and thankless role of being my constituency assistant. We were able to secure two adjoining rooms above the Spencer Dickie Drugstore on the main street, with a small private office for me and a larger room that doubled as a waiting room and space for Nova.

During the campaign, the only promise I can remember making was that I would make myself available in every town and small city on a regular basis. I decided the best way to do this was with a mobile office, so I leased an eighteen-foot trailer, covered it in signage and prepared to tow it around the riding with my pickup. The House of Commons paid the $200 a month lease payment. My gas bills were also covered.

As soon as the office in Williams Lake was organized, people started to come in with all sorts of problems. Nova and the women in Ottawa were able to handle most of them, and I met with many in my office. We immediately decided on a strategy that I think served us well: no one was to be turned away from our office without a sympathetic hearing, a solution, or a suggestion as to where to go to have the problem solved.

Our philosophy created a huge workload, though, because we were continually presented with situations that had little or nothing to do with the federal government. Problems were often personal, municipal, provincial, or concerning the Regional District—people never seemed to understand the difference between the levels of government, or how to make the various levels work in sync. They did learn, however, that we were good listeners, and could quite often resolve many of their concerns by applying a little effort and common sense.

In July, Phyl and I managed to take a couple of weeks off to spend at our Shuswap retreat before I was called back to Ottawa to serve on a task force created to review a situation concerning the import and export of beef. At that time, Canadian beef producers were feeling the threat of a US proposal to curb Canadian imports, as well as the increasing importation of Australian and New Zealand beef. The job of the task force was to call witnesses and to ultimately make recommendations for a new beef import law. I had a rough idea of how the North American beef market operated but, nevertheless, felt considerably out of my depth. Most of us on the committee were new members with a lot to learn but we did manage to get the job done.

Phyl found us an apartment on the fourth floor of a relatively new building on Sparks Street in downtown Ottawa, close to the House of Commons. We moved in on September 1 and Steven joined us with the intention of enrolling at Carleton University. He too had been bitten by the political bug!

In early September, I decided to make my first swing through the Interior part of the riding with my new mobile office. My first stop was in Lillooet, where I set up in the corner of the parking lot at a small shopping centre. I had arrived unannounced but, nonetheless, had a very busy day, and with some relief I was able to leave for Ashcroft in the evening. I crossed the bridge, reached the top of the hill and came around the corner only to be confronted by a sea of vehicles with flashing amber, blue or red lights. I stopped, assuming that there must have been a terrible accident, and got out to ask what had happened.

It turned out that Department of Fisheries officers had arrested several Native fishermen down at the river and were about to bring them, by helicopter, up the thousand feet or so to the highway. It was dusk and the light was fading fast, and as the helicopter arrived, including at least a dozen Fisheries personnel, it only barely missed a high-tension power line that crossed above the crowd.

I was surprised to see Chief Victor Adolf's son Roger, his hands cuffed behind his back, as the first to be pulled out. I had done a considerable amount of veterinary work for Vic and counted him and Roger as good friends. I rushed over to talk to Roger and saw how shaken he was. He quickly described how they'd been thrown, handcuffed, on the floor of the helicopter. They hadn't been belted in, the door of the helicopter had come open on the way up from the river, and he had almost fallen out. I must admit feeling pretty angry and when I was pushed out of the way by a Fisheries officer I gave him a good push back and told him, "Take care or I will have your job."

The result was that this episode was deemed important enough to make the CBC *National News* that very night. Of course, by the next day, the story wasn't quite so dramatic. In short order, I was contacted by the ministers' office in Ottawa to report to our minister, Jim McGrath, as soon as possible. Jim and I met privately and I recounted my interpretation of the events that had occurred. I got the impression that he thought the entire episode bordered on the hilarious. He and I became good friends throughout my years in Ottawa, and Jim later went on to become the Lieutenant-Governor of Newfoundland. But I was about to learn that it was not the politicians who made the decisions—it was the bureaucrats.

I went back to Williams Lake to complete my tour through the riding. Later in the month, pulled over at a rest stop, I was greeted by a pleasant fellow who said he had an envelope for me. He knew my name, which I thought was rather strange, but I accepted the envelope and continued on my way. I had never received a summons before but that's what the envelope contained. I had been charged with obstruction and a court date in Lillooet had been set. A few days later, on my return to Ottawa, I sought out my new friend Eldon Woolliams for advice. After reviewing the summons he said, "Son, go back to Vancouver and hire the best damn lawyer in the city." He gave me two suggestions: H.A.D. Oliver and Tom Braidwood. I took his advice and was fortunate in being able to retain Mr. Braidwood.

It's surprising, in retrospect, that most of the publicity I received regarding this incident was very positive. I was even given good marks by the newspapers in our riding. I don't think that would be the case today.

I met with Tom in his Vancouver office and told him my story, and he said that he would busy himself preparing a defence. On the court date, I picked him up at the Kamloops airport and drove him over to Lillooet, stopping on the way to visit the scene of the crime. When we arrived at the courthouse, the courtroom was jammed with people. Tom delivered a rather complicated but successful defence, and the judge dismissed the charges. We both believed that this would be the end of the case, but within days, we were informed that the department of fisheries had launched an appeal. This appeal was to be conducted before another judge in the Kamloops Courthouse. Tom went through the same procedure but this time we were less successful. The judge found me guilty but gave me an absolute discharge. As the proceedings concluded, the judge asked me if I had anything to say. I got up and stated, somewhat belligerently, "If I encounter the same situation again, I will do exactly the same thing." Tom pulled me back down into my seat by my jacket and told me to be quiet. The judge turned red in the face, banged down his gavel and dismissed the court.

Shortly thereafter, I received Tom's bill for $10,000. This really brought me down to earth but I had to admit that he had earned it. My good friend and mentor Ron Huntington was now a minister and his riding association contributed $2,500 to my cause. Phyl and I contributed another $2,500 and Tom, bless his heart, wrote off $5,000. There is no doubt that I learned a good deal from this incident.

In October I was selected by the prime minister to serve on two standing committees: Fisheries and the Environment, and Indian Affairs. My constituency had forty-three Indian Bands—more than any other riding in the country—so I wasn't surprised that I was listed to serve on Indian Affairs.

The PM came under increasing criticism for the long delay in opening Parliament but finally the day came in early October. There was much pomp and ceremony and that evening we were invited to the Governor General's, along with our wives, husbands, or partners, to the traditional and most enjoyable dinner dance.

For the newly elected, our main preoccupation was familiarizing ourselves with the House rules. We were each given a book that was probably quite easy to understand if you were a lawyer, and told to study it. We also had to give our maiden speech and, when my turn came, I must admit that I was frightened half to death. I wasn't the only one, and you couldn't help notice that even older, experienced members often seemed a little nervous when they were on their feet. The House of Commons is a very intimidating place and takes a good deal of getting used to. We began to serve on our committees and it was a busy time.

I made a trip out to the riding in November to attend the Armistice Day service in Williams Lake. I made a practice of attending the ceremony in a different town each year for the duration of my time in Ottawa.

Long hours at work and frequent trips to the riding made Phyl and I value our time at home.

The Clark government was in a minority situation and the five Socred members from Quebec held the balance of power. It was noted that Clark often seemed to treat Fabian Roy, their leader, with a fair degree of derision. Pierre Trudeau had resigned the Liberal leadership in November and the Liberals were somewhat preoccupied with organizing a leadership convention. In early December, Minister of Finance John Crosbie brought down the budget, which called for, among other things, a federal tax of eighteen cents per gallon on gasoline.

This was an extremely unpopular move and ultimately led to our downfall. The budget debate went on for a week and the gasoline tax was the main issue. Assuming that the Socred members would support the government, and with the Liberals leaderless, Joe decided—unilaterally—to call for a budget vote on December 17. Two of our members, Flora McDonald and Lloyd Crouse, were out of the country. The vote on the night of the seventeenth saw all five Socreds, who could hardly wait to get even with Joe Clark, vote with the Opposition and the government was defeated.

Initially Conservative House Leader Walter Baker took the blame for the defeat. The media delighted in accusing him of not being able to count. This was completely untrue, as he had nothing to do with calling the vote. The vote could have been postponed and the unpopular tax could have been modified or removed from the budget. I, along with many others, had no idea that we were going to be defeated that night; it came as a complete shock. As a matter of fact, Phyl and I had signed a purchase agreement on a house in Ottawa[1] that very day.

It HAD BEEN CLEAR all fall that Prime Minister Joe Clark had had difficulty finding his feet. The media had cast him as young, inexperienced and inept, especially when compared to Trudeau. In our weekly caucus meetings he faced a continuous barrage of suggestions on how to improve his image. George Hees had several times suggested that Joe consider weekly or monthly televised fireside chats à la President Roosevelt, and that he should appear in less formal attire, preferably in an open-necked plaid shirt. At a caucus meeting, he also suggested that Joe take up some athletic endeavour to be more of a man of the people. Chuck Cook, no fan of Joe Clark's, called out, "like hang-gliding," which made even Joe laugh.

The PM also suffered from the story that he had lost his luggage on a flight to Korea. This was grossly unfair, as his Air Canada flight was late arriving at the Narita airport in Japan, and the group he was travelling with had made a dash across the tarmac to catch their connection to Seoul, leaving their luggage to follow on a later flight. At no time was the baggage "lost." There was a fair contingent of media accompanying him, who knew exactly what had happened, but they appeared to take every opportunity to belittle Clark, casting him as a bumbling, fumbling leader in stark contrast to the debonair, polished, experienced Trudeau. We were down at least twenty points in the polls.

So the die had been cast and the election date was set for February 18, 1980. Almost immediately, Trudeau revoked his resignation and was reinstated as leader of the Liberal party. We were about to be involved in a nasty, cold, midwinter campaign—the kind all Canadians hate.

Phyl and I decided to spend a long weekend in Florida before heading out to Williams Lake for Christmas, hoping that a few days of sunshine would be a good tonic prior to the campaign ahead. We arrived in Tampa in the midst of one of the coldest spells in years— it might even have been warmer in Ottawa! We returned to Ottawa on the third day and shortly thereafter left for Christmas in Williams Lake. The entire campaign had been put on hold until the beginning of January. Nova took over as my campaign manager; we put our team together and suffered through a cold and miserable eight weeks. I won easily in our riding, but the Conservatives showed poorly overall and, once again, Pierre Trudeau and the Liberals took over.

AND SO WE BEGAN five years of Opposition. Phyl had been offered a job at Richardon's Securities in Ottawa before the writ was even dropped, and she was the only female stockbroker in the office. Since completing the basic Securities course, she had passed the Investment Finance courses and was studying towards her Certified Financial Analyst designation. She moved over to RBC Dominion Securities the following year. She was much happier there and, with a good deal of fortitude and initiative, she developed a formidable client list and became one of the company's top performers. We had moved into our house on Lewis Street and we both enjoyed walking to work. That fall, Phyl and I put ourselves in Kathy's hands for a trip to Italy, retracing her own trip in pseudo-backpacking style and creating some wonderful memories of picnic meals and drinking wine out of paper bags.

My time basically centred on my work on the standing committee of Indian Affairs, but every three weeks I made a trip to the riding and took as much time as I could meeting with people, trying to sort out their problems. In the winter, when I was unable to use the trailer, I set up appointments in hotels, motels, town offices and so on. We were always able to find some helpful person to make arrangements and set up appointments; we put notices in local newspapers stating when and where I would be located. I always tried to start at 9:00 a.m. and often ran through until late evening.

I was continually amazed at the number of people who came to see me and, invariably I would return to Ottawa with one or two large briefcases filled with notes and documents for my staff to sort out. It was a rewarding experience, especially if we could solve a particular issue, but those days were always exhausting. In warmer weather I used the trailer and moved from town to town, often at night. The trailer, with its highly visible signs, gave me good exposure and I was able to crawl into my sleeping bag instead of booking hotel rooms.

The riding was divided into three geographical areas: the north Cariboo, the south Cariboo, and Squamish/Whistler/Pemberton/ Mount Currie. I did my best to visit each of these areas every three months and spend a day in each major centre, as well as smaller centres such as Wells and Barkerville. I spent a lot of time doing phone consultations, and was called upon to appear at various functions throughout the riding, especially in the summer.

I also made a point of visiting aboriginal bands upon request or to investigate situations that had been brought to my attention. I soon discovered what really went on at many of the reserves and it wasn't pleasant. In many cases, it was the strong taking over to the detriment of those who were weaker. There was an almost universal lack of accountability; the modus operandi seemed to be to keep a lid on things by allocating sufficient money to prevent any disturbance. One could go on and on, detailing specific incidents of mismanagement, corruption and waste. Suffice it to say that, over the years, the Natives learned very well—by means of public protest and blockades, and with the assistance of an inept federal bureaucracy—to take advantage of the system.

The standing committee heard time and again of the evils of the Indian Act and at one point we spent several months working on legislation that would have rescinded and replaced the act. When word got out about what we were doing, aboriginal leadership across the country put pressure on the government to abort the process. The Native power was quite happy with the status quo. They were in control of the funding, continually available and in increasing amounts. The lack of accountability on many reserves seemed made to order for the corruption that so often occurs.

During one session of the Indian Affairs committee, Chief Billy Diamond of the Quebec Cree came before us and outlined a number of serious problems, some of which were tragic. I began to concentrate on the issues he raised and zeroed in on one in particular. On one of his reserves, the department had somehow installed a sewage system that emptied upriver from the water intake and there was an outbreak of E. coli diarrhea that resulted in the deaths of several infants. Monique Begin was the Minister of Health and I was able to question her on the issue during Question Period in the House. She initially denied any knowledge of the situation, which wasn't surprising, but in my subsequent question to her a week or two later she attempted to stonewall me. After several more questions, she admitted that the situation was untenable, and ultimately it was corrected. It was issues such as these that gave me a boost and made me think that perhaps this process wasn't as useless as it seemed.

I got another boost when my first motion in the House of Commons was passed unanimously. I had noted that veterinarians were not on the list of those who could endorse passport applications. My motion brought this to the attention of the House and veterinarians were added, to my satisfaction.

The next issue that arose came out of our own riding, mainly from the 100 Mile House area. It concerned Section 31 of the *Income Tax Act*. Many people around 100 Mile House lived on small holdings and worked in town in the service sector or the forest industry. They generally had some livestock on the property and were able to use certain

Mom and Dad celebrated their 50th wedding anniversary in 1982.

expenses pertaining to farming as tax deductions. Without warning, Canada Revenue Agency had decided to disallow these deductions. We received a deluge of correspondence and phone calls concerning this sudden change.

I was able to arrange a public meeting in 100 Mile House to which I invited the top Revenue Canada bureaucrat in BC. About one hundred people showed up and gave the poor fellow a pretty good going over. Meanwhile I was able to question the minister in the House, to his annoyance, and finally the department gave in—much to my satisfaction and to that of my constituents.

I SHOULD EXPLAIN HOW Question Period worked. When we were in Opposition, each morning at nine o'clock sharp you could attend a meeting chaired by Eric Nielsen and compete for a place if you felt that you had a burning issue. You put your question before Eric and if he decided that it was of some significance, particularly if it might be damaging to the government, his secretary would call later and tell you that you had been successful. Eric or the Question Period Chairman would then draw up a list that was presented to the Speaker. The Leader of the Opposition was always recognized first by the Speaker, followed by those with other questions who had been ranked according to their perceived importance. When the Speaker had completed the list there was usually time for one or two more questioners to be recognized. There was never a shortage of members competing for these spots and it was common to see five or ten members, all rising at the same time, hoping to be recognized by the Speaker.

Question Period is a very carefully orchestrated and structured gong show. No one ever asks a question unless they know the answer. There is no doubt that it is a very partisan and often distasteful, if not disgusting, part of our political process. There is also no doubt that allowing it to be televised has resulted in the spectacle that it has become.

One of Trudeau's goals had always been to repatriate our Constitution. The House was preoccupied with this issue for a year or so, culminating in a vote that I shall always remember. The 103 of us were invoked by Eric Nielsen to vote in favour of the legislation because it was popular in the country and, if we voted against it, we would lessen our chances in the next election. Eighteen of our members broke rank and voted against it and I wish I had been one of them. I have forever chastised myself for not having paid more attention to the legislation; if I had, I certainly would have voted against it. I was on Parliament Hill the day Queen Elizabeth and Trudeau signed the document.

JOE CLARK'S LEADERSHIP WAS continually questioned and, at some point, a petition calling for his resignation had been circulated by several MPs who made no bones about their dislike of Clark. Ultimately this and other actions led to the leadership vote in Winnipeg in January 1983, which resulted in his resignation. The Winnipeg Convention led to serious divisions within our caucus. There were considerably more of our members against him rather than for him. These included the old guard who had been passed over when Joe chose his Cabinet. Personally, I liked Joe but had seen enough behind the scenes to realize that he was not the person we needed to lead us to victory over the Liberals.

Subsequently the date was set for the 1983 leadership

Phyl and me at the 1983 Progressive Conservative leadership convention.

We managed to get everyone home and suitably attired for my House of Commons Christmas card, 1983.

convention, to be held in Ottawa. Joe Clark, John Crosbie and Brian Mulroney were the frontrunners. Brian Mulroney came to Ottawa and set up camp in the Château Laurier hotel. He invited members of caucus, a few at a time, to meet with him. At some point Ron Huntington and I, with our wives, went to meet him. I had watched his performance in the 1976 Progressive Conservative Leadership Convention and wasn't too impressed. Both Ron and I came away from that meeting with an uneasy feeling. He seemed to have surrounded himself with some people of questionable character and he himself seemed to be altogether too smooth. I remember going back to the office and having Pauline, my assistant, prepare a letter to Brian listing seven reasons why I couldn't support him, such as: he had never been an MP; he was from Quebec (as was Trudeau); I didn't care for the people who surrounded him;[2] and so on. As things transpired, that letter was my political death sentence.

At the time, however, Ron and I were very comfortable throwing our support behind John Crosbie. I ultimately spent several weeks campaigning with John, and the more I saw of him and his wife, Jane, the more I liked them. John was extremely bright and articulate but his Achilles' heel was his inability to speak French.

With John Crosbie and Mayor Ethel Winger of Williams Lake.

Any attempts he made to speak French were comic, bordering on disastrous. During the campaign, the media continually raised the subject. John was very popular with the Tory party members and wherever he spoke he drew overflow crowds. About three weeks before the convention he was leading the other two by twenty points. An evening meeting in Montreal sealed his fate. After the meeting the media descended upon him and continued to question him about his inability to speak French. This time the subject brought John to the boiling point, and his response was, "I don't speak Chinese either, but I can damn well run the country."

Brian Mulroney and his wife, Mila, travelled the country and spent an evening in Williams Lake. We had elected six delegates, at least three of whom he won over. At our delegate selection meeting I had encouraged delegates to keep an open mind, although everyone knew I was supporting John Crosbie. Many MPs insisted that elected delegates must all vote together for whomever that MP supported but I was naïve enough to feel that this was undemocratic. So our delegation split.

At the convention, before the first vote, I was amazed that many good friends of mine had jumped to the Mulroney camp. This, of course, was the savvy thing to do and the Mulroney group begged me to join them, but I stuck with John to the last.

After his win at the convention, Brian Mulroney was elected to the House of Commons in a hastily arranged by-election in Central Nova, a safe Conservative seat in Nova Scotia vacated by Elmer MacKay. With Mulroney in charge, things quieted down and our caucus, at least

Sharing a laugh with Flora MacDonald and Brian Mulroney.

on the surface, appeared to pull together. We began to gain strength in the polls and remained in full election mode.

It was during this period that I became involved in a prolonged investigation of Chief Ron Derrickson and the management of the Westbank Indian Band. My colleague, Fred King, the MP for Okanagan–Similkameen, whose constituency included the Westbank Reserve, brought the issue to my attention. It became an enormously complicated affair that ultimately led to the formation of a Royal Commission. Even then, I never felt that the allegations of corruption were satisfactorily concluded; however, I did take some comfort from the fact that Mr. Derrickson was defeated in the subsequent band election.

It was not often boring in the House of Commons, especially as practical jokes were common. I happened to be the butt of one of the best ones, played on me one day by a fellow Conservative MP named Lorne McCuish, from Prince George–Bulkley Valley. One morning, I was sitting in my place during Question Period when a parliamentary page handed me a note. It informed me that a constituent of mine, a woman, was sitting in the gallery. It said that she was wearing a pink sweater, wished to see me after Question Period, and that I should wave to her so that she would be certain to recognize me later in the rotunda. At the same time, McCuish sent a note to a rather good-

L–R: Ross Belsher, Chuck Cook, me, Ron Huntington, Benno Friesen, Bill
Clarke and Gerry St. Germain.

looking and well-endowed woman that read, "Madam, you have the
most glorious bosom and I would very much like to meet you. We could
meet in the rotunda after Question Period. I am going to wave to you
so that you will recognize me." He then scrawled my name on the note
and had it delivered by a page. I followed the instructions and waved to
her with enthusiasm, and couldn't understand why she seemed to scowl
at me. Of course, not wanting to offend a constituent, I waited for her
for ten or fifteen minutes after Question Period, not realizing that I was
being observed by a good number of my colleagues. They enjoyed a
good laugh at my expense. It's amazing that this prank didn't become
public because I'm sure the poor woman was deeply offended.

McCuish was an interesting fellow. He had been an insurance
adjuster in Prince George before being elected. He had inadvertently
angered a policy holder by turning down a claim and one night, after
his staff had left the office, this person came in and shot him point
blank over his desk with a 12-gauge shotgun. He somehow survived
but was nervous and sometimes quite unsteady. Shortly after he was

elected, his wife left him. He had a difficult time in the House and at one point in the middle of asking a question to a minister, he lost his train of thought and had to sit down. He was absolutely devastated and henceforth spent a good deal of time during Question Period sending humorous notes to various members. One day he passed around a very disparaging note concerning a female MP from Toronto. As soon as I saw it, I knew I'd found a way to get even with him for the woman-in-the-pink-sweater incident.

John Fraser, a good friend, was the Speaker of the House and I was able to obtain some of his personal stationery. I had Pauline type up a letter, supposedly from John, stating that this Toronto member had come across McCuish's note and was contemplating legal action. I, the Speaker, requested him to report to my office at 9:00 on Monday morning to discuss this issue with the hope that it could be resolved. It was easy to forge John's signature, and we had the letter delivered to McCuish's office on a Friday as he was about to leave for Prince George for a weekend in his riding. According to his staff, he was absolutely devastated by this letter, cancelled his trip, and spent the weekend in his apartment contemplating his future. Just before nine o'clock on Monday morning, a number of us concealed ourselves outside the Speaker's chambers and watched as McCuish slowly shuffled his way up the hall. Just as he reached the Speaker's door, we all jumped out laughing fit to kill. Once he realized what was going on, he almost fainted with relief.

Leading up to the election of 1984, our party continued to gain popularity. The main issue at that time was fiscal restraint and responsibility. The Liberal government was seen to be presiding over government spending that was out of control. Brian Mulroney and the Tories continually drove home the message that a Tory government would act responsibly and get spending under control. To this end, I joined a group of colleagues, under the leadership of Don Mazankowski, whose purpose was to review all government spending, especially the various programs that allocated grants, loans and government contracts, which were often politically motivated, especially in the Maritime provinces and Quebec. We drew up a list of what we felt should be scrapped and I remember feeling that at last we were going to make a worthwhile contribution.

Because the revenue ministry had come under continual attack, Mulroney and his advisers decided to strike a task force to hold public hearings in the major cities of all provinces. It was felt that the election was imminent and this task force, chaired jointly by Perrin Beatty and John Bosley, was given a month to travel the country and present a written report. Because of my interest in Section 31 of the *Act*, I was selected as one of the eight members to serve on the task force. Several tax lawyers from Toronto were seconded to travel with us, as well as necessary staff. It was a tough schedule but we were able to hold hearings in twenty-one centres in seventeen days and presented our report on time. The media closely monitored the hearings and the initiative was very popular with people right across the country. It proved to be a very good political move.

During our travels we heard from people representing almost every walk of life: individuals, small business owners, farmers, corporate CFOs, tax lawyers, and so on. I got myself into considerable trouble at the Kamloops hearing. A widow came to describe the most unbelievable and unreasonable encounter with Revenue Canada personnel. Some in the audience were moved to tears. I clearly recall John Bosley turning to Perrin Beatty and saying, "What can we do?" Perrin's response was, "I really don't know." Our microphones were open and everyone in the room heard this exchange and then I blurted out, "We need to take a few of these taxmen out and shoot them." Of course I didn't really mean it, but that's not the way the press saw it and my words made headlines across the country.

When we returned to Ottawa, I was immediately chastised for being so outspoken and Gerald Bean, president of the Public Service Alliance, stated publicly that I had endangered the lives of his employees and demanded an apology. I didn't pay any attention to Mr. Bean, as I liked to call him, and he continued his demand, finally contacting Mulroney. The result was that I was ordered to apologize, which I grudgingly did in a terse one-sentence letter, but Mr. Bean refused to accept it. He was upset because I showed no sign of remorse. He fussed around and threatened legal action but finally gave up and the situation blew over.

After the 1984 election, Michael Wilson became Minister of Finance.

WE WON THE 1984 election, scoring a huge majority and decimating the Liberals. Michael Wilson became Minister of Finance. I was made Chairman of the Fisheries and Environment Standing Committee, and later on, the Parliamentary Secretary to the Minister of Natural Resources. I was also elected Chairman of the BC Caucus, so it was a busy time for me. I still had to make my regular trips to the riding and I continued to use the trailer. As BC Caucus Chairman, it was necessary for me to attend public functions throughout the province.

In the fall of 1985 I was honoured to be on hand when Rick Hansen, a young man from Williams Lake, started his famous and very successful Man in Motion tour to raise money for spinal cord research. After his return to Canada in 1987, a reception was held for him at the House of Commons where he moved us all with his account of the experience, which took twenty-six months and saw him visit thirty-four countries around the world. At that time, many historical government buildings had formidable front steps, but Rick's efforts had lasting influence, instigating a long-overdue effort to make these buildings more accessible.

DURING THE TEN YEARS I was an MP, I was chosen a number of times to travel to various countries as a delegate representing our Parliament and/or country. I spent the better part of a week in Brussels and Mons undergoing NATO briefings. This trip was during the Cold War and I vividly remember the briefing dealing with the Russian threat that we had received from the NATO chief. At the time, Western Europe appeared to be very vulnerable to attack by the Russians and we were told that if the Russians wished to move, they could gain access to the English Channel in forty-eight hours. This was backed up by satellite photos taken via a process of which most of us were not even aware. We were shown large buildups of tanks and vehicles along the Russian border. What surprised me most was seeing large dumps of oil pipe that was to be rapidly laid down by special machines to service tanks, troop carriers and other vehicles.

Rick Hansen, from Williams Lake, took his Man in Motion tour to 34 countries.

I had joined the Canada–Japan Parliamentary Friendship Association, and during my last year in Ottawa I was chosen to make a trip to Japan. My particular interest was in promoting lumber sales from BC. The Japanese had an aversion to building wooden houses because several of their cities had been destroyed by fire, which they felt was due to their use of wood. The Council of Forest Industries (COFI) in BC had purchased a small building lot in downtown Tokyo for $750,000, upon which they proposed to construct a platform-type wooden house similar to those common in Canada. I visited the site with our Japanese contemporaries and took every opportunity to extol the virtues of wood frame houses. I probably didn't have much effect on the outcome but the use of lumber in Japan has certainly increased. I remember being amazed at seeing modular Japanese houses made of concrete and ceramics. They could erect these prefabricated homes in just a few days and they definitely were fireproof.

The chairman of our delegation was Bill Kempling, MP from Burlington, and over the years he and I had become good friends. Bill had owned and operated a large automotive parts store for many years and I remember him telling me of his exasperation when it came to dealing with all-too-numerous government requests for information about his business. He said he had considered hiring extra staff to deal with this annoyance. He hit upon a novel idea of having a large rubber stamp made that said "Not Applicable." From that point on every government request was stamped and returned to sender. He claimed that this practice had about an 80 percent success rate.

On this trip we visited the Japanese Diet Building, a Nissan plant that provided our introduction to the use of robots, a canola oil plant that used Canadian seeds, and many other interesting facilities.

One day, however, Bill didn't show up to lead us; in fact, he didn't appear at all until the next morning. Our Japanese hosts were busy that morning reading Tokyo newspapers, most of which carried a picture of Bill on the front page. Of course we couldn't understand the newspapers, but the most amazing story unfolded. During the war, for at least two years, Bill had been with a special unit that was dropped behind the Japanese lines in the jungles of Burma. This unit's job had been to harass and sabotage the enemy. One day they unexpectedly encountered a small Japanese force and were fortunate enough to win the ensuing firefight. While looking over the casualties, Bill came upon a Japanese soldier who was still alive. As Bill approached him, the enemy soldier slid his hand inside his tunic and Bill, thinking he was about to draw a pistol, shot and killed him. It turned out that what he had been reaching for was his wallet, which held his home address and pictures of his wife and children.

Bill had kept the wallet and brought it with him to Japan. He had mentioned this through an interpreter to his Japanese counterpart. Immediately, attempts were made, successfully as it turned out, to contact the dead soldier's family, and Bill, accompanied by several government ministers and a number of members of the media, left Tokyo to travel to a small rural community where Bill presented the wallet to the soldier's wife. Evidently most of the town turned out and it was a very moving event. Bill was a pretty private person and had not mentioned this to a single soul.

Other trips took me to the British Isles to visit the House of Commons in London; to Aberdeen, Scotland, to receive a briefing on the North Sea oil development; to Paris to visit our embassy; and to southern Germany to visit our military contingent at Lahr. I was invited to Taiwan on several occasions with a short side trip to Seoul, Korea, then to Singapore, and on to Jakarta where we opened a veterinary laboratory sponsored by the Canadian government. On this particular trip, our wives were able to accompany us, and when the formal business was completed, Phyl and I continued on to Papua New Guinea to visit Kathy, who was working at a small outpost hospital. Kathy had started

Phyl with Kathy and a group of her nursing students on our trip to Papua New Guinea.

calling herself "Kate" because there were so many other Kathys there; Phyl made the switch with more commitment than I did—I never could get used to it.

WHEN I WAS MOVED from committee chairmanship to the position of Parliamentary Secretary I became even busier, but the work was very interesting. I spent every morning with Minister of Forests Gerry Merrithew, who was a wonderful guy, being briefed by ministry officials. I was often asked to stand in for Gerry and to give speeches on his behalf. There was one experience I shall never forget. I was asked to go to London to give a speech on behalf of the Canadian government at the opening of the annual convention of representatives of the nuclear energy sector from countries all over the world. I travelled with a good friend who was on the minister's staff and we were put up at the Savoy Hotel, an experience in itself. The night before the convention was to begin, I delivered a speech to delegates at a dinner that was held in the famous Guildhall. I had a few minutes before the dinner began, and I was able to go through the room to find the guild mark of my ancestor, John Greenway, amongst the many others that adorned the walls. His mark dated back to the 1400s, so it made a considerable impression upon me.

In the spring of 1988, I was asked to deliver another speech at a conference in a small city in southern Ontario, the name of which escapes me, and I drove down with Phyl and Kathy. We had taken some tennis rackets and the hotel at which we were staying had tennis courts. We decided take a few minutes off to knock some balls around. Unfortunately, in going for a ball Phyl caught her heel and fell backwards onto the court. She was immediately in a good deal of pain and we took her to the nearest hospital where she was X-rayed and diagnosed with a compression fracture of her fourth and fifth lumbar vertebrae. We drove home as carefully as possible and she spent the next six weeks flat on her back in bed. This provided a completely unexpected—and unprecedented—time-out and gave Phyl an opportunity to contemplate the busy life we were leading. I guess we both felt that we were working too hard, not having much time to enjoy life and losing touch with friends in BC, and perhaps we ought to consider some changes.

Speaking in London's Guildhall at the international nuclear energy sector's annual convention.

I had become very disenchanted with the federal government and it was becoming more and more difficult to condone many of its initiatives. A good example was the moving of the F-18 fighter jet maintenance contract from Winnipeg to Montreal. It was also difficult for me to explain the decision to move the space agency from Ottawa to Montreal, or the construction of the new Museum of Civilization in Hull. Our government kept pouring more and more money into Quebec by way of shipbuilding contracts, grants and loans, all terribly difficult to rationalize as an MP from the West.

To assist us in resolving our situation, we made an appointment with a counsellor and, in short order, she reinforced our thoughts of leaving what we were doing and returning to BC. It was a simple decision to enact. I declined to run for re-election, and Phyl gave her notice at RBC Dominion. We left for British Columbia in August and moved to Victoria in September.

Trials and tribulations aside, I have to say that my time in politics and in Ottawa was interesting and even, at times, rewarding. I was not able to retain my idealistic views for very long, a common experience amongst those who seek to make changes on the federal scene. I was more fortunate than most, as throughout my ten years as an MP, I had retained my marriage and my health and had not begun to drink too much, all things that can impact many Members of Parliament. I certainly wasn't going to miss the monotonous and often difficult flights to and from Ottawa that had become a way of life for those of us from British Columbia.

IF I WERE ASKED for advice from anyone contemplating becoming a Member of Parliament, the following might be considered:

1. If you have a partner, make certain he or she understands the sacrifices that must be made.

2. It is not wise to become actively engaged in politics if you have a young family.

3. Become bilingual.

4. Work to become a good public speaker.

5. Morals and integrity are everything, not to be sacrificed under any circumstances.

6. Put your constituents ahead of pressures from Ottawa. You must not forget those who elected you.

CIVIL SERVICE: WALKING THROUGH THE MINEFIELDS

THE DECISION TO LEAVE Ottawa left both Phyl and me at loose ends, work-wise. I let it be known that I was looking for work and, before long, a headhunting firm approached me about a position in the BC government as Deputy Minister of Agriculture. There were evidently four of us being considered. I was invited to an interview and asked to undergo a written examination in Vancouver.

The political situation in BC at that time was not at all stable. Social Credit Premier Bill Vander Zalm had become quite unpopular and the NDP (under Glen Clark's leadership) was ahead in the polls. The job itself appealed to me but there was a risk that it might not last long.[1] Nonetheless, ever the optimist, when the position was offered to me, I accepted. I took it as a good sign when I was informed that I had won the competition on merit, not on political sympathy.

Meanwhile, since I was resigning as the MP for Cariboo–Chilcotin, it was incumbent upon me to leave in place a candidate who would have a good shot at replacing me in the upcoming federal election. Our association arranged a nomination meeting and two candidates came forward: Dave Worthy and Ron Harder, both good friends and loyal supporters. It was a very difficult decision to make and after a lot of soul-searching, I threw my support behind Dave. Dave went on to win the nomination, and that fall he was elected. I felt concerned for Ron and it's not clear to

I returned to BC in 1988 to become Deputy Minister of Agriculture.

me even now whether or not I made the right decision. Sometimes it seems that there is no "right" decision.

My appointment as Deputy Minister (DM) was to begin September 1, 1988, and that meant a move to Victoria. I was still serving as an MP until the end of August, so it was left to Phyl to look for our new home in Victoria while I worked in Williams Lake. She spent several days with a realtor looking at houses and finally settled on a beautiful home on an acre of land in Ten Mile Point. We had planned to be in Guelph that weekend for the thirtieth reunion of my graduating class, so I made a quick side trip to Victoria to look at the house, and then Phyl and I headed back east. In the midst of a very hectic weekend and a flurry of other potential buyers, we quickly secured the financing (through Phyl's old friend Peter Vale at the Bank of Montreal) and landed the purchase of one of the best investments we ever made.

We listed our house in Ottawa and began packing up ten years of our lives—the longest we'd stayed anywhere since our Kamloops days. We were fortunate to find that our new neighbours in Victoria, Christian and Monique Von Westarp, were going away for the month of September and were very happy to have us stay in their house.

In August, I was required to attend a swearing-in ceremony at the Lieutenant-Governor's house, along with the other new appointments. My experience with bureaucrats had always been pretty negative and now, suddenly, I was one! I met Minister of Agriculture John Savage, a farmer from Delta who was very popular within the agriculture community, and he and I quickly became good friends. It was no secret that the premier and Cabinet were contemplating phasing out the Ministry of Agriculture (MoA), responding in part to the strong sentiment that farmers didn't need to have government officials telling them how to run their business. The Ministry of the Environment was poised to take over. There were, however, forty pieces of specific legislation pertaining to agriculture that had always been administered by the MoA, so it seemed to me that there was more than enough work to be done.

At the time I took over, there were about four hundred MoA staff, about a third of them based in Victoria. To my way of thinking, the ministry was overstaffed, especially with people working in offices. I was much more in tune with those who worked in extension positions, providing direct assistance to farmers and ranchers with problems and presenting new and improved practices.

Our head office was located across from the Empress Hotel in an old five-storey building on the corner of Humboldt and Douglas. I had more personal staff than I'd had as an MP, with three assistant deputy ministers (ADM); a number of directors; an executive assistant, David Buchan; and a very capable secretary, Agnes Vollmeier, who had three young women reporting to her. With the help of Frank Rhodes—the premier's deputy minister and the government's top bureaucrat—I rearranged several positions at the ADM level. This caused some tension, but I felt I needed several people that I could depend upon.

My first major problem arose immediately. The previous deputy, who had been fired for irregularities related to his expense account, had been very interested in international trade and was convinced that there were many products of BC agriculture that could be profitably exported, so for the previous three years he had funded a very expensive exhibition of BC products at BC Place. Dozens of expensive show booths had been designed and were stored in a warehouse between shows, at considerable expense. Many of our own staff were seconded for the week to occupy the booths at the annual event.

Warning bells were going off in my head but it was my first month in a new job, so I resolved to keep an open mind. I spent a day visiting the show and meeting the staff, and on my return to Victoria I began to inquire about the results of previous exhibitions. I was surprised that there had been no orders from Asia, since exporting to that part of the world had been a central part of the strategy. The more closely I looked, the more I smelled a rat, as evidence of numerous overseas trips and unreasonable expense claims came to light. John and I unceremoniously dismantled the project, sold off the portable booths and fired the bureaucrat responsible.

Phyl (L), with three of her close friends.

I'd had a pretty stressful initiation to civil service, but fortunately things settled down and I had some time to learn the ropes. The single most time-consuming activity was meetings. Endless meetings, all week long, starting every Monday morning when all of the deputies met at 8:00 in the Legislature Cabinet room, presided over by Frank Rhodes. We each presented a brief report on the week's events along with identification of any potentially "hot" situations. I met weekly with my ADMs and the directors based in the Victoria office. Meetings with producer organizations, lobby groups, task forces and staff seemed to take up the rest of the week.

We settled into making a new life in Victoria. Phyl had a vision for putting an addition onto the house and doing some serious landscaping, which turned out really well and made the house perfect for us. She started playing tennis, joined the Saanich Newcomers' Club, met some wonderful people, and soon we had a really interesting circle of friends. I was still working long hours but, thanks to Phyl's efforts, we had a busy social life and took some memorable trips.

By then, Kathy seemed to have got travelling out of her system and was teaching nursing at East Kootenay Community College in Cranbrook, where she met and married Don Craft in 1989. Sadly, shortly after the wedding, my dad died after a long struggle with cancer. I still wish I'd spent more time with him and had been a more attentive listener to the stories he so anxiously tried to pass along in those final months.

Steven married Teresa Chew on September 14, 1991.

After Dad died in 1990, Mom lived in a small house in a Kelowna retirement community.

Terry was in Vancouver working for Northwest Music. Steven married Teresa Chew in the fall of 1991. Teresa was raised in North Vancouver and had worked for fifteen years at one of BC's largest advertising agencies, Vrlak Robinson. They moved to Kelowna the following year.

Over the next few years, Steven and Teresa had two children (Olivia in 1992 and Ben in 1993), and Kathy and Don adopted Udom Andrew from Thailand in 1992. Terry spent a few years in Yokohama, where he worked for a technology development company. In 1994, I took Mom to Bella Coola to attend the one hundredth anniversary of the arrival of the Norwegian settlers; Norwegians who'd been raised in Bella Coola came from all over the world and Mom saw people she hadn't seen since she was a little girl. She and I buried Dad's ashes with the family at the cemetery there.

Mom enjoyed several more years of relatively good health, living on her own in a small house in a Kelowna retirement community, until she suddenly collapsed and died in 1998. I took her ashes to Bella Coola as well, with a plaque I'd made to mark their plot. The cemetery (at Hagensborg) is tended by a small number of volunteers and I had to prepare a cement foundation for the plaque. The following day, when I

Kathy married Don Craft in 1989 and adopted a son, Udom Andrew, in 1993.

Steven and Teresa's first child, Olivia, born in 1992, was named for my mother.

returned to the site to remove the forms, I found two grizzlies sunning themselves in the cemetery, full of fish after a good feed at the river. I got out of the truck and looked at them for a minute, and then said, "Good morning, boys" to shoo them off. They heaved themselves lazily to their feet, snorted at me and ambled off into the bush, their healthy coats shimmering in the sun. Moments like that don't come along every day.

At work, one of my most heartfelt missions was to elevate women, based on merit of course, to higher positions as they became available. This was met with a surprising level of resistance in both professional circles and on the union front. The first of many battles in this small war was held at the famous Union Club.[2] The ADMs had convinced me that I should join the Union Club in order to have a place to take "important" people to lunch. The British-style club, exclusively for men, had been around for literally one hundred years. It consisted of a well-appointed dining room complete with liveried waiters, a bar, a smoking room, a billiards room, and sleeping accommodations on the floors above.

I joined the club and soon found myself involved in the debate about extending membership to women. Unbelievably, women were allowed only in the dining room and had to enter through the back door.[3] The debate raged on until finally a meeting was held, drawing almost the entire membership of nearly four hundred men. After a heated discussion, the members voted to maintain the status quo. I immediately resigned, much to the horror of several colleagues and friends, and I found myself under considerable pressure to reconsider. But I was truly incensed and wrote a strong letter of resignation saying that I would be ashamed to belong to an organization living in the dark ages, and that "it's what's between your ears that counts, not what's between your legs!" In the mid-'90s, the Union Club finally allowed women to become members.

At work, I was also determined to improve the relationship between the ministry and the industry it was meant to serve. To this end, I invited the executive manager of the BC Federation of Agriculture to attend one of our weekly meetings to give us his view of how the ministry was seen by the industry. I was surprised to discover that this was the first invitation ever issued to the federation and I think it helped to change the attitude in the upper levels of our ministry.

On the BC fisheries front, our attention was drawn to the Asian drift-net fishing practices and the damage they were doing in the Pacific Northwest. Drift nets are unimaginably destructive inventions. A fishing vessel would roll out up to forty miles of net hanging from buoys, letting it drift for some hours or even days before it was rolled in to disentangle and sort the catch. Almost everything that swims is caught and, even worse, a number of these drift nets break loose and drift unattended, ensnaring and killing fish for months, even years. Our ministry spearheaded a public relations campaign to garner support for the eventual ban on this type of fishing.

With grandson Ben at the Farmers' Market in Salmon Arm.

I was especially proud of the computerization of our ministry;

ours was the first in the government to achieve this. It was a bit ironic, though, since I was—and still am—completely computer illiterate. I had never learned to type and had been spoiled all my life by a series of patient, competent "girls" (administrative assistants) who took dictation, reconciled my expense claims and sent my emails. But Agnes, my executive assistant, was so embarrassed by her dinosaur of a boss that she set up a fake computer workstation on my desk as a decoy, the kind they have at Ikea, just a plastic shell. You couldn't even plug it in, but it didn't matter because I didn't know how to turn it on! It worked perfectly—made her happy and it sure made me look good.

During my tenure as deputy, the Ministry of Agriculture developed a detailed scheme to overhaul our grape and wine sector. People had been growing grapes and making wine in the Okanagan for years, but everyone agreed that the quality and variety of wines was inferior. We had put a very capable man, Mike Warren, in charge. He put together an excellent program that gave grape growers $10,000 per acre to pull out their old vines and replant with new varietal species. The program was a huge success and was the beginning of what is now one of North America's very highly regarded wine-producing areas.

My undying passion for all things equine led me to inquire about why we never did any extension work with the horse industry. Of course, there was no answer—as I'd seen in veterinary colleges, the government's priority was to support food-producing sectors. I had taken a liking to a young man in our Abbotsford office, Mark Robbins.[4] Mark and I discussed the importance of the horse industry to the BC economy—at that time, the BC thoroughbred industry provided an estimated five thousand jobs, just within the province. We decided that a ministry-sponsored weekend conference, with top-notch guest speakers from all over North America, might raise BC's profile and meet the needs of our equine community. Nothing like this had ever been done before, but Mark organized a wonderful program for over five hundred enthusiastic participants. Unfortunately this initiative was not a priority for the deputy minister who replaced me when I eventually left office.

The plight of the Okanagan tree fruit industry, especially the apple growers, had plagued successive provincial governments for many

years. The trouble had started in 1973 when the Dave Barrett government instituted the Agricultural Land Reserve (ALR), setting up an
untenable situation for fruit producers. Orchards that had been "by
luck" excluded from the ALR were often sold and subdivided into
residential lots, making their owners instantly wealthy. Most orchardists, however, struggled on, unable to either sell out or make a living.

The plan had been that they would be compensated or subsidized
by the government but, of course, subsequent governments tried to
ignore this commitment, resulting in continual and often quite nasty
demonstrations. Orchardists who had been able to afford to replant
with dwarf trees of new varieties, and then wait as they matured, had
a hope of eventually making a living, but many others found work
elsewhere and let their orchards go wild. Things came to a head in late
1989 when producers organized a huge meeting in a school gymna-
sium in Westbank. The minister was reluctant to attend and I was
requested to go in his place—somebody had to take the heat and it
wasn't going to be the minister! It was one of the worst experiences of my
life, walking into the meeting of about five hundred militant growers and
taking the brunt of their pent-up rage. I had no authority to accede to
their demands and, after taking a beating for two hours, I left the meeting
with the promise that I would take their message to the premier.

At about the same time, a new premier's deputy, David Emerson,
came on board, replacing Frank Rhodes.[5] David was a very capable
person whom I grew to respect and admire. I arranged a meeting with
him and the premier on behalf of the fruit growers and out of the blue,
David proposed that we set up an authority based on the Tennessee
Valley Power Authority model. The premier immediately jumped at
the idea and the BC Tree Fruit Authority was established. One of my
ADMs, Ross Husdon, became the executive director and immediately
began putting the authority's structure in place.[6] One of its first initiatives was a replanting program, similar to that used for grapes and,
much to everyone's relief, the perennial problem of the fruit growers
appeared to be at least partially resolved.

ONE OF THE BEST things about being back in BC was being closer to
our cabin at Shuswap and to our grandchildren. And although horses

We had many wonderful summer meals at Rex and Bea Mears' cabin, next to ours at Shuswap Lake.

had gone out of our lives, we had a wonderful series of dogs, both golden and black Labrador retrievers. Phyl and I went on some wonderful holidays, worked hard on developing our home and garden, and developed rich and lasting friendships.

As the election approached, it became more and more evident that the Vander Zalm government was going to be defeated. The premier had been involved in an enterprise (Fantasy Gardens) that was forced into bankruptcy after some questionable loans.

One morning that spring, quite unexpectedly, I was summoned to a meeting with the premier and David Emerson. They had prepared quite a tempting pitch, asking me to take over the management of the Agricultural Land Commission. They offered me a first-class office in Victoria, even though the headquarters for the Land Commission was located in Burnaby, with a generous expense account and access to the helicopter service for flights between Victoria and Vancouver. It was made obvious that maintaining the status quo was not an option: with a change of government, I would be terminated as deputy minister. In fact, my successor had already been selected.[7] At some level, I knew I was lucky to be able to maintain my salary, status and benefits, and the idea of job-hunting held little appeal. So more by default than by choice, I became chairman of the BC Land Commission.

The Victoria MoA staff put on a surprise farewell party for me, and shortly thereafter I was installed in a suite of offices on the top floor of a brand new building on Douglas Street. I was given a very competent secretary and kept my government vehicle.

I can't claim to have been unfamiliar with the problems I was about to inherit, but I was definitely naïve about the potential for sorting them out. The ALR had been set up in a hurry, almost overnight, to prevent landowners from taking advantage of any advance information. The boundaries had been very hurriedly drawn and, in many cases, barren land had been mistakenly left within the boundaries and good farmland left out. This caused continual controversy and the succeeding governments had never had the fortitude to put it right.

The commission board consisted of the chairman and five appointed members,[8] and the members I inherited were strong, practical and fair. They were informed by a staff of forty, which included the manager and a half-dozen experienced land use specialists. The commission was tasked with holding regular meetings to address petitions from landowners, most seeking exclusion from the reserve, usually for development. The staff was generally "pro-retention"—green space appeared to be of primary importance—but the board was remarkably even-handed.

Landowners whose exclusion requests were rejected had the option of going before a special committee of Cabinet—a loophole for good government supporters—where decisions made were often political and usually disadvantageous to the surrounding landowners. Especially in the Kelowna area, the excluded land caused visible disruption to continuity of the surrounding agricultural area, an effect called "hopscotching." This resulted in much bitterness and charges of political favouritism.

I was only in place a few months when the election was called and, as expected, the NDP were returned with Glen Clark as premier. A very good high school friend and well-known BC historian, Bill Barlee, was elected and made Minister of Agriculture. Bill and I had been in regular communication over the years, and I had more or less expected that if he did become Minister of Agriculture he would make me his deputy. How wrong I was.

Within a week of the election, the knives were out and two very capable deputies, Bob Plecas and Doug Horswell, good friends of mine, were fired. I was fired a few days later, taking some solace in being number three on the hit list but nevertheless it did sting. When you treat people with respect all your life, you come to expect it in return, so it was a shock to be informed so brusquely by two former employees whose main interest was to recover the keys to my vehicle. So that, more or less, wrapped up my tenure as a provincial civil servant.

So I UPDATED MY CV—again—and spent some restful days working in the garden and catching up on things around home. Within a couple of weeks, I received a phone call from Doreen Mullins, who asked if I would be interested in working for the federal government in the land claims area.

It was the spring of 1993, and both levels of government were under pressure to get BC First Nations land claims issues sorted out, once and for all. The Nisga'a negotiations had been going on for some time and other First Nations in BC were demanding attention. Almost the entire province was under claim, as there had been only a few small treaties concluded on Vancouver Island by Sir James Douglas. The situation was becoming untenable, with action threatened by many First Nations and the BC economy under threat.

It was Doreen's job to prepare for the federal government's participation in the anticipated negotiations. She was knowledgeable and very personable, and within a few days I went to work for her. Initially based in Victoria, it soon became evident that a more sensible location for the office would be in Vancouver. With the move, the staff expanded and the office became known as the Federal Treaty Negotiation Office. I stayed in Victoria, working from home and travelling to Vancouver and around the province as necessary.

In the meantime, an independent body was needed to oversee negotiations, which would support the development of both federal and provincial legislation. Each government put forward a team, headed by deputy ministers, to hammer out the legislation. I was seconded to

Grandchildren Ben, Udom and Olivia at a family dinner at Shuswap in 2001.

the federal team in an advisory role. The federal government had underestimated the complexity of the BC situation. With 95 percent of BC owned by the provincial Crown, they anticipated simply giving large tracts of land to First Nations, backed up by federal government cash on a quid pro quo basis. What they didn't realize was that most Crown land in BC was under licence, permit, or lease to forest and mining companies, cattle ranchers and others. Understandably, there was great uneasiness among these groups as the land claims issue became public.

After numerous meetings, the Treaty Commission legislation was put in place. It called for five members, one from each government, two from First Nations, and an independent chairman. I was asked by the federal government to be its representative, or commissioner. The chairman was Chuck Conaghan, a well-known Vancouver businessman with expertise in arbitration and negotiation. I got to know Chuck very well and we became good friends.

The five of us met regularly in Vancouver, sometimes for two or three days, as we worked out the details for the anticipated negotiations. We also travelled the province individually and met with First Nations and third-party groups to explain the six-step treaty-negotiation process. In the meantime, Doreen and her team met with the same groups to try to build support for, and trust in, the process.

Once again, politics superseded common sense. The 1993 election brought the federal Liberals back into power and my position came to an abrupt end. Within a few days, however, Lorne Leach contacted me with a request to act as a land claims consultant for the BC Cattlemen's Association. I was to represent the association at meetings and keep cattlemen informed through their meetings and a monthly information column in their magazine. I was offered a generous per diem and expense account and, as I knew many of the cattlemen throughout the province, I was more than happy to accept the offer.

I continued with this for the better part of two years, but became increasingly disillusioned and frustrated with the lack of progress. Both governments and the First Nations groups often refused to take positions on key issues, especially on the apparently intractable issue of the extinction of aboriginal rights.

In the meantime, the Nisga'a negotiations, which were separate from the Treaty Commission process, were reaching conclusion. Some aspects of the settlement were causing considerable anxiety in the non-Native community, such as the level of ongoing government funding after treaty conclusion and the proposed third level of government. While the governments continually denied that the Nisga'a Treaty would set a precedent for the fifty or sixty negotiations in the treaty process, skepticism was rampant. Opposition heightened and The Citizens' Voice group emerged, founded by John Pitts, retired CEO of the MacDonald Dettwiler Corporation, a very highly respected and influential person. He had put together a powerful board of lawyers and businessmen, including Ron Huntington, an ex-federal cabinet minister and my old political mentor, and he hired Martyn Brown as full-time manager of the group.[9]

When Ron invited me to join The Citizens' Voice team, I was so frustrated and disappointed with the treaty process that I agreed. I left my job with the cattlemen and threw myself into working with John Pitts. There was no salary involved but I was much happier working with like-minded colleagues.

Rex Mears gave me a hand fixing the deck at the cabin.

We were proud of our lovely home and garden on McAnnally Road in Victoria.

We published one-page ads in the *Globe and Mail* and the *Vancouver Sun*, pointing out the perceived mistakes that were going to be written into the Nisga'a Agreement. This branded me "an enemy" of the Federal Treaty Negotiations Office and to this date, sadly, I have not spoken to anyone from that office, including Doreen Mullins.

It's not surprising to note that in the ten-plus years that the treaty process has been in place, only two or three out of fifty or so negotiations have been settled. The process *alone* has cost $1 billion. Economic development in the province continues to face ongoing uncertainty.

So that concluded my working career and I settled into a busy retirement, gardening, playing tennis and bridge, keeping up the cabin, enjoying our dogs and, most of all, catching up on loving my wife.

THE GOLDEN YEARS

THE LATTER YEARS OF my life were much like the first ones, surrounded by the people I loved and enjoying the freedom of retirement. I spent a lot of time working to bring our huge garden into a semblance of order. Phyl and I took some wonderful trips (a credit to Phyl's careful research and planning) and spent several weeks every year at Shuswap. The climate in Victoria was perfect for a year-round garden so it kept me really busy. I started playing tennis and worked on my bridge game: these two pursuits kept Phyl and I very busy all year round. I began to enjoy bridge so much that Phyl and I celebrated our fiftieth wedding anniversary by taking a bridge cruise to the Caribbean in 2006.

We also had a lot of fun with an old family tradition adopted from Phyl's childhood. On the first day of a new month, the first person to say, "Rabbits, rabbits, rabbits," gets a prize. A small prize—an extra helping of dessert, a flower on their bedside table, relief from kitchen cleanup—just something that will brighten their day. Over the years this tradition morphed from a simple verbal "rabbits rabbits rabbits" to stuffed, carved and porcelain rabbits, from handwritten notes to elaborate drawings, from rabbit cards (mailed well in advance) to faxes, emails and text messages. Over three generations, Greenaway family "rabbits" messages have crossed borders and continents, households and workplaces, reliably bringing us together across the miles once a month with a laugh and a smile.

Our kids, now adults of course, continued to give us a lot of joy. Kathy, her husband, Don, and their son, Udom, moved to southern Africa where they spent eight years doing development work, with a focus on HIV/AIDS. We missed them terribly but Phyl kept up with them

Phyl and I spent several weeks every year at our beloved retreat at Shuswap Lake.

through email, and we spent several weeks with them in Zambia in 2001, which we thoroughly enjoyed. We had the best of both worlds there: an amazing safari and a first-hand look at the work that CARE was doing in Zambia—a real eye-opener. If I'd been ten years younger, I'd have packed up and gone to join them there. Kathy joined us in France for a week where we had a wonderful time just catching up, doing a lot of wine-tasting... By the time Kathy and Don came back to Canada in 2005, Udom was a young man. They settled in Kamloops, from where Kathy now consults in HIV all over the world and still travels—too much for my liking. Don has a tough job as the manager of a residence for low-income seniors, overseeing the transition to a brand new and expanded facility, and amassing a wealth of touching and humorous anecdotes about working with seniors. Udom is a prep chef in an upscale restaurant, still working on his life plan, but productive and responsible.

As for Terry, he met the love of his life, Jeong Ah Kim, in 2008 and they were married in Salmon Arm in 2009. With Jeong Ah's father too ill to travel from Korea to Canada for the wedding, I had the honour of walking her down the aisle. They had a wonderful reception at our Shuswap cabin. Jeong Ah has been a wonderful addition to our family and has managed to fit right in with us in spite of all our warts.

With Kathy in Beaune, France, on one of our wonderful trips.

Steven and Teresa settled in Kelowna just after their daughter, Olivia, was born on June 12, 1992. I was delighted they chose to name her after my mom, and it was nice that Olivia got to know and still remembers her great-grandmother from the many times Mom and my Aunt Helen would babysit her.

Steve and Teresa started their own advertising and corporate communications firm and have had a wide range of interesting clients over the years. I know that they have experienced all the challenges—and successes—of owning a small business over the years, many of them similar to ours establishing the veterinary practice in Kamloops.

Enjoying a break, with Phyl, over a beer.

Olivia was soon joined by a younger brother, Benjamin Lorne, who was born—all eleven pounds, four ounces of him—on November 22, 1993. Now sixteen, he's six foot three and two hundred pounds.

We spent many wonderful Christmastimes at Steve and Teresa's over the years. One cold year, after a great Christmas dinner, they ran out of room for the turkey in the fridge. They chose to leave it overnight on the workbench in the garage. Much to our surprise, a raccoon came in over the outdoor dog kennel and through the small "doggy door" and stole what was left of the twenty-pound bird. Not a foot-

The "rabbits" faxes to Kathy's office in Zambia raised a lot of eyebrows among her co-workers!

print. Not a bone on the ground. Just gone! Poor Teresa had planned on serving turkey sandwiches, but Terry and I managed to find a store open on Boxing Day, and bought a ham instead.

Olivia and Ben have matured into thoughtful and hard-working young adults. After Olivia graduated from high school, she started at the University of Victoria in 2010 in sciences and is on the women's rowing team. Now in Grade 11, Ben's first love has always been hockey and he's playing with the Kimberley Dynamiters, and hopes to play Junior A as his next step.

Phyl and I have had a wonderful circle of friends and did a lot of entertaining (and a lot of *being* entertained!). I found a small group of friends to play poker with, and, for several years, went salmon fishing every fall. I never lost my affinity for playing practical jokes on people and continued to harass my friends with my warped sense of humour.

One of my favourite tricks of all time was to leave a plastic spider or cockroach lying around for some unsuspecting person to discover. One of my biggest successes was with Chris Siller and John Kilburn. Chris

Kathy's husband, Don, and me in South Luangwa National Park, Africa, evaluating an elephant femur.

Udom and I had great tennis matches.

had arranged a fishing trip for John, himself and me at Port Renfrew. Our regular accommodation fell through at the last minute and we ended up in a rather dilapidated little cabin. While John and Chris were making dinner, I put a plastic cockroach on the drain board and Chris, spotting it, picked it up with a dishcloth and threw it outside in the bush. Having

Terry married Jeong Ah Kim in July 2009. I had the honour of walking her down the aisle.

Our children, Terry, Kathy and Steven,
at Terry and Jeong Ah's wedding.

Steven and Teresa's daughter, Olivia,
celebrated her high school graduation
in June 2010.

failed to get a rise out of him with the cockroach, I tried again with a plastic spider on his pillow.

When Chris saw it, I warned him about poisonous spitting spiders so, once more using a dishcloth, he carefully collected it. However, instead of simply throwing it outside, he stormed to the manager's house and launched into a tirade about the cockroaches and spiders, and the generally unsanitary condition of the cabin. The manager asked to see the spider and when Chris unfolded the dishcloth the manager immediately exclaimed, "It's plastic!" An embarrassed Chris came back to the cabin with his tail between his legs and found John and me practically wetting ourselves laughing (though Chris is a pretty big guy and I was a little worried he'd take me out). He cursed at us for a while, but he's very good-natured, and eventually laughed it off.

I also got John Kilburn on his own home turf with a bit of mischief that I just couldn't resist. John is a celebrated amateur golfer, the winner of numerous championships, and a highly esteemed member of the Royal Colwood Gold Club, and he

Grandson Ben and I swapping stories in June 2010.

invited a number of us to a dinner there. As dinner got underway, I contrived a reason to get up and pass John's table and covertly slipped a spoon from my table into his jacket pocket. When I sat down again, I whispered to the waitress, "Maybe you could have a word with the manager. I've seen the man, sitting there," as I pointed to John, "putting silverware in his pocket." After a few minutes, the head waiter came out and tapped John on the shoulder. John put his hand in his pocket and came up with this spoon—utterly dumbfounded! He caught my eye across the room, where I was beside myself laughing, and knew he'd been had.

We sold our beautiful home at 10 Mile Point and moved into something smaller, all on one level. It was a real wrench for both of us to let go of the house we loved, but it was getting to be too much to manage. It was fortuitous that we moved when we did because only a year later, I was diagnosed with ALS (Lou Gehrig's disease). That seemed a pretty low blow since we'd spent so much time with Ken Randall (who also had ALS) and his wife, Dianne. Ken died right around the time that I was diagnosed.

I joined John Kilburn (L) and Chris Siller (R) on a fishing trip to Port Renfrew in 2009.

Slowly, but without reprieve, ALS has chipped away at my life and lifestyle, taking first—and perhaps hardest to bear—my hands. My experience of overwhelming fatigue has been directly incompatible with my sense of urgency to put my life in order. This past year has been a relentless series of "lasts": last time to drive the car, last time to unload the dishwasher, last time to feed the dog, last cup of coffee... I live with the guilt of my increasing dependence and the dread of an undignified end to my days.

The silver linings, however, deserve mention. Although intensely frustrating, ALS is not painful. Nor does it demand that you expend valuable time and energy seeking treatment or cure, since there are

Rex Mears' wife and my dear friend, Bea, entertaining us in August 2010.

During the last six months, Nick was my daytime companion and afternoon sleeping buddy.

none. Knowing you're going to die gives you a chance to say what you want to say, and do what you want to do. I am grateful that ALS chose to manifest itself near the end, rather than the beginning, of my life; so many with ALS are stricken in their prime.

Phyl and I went on a wonderful final holiday, a cruise from Moscow to St. Petersburg. I have been able to focus with pride on each of my children and my grandchildren, as their lives have unfolded in meaningful and productive ways. Our friends have been truly generous and thoughtful, providing an endless stream of wonderful food, good-humoured visits and practical help with jobs around the house that I can no longer do. Our black lab, Nick, now three years old, has settled down into an intuitive, gentle dog that will be a great companion to Phyl after I go.

And of course, I finally sat down to create this memoir. I enjoyed, at least most of the time, getting these stories down on paper and going through all our old photos and memorabilia. The use of voice-activated computer software (Dragon Naturally Speaking) allowed me to dictate rather than type, which, for me, would have been a hopeless endeavor even *without* ALS. I certainly never dreamed I'd fill so many pages!

Bringing this book to a close has been almost as difficult as it was to start it—I still have more to tell, but one has to stop somewhere. So today, I draw that line and call it done. I turn it over now to family and friends with the hope that these stories bring them together over a laugh and a fond memory or two.

For when the One Great Scorer comes
to write against your name,
He marks not that you won or lost
but how you played the game.

Relaxing with a libation on my birthday in May 2010.

LORNE DIED AT HOME on September 13, 2010, at peace and surrounded by his loving family. He appeared to have had a stroke on September 10, which, mercifully, helped him to slip from the grasp of ALS before it had a chance to run its full course. His presence is deeply missed by his family and all who knew him. In Williams Lake, the city flag flew at half-mast. Phyl has received countless cards of condolence and more than forty donations were made to the ALS Society in Lorne's name. A celebration of Lorne's life, held in Victoria on October 2, 2010, was attended by more than 250 people.

His legacy endures in these pages and in our hearts.

Dr. Lorne Greenaway, DVM

At home peacefully on September 13, 2010 after a courageous battle with ALS, surrounded by his loving family and with the support of his many friends.

Born on May 8, 1933, in Bella Coola, son of the late Everett and Olivia (nee Nygaard) Greenaway. Husband to loving wife and best friend, Phyl, wonderful Dad to Kate (Don Craft), Terry (Jeong Ah Kim), Steven (Teresa) and Tom, proud "GG" to Udom, Olivia and Ben.

Lorne led a truly remarkable life, full of achievement, rich in family and friends, and always guided by his renowned integrity, kindness and indomitable sense of humour.

His career was highlighted by his election in 1979 to the House of Commons as the Progressive Conservative Member of Parliament for Cariboo–Chilcotin, where he served until he resigned in 1988. Throughout his time in Ottawa, representing his constituents was always his primary focus. He was known and respected for his commitment to listening and applying common sense solutions to everyday problems.

From his early days in Bella Coola, Naramata and Kelowna, Lorne developed an enduring attachment to his native British Columbia and a practical knowledge of all things outdoors. He owned, trained and loved many horses and became an accomplished rider. After graduating from Kelowna Senior Secondary in 1952, Lorne attended Ontario Veterinary College in Guelph, where he graduated with first-class honours and served as class president.

Lorne established a small and large animal veterinary practice in Kamloops where he served the needs of many of BC's largest ranches, including the historic Gang Ranch and Douglas Lake Cattle Company. It was also during this time that Lorne and Phyl built the family cabin at Shuswap Lake that has brought so much joy to family and friends.

In 1968, Lorne was appointed Associate Professor, Western College of Veterinary Medicine in Saskatoon where he served for one year until his yearning to return to BC led him into ranching, first in Kelowna and then in Williams Lake, where he and Phyl owned the Soda Creek Ranch.

In 1974, Lorne moved the family to Vancouver where they lived in Southlands and he built and operated a small animal veterinary practice in Steveston.

After leaving elected office, Lorne continued his career in public service as the BC Deputy Minister of Agriculture, Food and Fisheries and Chair of the BC Land Commission. He later represented the federal government as one of the first Commissioners on the BC Treaty Commission.

Lorne enjoyed his retirement years in Victoria amongst many friends, playing tennis and bridge, travelling and walking his dogs along the streets of Ten Mile Point. He got tremendous joy from designing and caring for a beautiful garden and was known far and wide for his practical jokes and his gift for telling stories. His dahlias, like his legacy, live on. The accomplishments of his children and grandchildren make him tremendously proud.

The Greenaway family would like to express our heartfelt thanks to Lorne's wonderful caregiver, Roy Neville, and to our many friends who understood our journey and responded in so many practical ways.

A celebration of Lorne's life will be held in Victoria at 1:00 pm on Saturday, October 2, 2010 at the Uplands Golf Club. At his request, there will be "no sniveling allowed!" In lieu of flowers, donations may be made in Lorne's name to the Canadian ALS Society at als.ca.

—Lorne's obituary as it appeared in the *Times Colonist*,
September 16, 2010

APPENDIX: RANCHES AND CLIENTS

1/2 Way
105 Mile
6 Mile
70 Mile Ranch
A&K Cattle
Art Bowers
Ashcroft Estates
B. Hursley
Bar HH
Bar Q
Basque
BC Cattle Company
BC Livestock
Big Bar
Bill Charleton
Bill Cook
Bob Steeples
Bob, Rudolph and Stan Creach
Bonaparte
Bostock
Bud Fox

Bulman
Burt
Cedric Dorrell
Charlie Dougharty
Chataway
Cherry Creek
Chilco
Christian
Clemitson
Corbould
Cordonier
D. Lake
Danielson Quarterhorses
Dave Perry
Davy Jones
DeLeeuw
DeMarni
Diamond S
Dot Ranch
Doug Bowers
Douglas Lake

Earlscourt
EM Hall
Empire Valley
Evander McLeod
F. MacDonald
Falkland Ranch
Fountain Indian Band
Frank Devick
Fred Dey
Froler
Gang
Gaston Gardi
Gottfriedson
Green Acres
H. Robertson
H. Threlkeld
Harper
Hat Creek
Haughton
Haven
Henry Schneider
Hook Ranch
Ike Lehman
Indian Gardens
Iver Edwards
Jack Stewart
Jim Cobb
John Benedict
Johnny Danley
Lindo Giacamulli
Lloyd West
Loon Lake
Lytton Residential School
Maber
Martin Forbacher
McLeod at Bestwick

Mesa Vista
Mitchell
Mound
Nicola Livestock
OK Ranch
Pasco
Perry
Piva
Pollard
Pozzobon
Ralph Devick
Red Rock
Rod Black
Russel Ross
Schebauer
Semlin
Shannon
St Gerges
Stump Lake
Tom Meeks
Tranquille Farm
Whispering Pines
Whitecroft

ENDNOTES

Chapter 1

1. Dad's father, Samuel Greenaway, and his five brothers emigrated from Ireland to the USA in the 1880s. One of his first jobs was to work and travel for several years as a sparring partner with the famous boxer John L. Sullivan. He met Ann Jennie Clarke, who was working in Wannamaker's Department Store in Philadelphia, and they were married soon after. Samuel was an accomplished ventriloquist and supplemented his income by performing.

2. At one time he was a cook on George Biern's pack train that was contracted to carry wire for the Yukon telegraph line.

3. Mom was the oldest daughter; her sisters were Thelma and Helen. Her brothers were John, Olaf, Melvin and Alger.

4. Aunt Margaret's house was in good repair when Mom and I went through it in 1994 on a visit to Bella Coola for the one-hundredth-year reunion of Norwegian settlers. A few years ago, it was moved down the valley to Hagensborg where it became a pottery workshop and

display/sales room. Very few of these houses remain in Bella Coola now. Over the years they've been purchased, dismantled, shipped to the US and rebuilt.

5. The Natives coming down from the Chilcotin were referred to as the Stick Indians because they came from jack pine country.

6. In the summer, these small sardine-like fish came up the inlet where Natives gathered them in nets and dumped them in large pits. The fish were extremely oily and when they fermented in the pits, the oil and fat rose to the surface and could be scooped off and put in containers. You could smell the decaying fish in the pits for miles around, so everyone always knew when it was oolichan time at the Native village. Trading in oil followed a route known as "The Grease Trail," used by Alexander Mackenzie in his explorations of the West Coast.

7. Lillian Stranaghan was Mom's cousin. Her son, Ken, later became a well-known West Coast bush pilot.

Chapter 2

1. Unfortunately, during one of our moves, the labels came loose from their eggs. I still have my collection of eggs in a beautiful display case but they aren't labelled.

Chapter 3

1. My Uncle Bob was from the Nygaard family, and was married to Mom's sister, my Aunt Helen. At that time they had one son, David, and later had three more children: Sharon, Dale and Rosalie.

2. Finley later retired to Ashcroft and I got to know him and his wife really well. She was a telephone operator in Ashcroft and I often spoke to her when making calls to clients there. In the 1980s, we renewed our acquaintance when I became an MP and Finley was a staunch supporter.

3. I say "Yukon" deliberately, having been chastised by Erik Nielson for saying "The Yukon." Erik served as MP for Yukon for over three decades—he should know!

4. Mr. Eden had driven the stagecoach that made the last trip down the Cariboo Road to Ashcroft. He later became a good friend and ran the Kelowna Rodeo every Labour Day weekend for many years. He hired me during the rodeo to run errands for him, which was great fun, especially because I got to hang out with the cowboys behind the chutes when I wasn't busy.

Chapter 4

1. By amazing contrast, the class of 2009 graduated only 11 men among 115 students!

2. We called him Coonhunter because he and his brother, father and various uncles used to hunt raccoons with dogs.

3. Harvey's surname was often mistaken as Green or Grinn. At some point we hit on "Groin" which, over time, morphed into "Harvey the Crotch." Awful name, now that I think about it.

4. Neil was studious and spent hours in the library looking up strange material, like photographs of African men with elephantiasis who had to carry their testicles in wheelbarrows.

5. In those days, dealers received new cars by rail only. To save time and money, it was common practice to have cars driven to dealerships if willing drivers could be found.

6. We found out later that the event had been plotted by a senior student, Bill Whittick, who is still famous among veterinarians for the tricks and practical jokes he played on colleagues and drug salesmen during the many years he practised in Toronto. That initiation ceremony was evidently the worst that aspiring members ever had to endure and,

as the details leaked out, senior members of the fraternity were warned to tone things down in future years.

7. Dr. Talbot and his family had moved to Vancouver where he set up a successful equine practice, primarily serving the thoroughbreds at the two racetracks.

8. The Guisachan Farm was originally owned by the Earl and Countess of Aberdeen, who established the first large-scale planting of fruit trees and hops in the Central Okanagan. Lord Aberdeen, later Governor General of Canada, and Lady Aberdeen, founder of the World Council of Women and the Victorian Order of Nurses, named the ranch Guisachan after an estate of Lady Aberdeen's father in Inverness-shire, Scotland. The Cameron family bought the property in 1903 and lived there for eighty-one years. Paddy Cameron operated a dairy farm for many years and was noted for his love of horses. The Cameron house now functions as the Guisachan House Restaurant, and has rooms set aside to display many photos and artifacts dating back to the 1890s. The surrounding parks, buildings and the "Avenue of Cedars" still stand.

9. We had been offered an apartment in Miami by the Fishmans, which we would have loved, but had to turn it down because we couldn't afford to get there. Evidently they were hurt by our refusal and we didn't get it straightened out until some years later.

10. Facilities at Guelph for handling equine cases were very primitive. Anytime a horse had to be anaesthetized, mats were laid out on the surgery floor. That set-up worked for handling cattle, which were by far the higher priority for the college's government funders, but not for horses.

11. This instrument, if you can call it that, was designed to catch pigs. It's a piece of pipe about two feet long with a loop of cable through it. When you snared something in the loop you could pull it tight. It was perfect for getting nasty dogs out of a kennel.

12. Uncle Milton had been fifteen at the time he and Dad were separated, but lied about his age in order to join the army. He served in Europe in World War I. He owned a shoe store and brought me a wonderful pair of boots for hunting. After leaving Guelph, they went on to visit their birthplace near Owen Sound and the cemetery where their mother, father and some other relatives rested. It was such an honour and a privilege to have them come all that way for my graduation. Uncle Milton died a year or so later.

Chapter 5

1. The National Housing Act (NHA) offered mortgages backed by the Government of Canada, which could be obtained through the local bank after meeting the financial application requirements.

2. Vic Spencer and Dale spent a lot of time drinking Carrington's Rye, which came with a fancy gold top, and their habit was to throw the tops into a big box in the woodshed behind the kitchen. One weekend, one of them had the bright idea that these golden ornaments would make a fitting top for fence posts, so off they went in a pickup and spent the day nailing golden caps on over seven hundred fence posts! Dale and I became good friends but, unfortunately, Dale's life came to a sad end a few years later. For Dale, living on the ranch with only the cook and the ranch hands for company was a pretty lonely experience. He drank a lot, but somewhere along the line he met a very good-looking woman, a real knockout, and before long they were married. Most of us who knew him were concerned that he had made a mistake and, sure enough, after a few months, she took off and left him with some large bills. Dale took this pretty hard and, before long, he left the Diamond S.

3. Jump Canada is the committee of Equine Canada responsible for all hunter, equitation and jumper activities in Canada, from the grassroots to the international level. Jump Canada is governed by a board, with the majority of members elected by stakeholders in the sport.

4. At that time, the Spencers owned and operated four ranches: the Diamond S at Pavilion, the Circle S at Dog Creek, Greenacres at Pritchard and Earlscourt at Lytton. In addition, Col. Spencer and Mr. Ross (a former Lieutenant-Governor) jointly owned the Douglas Lake Cattle Company.

5. In one moving Depression-era tale, Harry described raising turkeys because they were easier to sell than cattle. Late in the fall, he and Peg would head for Vancouver with a load of turkeys all done up and ready for Christmas. They would go door to door along Marine Drive and in Shaughnessy, peddling the turkeys for a little cash that helped to keep them on the ranch.

6. The buyers I worked for included Slim Dorin, Lew D. Williams, Tommy Wilson, B. Nielsen, Dale Miller, Henry Koster, Jack Paul, Henry Chung, Colin Bakey and, of course, Gary Hook and several others.

Chapter 6

1. Over my years in practice in Kamloops, my client list grew to over a hundred ranches. These are all listed in the Appendix.

2. I got a lot of help with this from the animal husbandry branch of the Faculty of Agriculture at one of the large California universities.

3. Bud was from the Diamond S Ranch, Charlie was from the Loon Lake Ranch, and Loy was from the Mound Ranch.

4. Brigadier Bostock was the son of Senator Bostock who, for some years, had represented BC in Ottawa. The Brigadier's two sisters lived in the old ranch house at Monte Creek. At some point, the family had built a church on the ranch near the old highway. When the government wanted to widen the road, the church was slated to be moved or demolished. The old sisters made such a fuss that, in the end, the highway was rerouted around the church. There it sits to this day, on an isolated hilltop, caught between the old road and the new one.

5. The Bostock foreman, Fred Nichol, had lived on the Bostock Ranch almost all his life and, as a boy, had been there when Bill Miner pulled his famous CPR holdup. He told me how the posse had hoped to catch Miner hiding at Bostock's by checking all the horses to see if any of them were warm and sweaty, but Miner's crew had moved on to Douglas Lake.

Chapter 7

1. As in Guelph, the main funders of the College (the provincial and federal governments) were interested primarily in the care of food-producing animals, so a suitable up-to-date facility for equine patients had not been included in the design of the clinic.

2. ROYGBIV is a mnemonic for the colours of the rainbow: red, orange, yellow, green, blue, indigo, violet.

3. He had come close to winning the Kentucky Derby with a filly called Indian Broom.

4. In a visit several years later, I found a very fancy concrete structure had been built after all.

Chapter 8

1. The Eldorado, or ACT Ranch, is located between the Kelowna Airport and the south end of Duck Lake, and was one of the first cattle ranches established in BC. In the 1850s, the Parsons brothers—squatters—farmed some of the property. Frederick Brent took up the land by pre-emption (a government scheme) and later sold to George Simpson. In the autumn of 1859, Father Pandosy and his group arrived at the south end of Duck Lake and spent a miserable winter there in a crude shelter. It was then taken over by the Posthill family who later sold to a Mr. McLellan. From there it was owned by Countess Bubna, the McNair brothers, and finally by a Vancouver businessman, A.C. Taylor. The first telephone in the BC Interior was set up

in 1891 between the Posthill Ranch and the home of Tom Wood, a distance of five miles.

Chapter 9

1. John Kelly had logged the property for railway ties before putting in the hayfield and irrigation.

2. The Pacific Great Eastern Railway (PGE) changed its name in 1972 to BC Rail.

Chapter 10

1. The group comprised Neil Woolliams, manager of the Douglas Lake Cattle Company; Jim Stewart, a purebred breeder from Kelowna; Bill McFaul, an auctioneer from Chilliwack; Wayne Everett, manager of the Perry Ranch; Morrie Thomas, rancher and manager of the BC Livestock Co-op Yard at Okanagan Falls; a couple of seasoned ranchers, Stan Towers from Kelowna and Gordon Parke from Cache Creek; Spud Heustis, a prospector who had discovered the huge Bethlehem copper deposit near Ashcroft only a few years earlier; Harry Bailey, who raised purebred Holsteins at Chilliwack and had already exported a number of loads of Holstein heifers to Korea; and me.

2. It had been decided at the company's inception that each member should put in $10,000 as start-up funds. In addition, because so many of the members of our company were well connected and successful, it was not difficult for them to arrange an open-ended line of credit on our collective behalf. I had a line of credit with the Bank of Montreal in Williams Lake and wrote a cheque on our ranch account.

Chapter 11

1. John Taylor was the son of the famous hockey player, Cyclone Taylor, and had been an MP in the Diefenbaker government.

2. The hotel was not impressed with this, especially since the Riding Association didn't have any money to repair the damages.

Chapter 12

1. It was Dr. Bigland who had recruited me to head up the large animal clinical division at WCVM.

2. The first project for VIDO was the problem of diarrhea ("scours") in newborn beef and dairy calves. The most common cause of this condition turned out to be E. coli, which not only affects animals but also humans. VIDO researchers were able to come up with a successful vaccine, Vicogen, and since then have developed several other VIDO vaccines that are the world's first in their type. In 2003, VIDO changed its name (Vaccine and Infectious Disease Organization) and opened an expansion to its building, which now provides 80,000 square feet of ultramodern laboratory space for a staff of 145 researchers. It uses the most modern research tools of genomics and bioinformatics to develop new vaccines and vaccine delivery technologies.

Chapter 13

1. We were unhappy apartment dwellers and Phyl had found a wonderful property, a completely renovated house built in 1870, ten blocks from the House of Commons.

2. One of them was Michel Cogger, later made a Senator by Mulroney and who finally resigned from the Senate after becoming involved in some nefarious affair.

Chapter 14

1. While government bureaucracy is supposed to be apolitical, deputy ministers are usually appointed by the premier and, with my political background, if the NDP did form a government, I knew my days would likely be numbered.

2. The Union Club was a frequent setting for Len Norris's cartoons in the *Vancouver Sun*.

3. It had long been rumoured that in the last century, a tunnel had been constructed under the street between the Empress Hotel and the Union Club, thus providing ladies of the night with discreet access to men using the club as a residence.

4. Mark was the son-in-law of Diane Braidwood, a girl I went to school with in Naramata. Diane had married Bud Tidball, owner of the Keg and Cleaver steakhouse franchise. Diane and Bud were well known in the equine fraternity and owned the Thunderbird Equitation Centre.

5. Frank had seen the writing on the wall and left to become president of the BC Ferry Corporation.

6. Several years before, the federal government (in response to continual lobbying by the fruit growers) had built a very expensive and state-of-the-art laboratory to research tree fruit problems and create new apple varieties. This building was located in Summerland and a good part of it was not in use. The province made a deal with the federal government and leased office space in it for the new authority.

7. One of my ADMs, Bruce Hackett, was to take my place. As a long-time civil servant, his position would be secure even with a change in government.

8. Two representatives were drawn from the fruit growers (who had been the most affected), one represented cattle ranchers, another the farming community at large, and the fifth was not connected with agriculture.

9. Martyn was well known for his political acumen and his energy. He eventually left to take a full-time position as Gordon Campbell's chief of staff.

ACKNOWLEDGEMENTS

THERE ARE SEVERAL PEOPLE who participated in the preparation of this memoir.

First and always foremost, Phyl, who has encouraged me for years to put these stories down on paper and who allowed me to spend countless hours of our final months together absorbed in dictation.

Our daughter Kathy (or Kate, as she is now called) edited and massaged my sometimes dry, linear dictation style, with the interest of the reader in mind.

Our son Terry introduced me to voice-activated computer software and scanned hundreds of family photos to create a rich archive of our history.

Our son Steven edited the more contentious sections to protect us from litigation.

Our good friend Maggie Kortes edited the entire document for structure and grammar when I couldn't possibly re-read it again.

Jeong Ah Kim, Don Craft, Trevor McLorg and Catrina Crowe assisted Kate with the final editing and formatting.

And our dear friend Neil Woolliams, whose enthusiastic response to an early draft gave me the encouragement I needed to see it through to the end.

LORNE GREENAWAY

LORNE GREENAWAY WAS BORN in
Bella Coola in 1933 and grew up in
the Okanagan. He studied veterinary medicine at Guelph University
and set up a practice in BC's Interior; he went on to ranching in the
Cariboo and exporting cattle before
becoming a Member of Parliament
for the Progressive Conservative
Party. Lorne suffered from Amyotrophic Lateral Sclerosis (ALS) and
died on September 13, 2010.

KATE GREENAWAY

LORNE'S OLDEST CHILD AND only
daughter, Kate Greenaway, worked
side by side with him as he dictated the
stories of his life, serving as secretary,
computer technician, editor and cheer-
leader on Lorne's memoir project. She
currently lives in Kamloops with her husband and son, where she works
from home as an international HIV specialist.